ARTIFICIAL WHITENESS

Columbia University Press
Publishers Since 1893
New York   Chichester, West Sussex
cup.columbia.edu

Library of Congress Cataloging-in-Publication Data
Names: Katz, Yarden, author.
Title: Artificial whiteness : politics and ideology in artificial intelligence /
Yarden Katz.
Description: New York : Columbia University Press, 2020. |
Includes bibliographical references and index.
Identifiers: LCCN 2020017166 (print) | LCCN 2020017167 (ebook) |
ISBN 9780231194907 (hardcover) | ISBN 9780231194914 (paperback) |
ISBN 9780231551076 (ebook)
Subjects: LCSH: Artificial intelligence—Moral and ethical aspects. |
Artificial intelligence—Political aspects. | Male domination (Social structure) |
White supremacy movements—Philosophy. | Imperialism and science. | Logic—
Political aspects.
Classification: LCC Q334.7 .K38 2020 (print) | LCC Q334.7 (ebook) |
DDC 303.48/34—dc23
LC record available at https://lccn.loc.gov/2020017166
LC ebook record available at https://lccn.loc.gov/2020017167

Columbia University Press books are printed on permanent
and durable acid-free paper.
Printed in the United States of America

ARTIFICIAL WHITENESS

POLITICS AND IDEOLOGY
IN ARTIFICIAL INTELLIGENCE

YARDEN KATZ

Columbia University Press *New York*

*For Azoul, our embodied marvel who loves
the earth and the sun*

CONTENTS

PREFACE

This book is rather personal for me. It is the outcome of a zigzag path that began while I was a teenager and got interested in computer science, and then philosophy, and what I think I thought then, with some hesitation, was their "intersection": "artificial intelligence." My subsequent experiences doing research around the academic field that goes by that label, after having taken too many analytic philosophy courses in college, cultivated this misunderstanding. It took years of unlearning to come to a different view, which this book attempts to synthesize. I hope my idiosyncratic presentation will be useful to some, especially those already suspicious of fields and their labels.

Thinking about the phenomena described in this book hasn't really been a pleasant experience. It reminds me of a story about the journalist Seymour Hersh. When Hersh completed his book on the notorious strategist of American empire, Henry Kissinger, he sent a copy to one of Kissinger's vociferous critics, Noam Chomsky. Chomsky wrote Hersh back that his book was "really fabulous, apart from the feeling that one is crawling through a sewer." While Kissinger the man plays only a small role in my book—though what he represents certainly looms large—in writing it, I also felt like I was crawling through a sewer. Reading the avalanche of "AI" propaganda is a demoralizing experience (regrettably, some of that ugliness is reproduced in these pages). And propaganda aside, the developments described here are not positive.

Hardly hidden in this work is a tale about the American academy and its world of "knowledge production," which suffers under slow violence as it fuels faster violence nearly everywhere. There is a depressing willingness on the part of academics to serve empire and the corporate world with remarkable flexibility. The services are provided under the banner of working for the good of all, and while unblinkingly appropriating the language of radical social movements and struggles (the discourses on AI that this book examines provide another example). The realms of computing that this book is concerned with feel particularly compromised. Nonetheless, I have tried to highlight the cracks and openings to alternatives within this system.

ARTIFICIAL WHITENESS

INTRODUCTION

A pall of sadness becomes almost a constant presence for anyone who wishes to revisit the corrupt association between American science and race in the century—the nineteenth—which ended with the appearance of moving pictures. In a better world, a world so different from the one this science helped to create, one might avert one's eyes. But good manners are a luxury which these scientists forfeited, willfully and frequently. They gave little quarter to those whom they regarded as their inferiors, dismissed and hounded those critics whom they could not summarily dispatch, and thoroughly enjoyed their social standing and each other.

—Cedric Robinson

A rtificial intelligence (AI) is capturing many minds. The famed physicist Stephen Hawking said the creation of "effective AI" may be "the biggest event in the history of our civilization, or the worst."[1] Vladimir Putin declared, "Whoever leads in AI will rule the world."[2] The United States, Britain, France, Russia, and China (among many governments) have drafted national plans on AI. Museums, too, have begun exploring the nature of art and creativity in what is widely, and nonchalantly, described as "the age of AI."[3] The fashion industry is asking how AI will "reprogram" clothing lines, and even human rights organizations are incorporating AI into their discourse.[4] AI has become a global media phenomenon.

An industry of experts from the academic and policy worlds has emerged to interpret AI's significance. According to the experts, AI could grow the economy and free people from labor burdens, help address climate change, remove the "bias" from the courts of law, automate scientific discovery, reinvent journalism (and hence democracy), and potentially produce, not long from now, "superhuman" intelligent machines that may launch new "civilizations" across the galaxy.[5] But if AI is misapplied or improperly cultivated, experts anticipate dismal outcomes. AI could widen social inequality, create a global underclass, catalyze trade wars, launch a "new" arms race, and bring about bloodier wars through "autonomous" weapons.[6] Media reports even consider the possibility that AI will "kill all of us," perhaps sooner rather than later.[7]

As is often the case with matters concerning science and technology, the ensuing conversation has been largely ahistorical. Many are willing to ponder the awesome benefits or perils of AI, but few ask what it actually is. And even if we presume to know what it is, why is it being talked about so much now? In other words, what were the developments—political, material, and otherwise—that made "AI" a mainstream focal point?

To the extent the latter question arises, it tends to be shrugged off as obvious. The ready-made answer is purely technical: larger data, faster computers, more advanced algorithms. These breakthroughs have supposedly led to a state where machines rival, and may soon exceed, the capacities of human thought.

A received wisdom thus formed: AI is a coherent and powerful force, made possible by recent breakthroughs in computing. It is a force poised to change everything, to bring about utopia or disaster.[8] For reasons elaborated in the pages that follow, this received wisdom, like so many others, obscures the phenomena it purports to explain. Moreover, the fact that these critical questions about AI are hardly raised—yet conversations continue at full speed—seems as important to making sense of AI as anything having to do with computers, data, or algorithms.

AI'S CONSTITUTION

The mathematician and philosopher Gian-Carlo Rota noted that "every concept is a drama which conceals the backstage of its constitution, a drama that followed a tortuous path of remembrance and oblivion, through cataclysms and reconstructions, pitfalls and intuitions and finally arrived at a construct, the object, which naively believes itself to be independent of its past."[9] This book is an attempt to step away from the self-evident discourse on AI and into the backstage of its constitution. I want to read AI's present through its past and by examining the political and ideological projects served by its reappearances.

The term "Artificial Intelligence" was coined by the American mathematician and computer scientist John McCarthy in the 1950s. It quickly became an evocative label for an academic field, a concept, and an industry. AI often drew great media attention. Yet this pursuit was also under scrutiny by both computing insiders and invested outsiders. Critics asked: Was AI a "science"? Or simply a quest to automate well-defined tasks of industrial production? And when would AI deliver the "human-level intelligence" in machines that invested military patrons so desire? According to conventional accounts, this skepticism led to the so-called AI winter (typically dated to the 1980s), a period when interest in the endeavor had purportedly waned. Recent commentators say AI has recovered at full strength, entering an "eternal spring."[10]

But what is AI and how does it work? What drives and sustains AI's reappearances, its so-called springs and winters? What are the continuities and divergences between invocations of AI across the decades—or in Rota's words, what were the "cataclysms and reconstructions" on this concept's path? And who and what is served by AI's iterations?

Answering these questions requires looking at AI's formation in the American military-industrial complex—and not from the perspective of awe. Many accounts of AI's history, written by practitioners and invested onlookers, present it as a march of progress. AI is often treated as a philosophically charged but autonomous technical pursuit, a product of great men's imaginations.[11] My point of departure, by contrast, is one that many scholars of science and technology have argued for: that developments in computing are shaped by, and in turn shape, social conditions. AI imbibes this circularity: it has been animated by, and has in turn refueled, the imperial and capitalist projects of its patrons. It is crucial to examine how an industry of experts, operating across academic, corporate, and state-military lines, employ AI in the service of these projects.

But it is also essential to examine AI's computing systems and their epistemic underpinnings. Many commentators speak of the age of "superhuman" machines that exceed the capacities of human thought in many domains. What those declarations mean, and the understanding of human life on which they rest, are important—especially when there is fear about people being subordinated by machines. Confronting these claims requires engaging with the substance of AI's computing systems and seeing how they fit into a broader political picture.

This book combines these elements to shed light on AI's reappearances and the functions they serve.

THE SELF, EPISTEMIC FORGERIES, AND THE MAKESHIFT PATCHWORK

From the start, AI was nebulous and contested. To cope with attacks on its incoherent basis and skepticism from patrons about its power, AI's promoters had to continually reinvent what it was about and explain how it advances the aims of empire and capital.

Yet throughout, AI was concerned with models of "the self": statements about the kinds of beings we are, our limits, and capacities. AI's aspiration to pin down the self has made it controversial, as even its advocates have recognized. In 1980 Allen Newell, then president of the Association for the Advancement of Artificial Intelligence, stated that AI's mission to grasp "the nature of intelligence" has "unsettling aspects," which unite AI with the controversial wings of psychology and biology.[12] Even practitioners who claim to only be interested in solving practical problems cannot escape the fact that appeals to AI are invariably interpreted as, or against, models of the self.

Each of AI's iterations brought somewhat distinct models of the self. Practitioners, cognitive scientists, and philosophers have tried to order this messy trajectory by creating taxonomies of AI's computing systems and epistemic styles. Distinctions are commonly made between AI that is "symbolic" versus "statistical," or "centralized" versus "emergent," or between AI systems in which "knowledge" is manually encoded by experts versus those in which it is learned from data, and so on. These different epistemic styles come with different models of self. Practitioners in the 1970s, for instance, offered visions of the self as a symbol-processing machine, rich with handcrafted internal structure. In the late 1980s and early 1990s, by contrast, the prevailing "self" started looking more like a statistical inference engine driven by sensory data.

But these classifications mask more fundamental epistemic commitments. Alison Adam has argued that AI practitioners across the board have aspired to a "view from nowhere"—to build systems that apparently learn, reason, and act in a manner freed from social context.[13] The view from nowhere turned out to be a view from a rather specific, white, and privileged place.

A different way into AI's epistemologies would be to see how computing systems help produce epistemic forgeries such as a "view from nowhere," and how such myths fit in a broader political context. I draw inspiration here from Toni Morrison's critical literary analysis. Responding to debates about the Western literary canon, Morrison urged critics to ask how a literary text functions.[14] Rather than dismissing the "universality" of a literary work because of its author's identity, Morrison asks: How does the text masquerade itself as universal? What are the mechanisms it uses? And where does the text slip and reveal its situated perspective? In the case of the American literary canon, as Morrison argued, this is a perspective imprinted with white supremacy—which, following Cheryl Harris, I understand as "a political, economic, and cultural system in which whites overwhelmingly control power and material resources, conscious and unconscious ideas of white superiority and entitlement are widespread, and relations of white dominance and non-white subordination are daily reenacted across a broad array of institutions and social settings."[15] Morrison reads the literary canon with this system in mind.

This book applies Morrison's reframing to computing systems, which come with their own narratives. Like the texts Morrison analyzed, AI's celebrated computing systems developed in a society premised on white supremacy and have worked to refuel its myths. Each of AI's iterations has produced racialized, gendered, and classed models of the self, delivered with imperialist rhetorics of colonization and conquest. Following Morrison, rather than simply negating the claim to universality, I am interested in asking how universality is forged and where the forgery fails. How does a view from *somewhere* creep into AI's computing systems and haunt the endeavor? And how can such systems be probed to reveal their service to the social order?

These questions require us to confront the ideological flexibility and incoherence of a social order based on white supremacy. As Cedric Robinson has argued, societies premised on white supremacy are inherently unstable. They constantly respond to changing social conditions and resistance struggles by employing a "makeshift patchwork": concoctions of science, law, and other bodies of knowledge that are invoked to maintain relations of power. Though the patchwork is changing and inconsistent, it can still serve a stable set of interests. AI's offerings—like those of the overtly biological sciences of "race," such as anthropometry or eugenics—are part of the patchwork, and they also don't have to be accurate or coherent in order to be politically useful.

The pursuit of AI, then, cannot be deflated by simply exposing its epistemic forgeries or knocking down its models of the self. Here, I would like to borrow a point from Edward Said's critique of Orientalism. Said cautioned against seeing Orientalism as "nothing more than a structure of lies or of myths, which, were the truth about them be told, would simply blow away." Said argued that, perhaps counterintuitively, Orientalism is not an attempt at a "veridic discourse about the Orient," contrary to what academic Orientalists might say, but rather "a sign of European-Atlantic power" and should be analyzed as such.[16] Similarly, my premise is that AI isn't an attempt at a "veridic" account of human thought nor a technology for reproducing human thought in machines. AI is better seen as a mirror of the political projects of its practitioners and invested powers.

If AI is indeed an expression of power in that way (as Orientalism was for Said), then it isn't just "a structure of lies or of myths" that will "simply blow away" when exposed. My aim in this book is therefore not an exposé but a better understanding of how AI—as a concept, a field, a set of practices and discourses—works to flexibly serve a social order premised on white supremacy.[17]

AI AS A TECHNOLOGY OF WHITENESS

Having formed in the largely white military-industrial-academic complex, AI has served the dominant interests of that world. As we will see throughout this book, it has been a tool in the arsenal of institutions predicated on white supremacy. But beyond that, AI also reproduced the shape of whiteness as an ideology.

As an ideology, whiteness has always had a nebulous and shifting character. Who is "white," when, where, and how is historically a contradictory and dynamic affair, one that cannot be reduced to a simple phenotypic matter of "white" versus "nonwhite." Yet the shifting trajectory of whiteness as an ideology has been consistently steered by the aims of empire and capital. Whiteness has been shaped by the need to accumulate land, maintain the supply of unfree labor, and, in settler-colonialist societies, erase indigenous peoples. The nebulous and shifting character of whiteness helps it to flexibly cater to these tangible aims—and to do so while reinforcing, as projects of empire and capital always have, patriarchy and heteronormativity.[18] When overt white supremacy became less tenable as a result of resistance, a logic of white supremacy manifested in other ways, from how the bureaucracies of banking and housing operate to how "merit" is understood in the school system—facts that induce individuals to become more invested in an artificial "white" identity.[19] Whiteness is therefore simultaneously a fiction that lacks coherent grounding and a devastating reality that shapes tangible relations of power.

To understand AI's formation, trajectory, and function, I will argue that it should be viewed as a *technology of whiteness*: a tool that not only serves the aims of white supremacy but also reflects the form of whiteness as an ideology. AI takes the form of a makeshift patchwork; its nebulous and shifting character is used to serve a social order predicated on white supremacy.

This book thus makes two related claims:

1. AI is a technology that serves whiteness by advancing its imperial and capitalist projects. In the hands of a flexible expert industry, AI has been used to advance neoliberal visions of society, to sanction projects of dispossession and land accumulation, and to naturalize mass incarceration and surveillance. These projects are assisted by AI's epistemic forgeries, which include the notions that AI practitioners offer a "universal" understanding of the self and that their computing systems rival human thought.

2. AI performs this service by mimicking the structure of whiteness as an ideology. It is isomorphic to whiteness in being nebulous and hollow, with its shifting character guided by imperial and capitalist aims. In computer parlance, AI's

nebulosity is a feature, not a bug. Nebulosity has made this
endeavor amenable to reconfigurations in the service of powerful interests. Like whiteness, AI has been reworked to meet
new social conditions and challenges. And like whiteness, it
aspires to be totalizing: to say something definitive about
the limits and potential of human life based on racialized
and gendered models of the self that are falsely presented as
universal.

The linkage to whiteness sheds light on AI's trajectory. It
helps explain how AI gets continually remade, with each iteration bringing a contradictory mix of narratives about the self.
Relying on this nebulous and shifting character, AI has indeed
moved far from its overtly militarized 1950s context.[20] AI's projects have since been shaped by social movements struggling
against racism, economic inequality, state surveillance, and the
criminalization of migrants. Such movements have changed
mainstream political sensibilities; precisely the kind of change
that the "makeshift patchwork" of whiteness must cope with.[21]
So when AI reappeared in the 2010s, it became the purview of
"critical AI experts" concerned with issues like racial and economic injustice. With a progressive veneer, these critical experts
ended up serving the same imperial and capitalist projects—
notably, helping to sustain mass incarceration—but in more
subtle ways than AI's prior iterations. This was a case of adaptation: using AI's nebulosity to reshape projects and narratives in
response to challenges by social movements.

The linkage to whiteness also illuminates the institutional
fabric that holds AI together. The experts and institutions that
help to remake AI in the face of new challenges become invested
in it much in the same way they are in whiteness. In their professional and privileged milieu, "AI" can therefore be invoked

seamlessly. But as with whiteness, these investments imply that AI's incoherent underpinnings must remain invisible. As George Lipsitz puts it, "As the unmarked category against which difference is constructed, whiteness never has to speak its name, never has to acknowledge its role as an organizing principle in social and cultural relations."[22] And just as with whiteness, the act of questioning AI's universality or its ill-conceived basis exposes a kind of "white fragility"[23] on the part of those invested. These ties between AI and whiteness suggest that AI cannot simply be lifted from its historical and institutional context and claimed as a liberatory technology.[24]

Nonetheless, I try to highlight the dissent in AI's orbit, and the points where practitioners reneged on their service to empire. Some AI practitioners challenged their field's militarized agenda as well as its prevailing epistemic premises, including the very concept of "AI." Some of these dissenting streams were motivated by visions of world building and caring for others. These alternative streams are not without their problems, but their record is valuable for making sense of the present, and for gauging the prospects of a radically different science of minds and selves.

ORGANIZATION

This book can be read as one long argument, built in three parts, that moves forward and backward in time.

Part 1 examines the formation of AI and how it has consistently been employed to serve imperial and capitalist projects. Chapter 1 looks at the trajectory of AI from its formation in the bowels of the American military-industrial-academic complex in the 1950s through the 2000s. It argues that AI has been nebulous and contested from the start, but the endeavor's nebulosity has allowed it to be continually remade to serve a consistent set of imperial aims. Chapter 2 considers AI's forceful reappearance in the 2010s, at a time when Silicon Valley's vision of world governance through "big data" was under attack. The chapter looks at how the rebranded AI gave new gloss to this familiar vision, and how newly formed AI initiatives helped sanction long-running capitalist projects.

Part 2 examines AI's epistemologies and models of the self, situating these in a political context. Chapter 3 explores AI's recurring epistemic forgeries, such as the notion that machines exceed the capacities of human thought, and how these support larger political projects. Chapter 4 focuses on the "progressive" wing of AI commentary, which emerged during AI's rebranding in the 2010s. Through examination of debates on mass incarceration, the chapter explores how a new class of "critical AI experts" used progressive veneers to advance familiar agendas, notably to naturalize the prison-industrial complex. Chapter 5 argues that AI is a technology of whiteness, synthesizing the threads from earlier chapters. Through the lens of whiteness, this chapter sketches a picture of AI that ties together its imperial origins, historical trajectory, and epistemologies.

Part 3 examines alternatives to AI's dominant visions and epistemologies. Chapter 6 considers the prospect of an alternative science of the mind and body. In search for alternative formulations, it revisits dissident voices and streams within AI's orbit and analyzes their relation to imperial projects and the military-industrial complex. Finally, Chapter 7 discusses ways to resist and refuse the troubling phenomena outlined in this book.

Before continuing, a few clarifications. This book is not a detailed intellectual history of the academic field of AI and the computing practices found within it. My concern here is with the concept of AI and how it functions politically. And as far as AI's history goes, in this short book I can provide only an illustrative tour, not a systematic review.

This book is also not too concerned with robots or cyborgs. The leap to depict AI with such imagery is misleading. For one, the futuristic frame can mask the rather concrete political projects that AI serves. Furthermore, enthusiasm for the emancipatory potential of cyborgs and AI (and many things "cyber") when it comes to race, class, and gender has been deceptive, habitually leading to what Judith Squires called "technophoric cyberdrool."[25] Last, the focus on robots is out of touch with actual practices. AI can do political work, as we will see, without ever finding physical embodiment in anything like what popular depictions of robots suggest. Much of what goes under the label "AI" looks more like a convoluted statistical bureaucracy than robots falling in love, robots rebelling, or various associations of the line "I'm sorry Dave, I'm afraid I can't do that."

For similar reasons, I give little room in this book to predictable humanistic attacks on AI. In that genre, we have the psychoanalyst and neurologist Oliver Sacks, who once reprimanded himself for being awed by AI after a 1960 visit with its evangelist at MIT, Marvin Minsky. Upon reflection, Sacks wondered how Minsky, talented in music as he was, could promote such an impoverished view of human experience. For Sacks, AI was an insult to human dignity and depth, which at best could perform "Pavlov's puppet theater," and the understanding of humans as machines merely a ticket into "the empty labyrinths of empiricism."[26] On these points, I am with Sacks (and many others).[27] But staging a head-on collision between the humanistic literary imagination and the coldhearted reduction of human experience to information processing doesn't go very far in explaining how AI works politically and ideologically.

ENTANGLEMENTS

In more than one way, I am also implicated in AI, and not just as an onlooker. I worked in AI's academic arena during the early 2000s, long enough to appreciate the discursive sea-change when AI forcefully reappeared in the mainstream a decade later. From the beginning I have been both puzzled and dismayed by the field's ambitions and ideologies. It took years of distance and the help of work by others to articulate what intuitively felt disturbing.

This book arose out of a need to reckon with the political projects AI serves, while searching the worlds of computing, cognition, and biology for alternative perspectives. My own scientific work in computing and biology has been a slow process of shedding the dominant epistemologies of AI and related fields. My trajectory was shaped not just by critical inquiries into science and technology but also by the work of scholars and activists concerned with whiteness and white supremacy. They have given me some of the language to make sense of AI's irregular contours, as will become obvious.

I feel compelled to explain the emphasis of this work on race and gender, which may surprise some (particularly my colleagues in the sciences). The surprise may be heightened when it all comes from an author who is the beneficiary of so many white and male privileges. But for me, the simple truth is that whiteness is also white people's business—chiefly of those who, with George Lipsitz and others, want to forgo their whiteness.[28]

There is also a more personal motivation that illustrates a theme of this book. It involves my grandfather, who was born in Algeria and grew up in the coastal city of Oran. For reasons that remain unclear, but likely under the influence of some strand of Zionism, Roger Azoulay left for Palestine to join in making it into the State of Israel.[29]

Although my grandfather had basically internalized French colonialism—even declaring to the authorities that he was from "Oran, France"—he was hardly white in the eyes of the Jewish community he met in Palestine in 1949.[30] A dark-skinned man, some say a brown man, with curly hair slicked back with brilliantine, his kind were slurred with the Hebrew and Yiddish analogs of "negro." Perhaps to further bury the Arab and North African elements of his own identity, he harbored racist views of Jews "lower" than him in Israeli society's racial order: Moroccan Jews, Yemeni Jews, and later Ethiopian Jews—not to mention the non-Jewish Palestinians, the base of the hierarchy of privilege. When my grandfather wanted to marry the blonde and green-eyed woman who would become my grandmother, that was a problem. Her family, for one, did not believe he was unmarried and asked for certification from the French authorities. He complied.

My grandfather would never be white. But marrying my grandmother, having three light-skinned daughters, establishing a small but respected shop in his town, and wearing his racism against more marginalized nonwhites on his sleeve all got him closer. At the very least, all these made his nonwhite identity recede into the background in some contexts (after all, it was being recognized that even Ashkenazi Jews from Poland can be quite dark, especially under the sun of the Levant). Yet, in another twist, my grandmother—despite her phenotype—was

actually white of a lesser shade in the eyes of the European
Ashkenazi Jews that formed the elite of her society. Though born
in Palestine, she was a Sephardic Jew of Bulgarian origin; a lower
rank by the settler-colonialist coordinate system connecting Jew-
ishness and whiteness.

I share this anecdote to say that who is "white," when, where,
and how, is an elastic affair. It is an affair with real and devastating consequences, but the elasticity of whiteness is real too. To
recognize the elasticity is not to diminish the devastation; on
the contrary, it is part of seeing how whiteness is used to sustain
oppressive relations. Beyond my family's history, much of the
world seems animated by destructive and elastic concepts like
whiteness—including the ostensibly "technical" zone of computing. For me, unraveling the elasticity and situating it within
broader structures of power is part of learning to see the world.
This book attempts to understand how such elasticity capitalizes
on the language of computing via the prism of AI—an understanding that is meant to be in service of opposing white supremacy in all its manifestations.

Last, a note on relevance. While writing this book, I was
warned that "AI" is a fad that may be forgotten shortly after this
project's completion (maybe even before). If that turns out to be
true, let this book be another case study of the reconfigurability
of professional knowledge production. But my tentative sense is
that, like whiteness, AI strikes a chord with power, and that its
nebulous engines, poised for reconfiguration, will not be shut-
ting down very soon. At least not without challenge.

I

FORMATION

1

IN THE SERVICE OF EMPIRE

It is some systematized exhibition of the whale in his broad genera, that I would now fain put before you. Yet is it no easy task. The classification of the constituents of a chaos, nothing less is here essayed.

—Herman Melville, *Moby-Dick*

Cherish the name Artificial Intelligence. It is a good name. Like all names of scientific fields, it will grow to become exactly what its field comes to mean.

—Allen Newell

I n Herman Melville's *Moby-Dick*, Ishmael surveys the formidable scientific efforts to capture the essence of the whale. As Ishmael shows, however, these efforts proved futile. The science of cetology remains confused and incomplete, forever befuddled by conundrums such as whether a whale is a fish. The diversity of whales simply defies physiological and anatomical taxonomies; one cannot classify "the constituents of a chaos."[1] The whale that Melville's Ahab was after could not be reduced to its innards because the animal's significance lies elsewhere.

This chapter explores the origins and scope of another messy arena, that of "Artificial Intelligence," which I will argue also cannot be captured by technical taxonomies. What has counted as "AI" since the term was coined? How have both AI practitioners and interested "external" powers used the label? In examining these uses, I don't claim any essentialist definitions. AI is simply what practitioners working under the label produce; the work that appears in academic conferences and journals by that name; what companies buy and sell as AI; what newspapers write about as AI; and so on. I want to explore how AI is invoked, how it shifts, and what gives the endeavor its presumed coherence and force.

As I will argue, AI has been nebulous and contested from the start. The pursuit never attained coherence around a set of frameworks, methods, or problems, as critics would sometimes remind AI's advocates. Yet AI's nebulous character made it perfectly suited to reconfiguration to meet the needs of imperial powers. My argument in this chapter—and throughout the book—is that AI is continually being remade to be that which can serve empire. Those invested in AI have consistently reorganized their endeavor around an imperial agenda, especially when AI's coherence and powers were called into question. They presented AI as critical to American political and economic hegemony, using imperialist narratives that invoke racialized and gendered tropes. This practice transcends the epistemic classifications (e.g., "symbolic" versus "statistical") that are often used to narrate AI's history. So while the computing systems and epistemologies being served as "AI" change considerably, the political aims, surrounding narratives, and animating ideologies persist.

The historical tour that follows sets the stage for a look at AI's recent reemergence (the topic of the next chapter).

NEBULOUS FROM THE START

The U.S. military is always on the prowl for new war technologies, and by the mid-twentieth century, computing was of paramount interest. By the 1950s the idea that computers could automatically control weapons, surveil, and simulate strategic decisions—and do so through sophisticated calculation inspired by nervous systems, as cyberneticians had suggested in the 1940s—was familiar to high military ranks.[2] In 1958, for example, Colonel W. H. Tetley reflected on the merits of different computational paradigms in implementing surveillance and weaponry. Cybernetic feedback mechanisms, which work in distributed fashion, might be too brittle; Tetley argued instead for "more sophisticated solutions along the lines of Descartes' 'reasoning machine,'" or a chess-playing program developed by Claude Shannon, which are centrally controlled.[3] In Tetley's vision, military systems would become one "vast computer system under centralized control," where the controller is yet another computer. As Paul Edwards has argued, U.S. military elites thought that the chaos of the battlefield, and political conflict in general, can be made "orderly and controllable by the powers of rationality and technology"—powers which the computer imbibed.[4] AI came into being in this atmosphere.

AI would be entwined with psychology, another discipline that was no stranger to war, particularly when it came to notions of "intelligence." During World War I, for instance, the American Psychological Association decided to give "all possible assistance" to the U.S. government with psychology-related affairs.[5] The psychologists working for the military included the field's most prominent figures, such as Robert Mearns Yerkes and Edward B. Titchener. As part of their efforts, more than 1.7 million soldiers were subjected to psychological tests that assigned each soldier an "intelligence rating." These ratings were used to classify men into five constructed intelligence categories, which in turn determined whether soldiers would be deployed or discharged.

Thus psychology and computing, poised for war, were two streams that contributed to the formation of AI. But the question "What is Artificial Intelligence?"—and how it differs from the many disciplines already nestled in the war machine—has plagued the endeavor from the start. Yet the term "AI" captivated the Pentagon's planners, with whom AI practitioners formed an alliance. Practitioners then worked hard to present AI as crucial for American political and economic hegemony, capitalizing on their endeavor's nebulous character to do so.

The American logician John McCarthy coined the label "Artificial Intelligence" to describe a meeting (with all men attendees) he co-organized in 1956 at Dartmouth College in New Hampshire. McCarthy never defined the term explicitly and had in fact considered several options before picking "AI." He thought of using "cybernetics" but decided against it, because that would mean embracing MIT mathematician Norbert Wiener, who coined the term, as the field's "guru."[6] Cybernetics was already too close to the field McCarthy was trying to claim. Cybernetics was loosely structured around the notion of feedback—when systems react to their own actions—which was presented as a unifying principle for how both organisms and machines operate. Like many other cyberneticians, Wiener thought that these conceptions of feedback could help explain "intelligence." And like AI, cybernetics catered to war.[7]

McCarthy tried to distinguish his pursuit from cybernetics, and a term that flaunts "intelligence" could help. The meeting in 1956 was in fact his second try at gathering colleagues around the concept of "intelligence." In 1952 he had asked Claude Shannon, then at Bell Labs, to coedit a collection of papers on "machine intelligence," but Shannon declined, apparently because he considered "intelligence" too loaded a term.[8]

The Dartmouth meeting turned out more successful on this front. Claude Shannon had agreed to sign on as co-organizer and the meeting drew participants who would become prominent figures in AI, like Marvin Minsky (who co-organized the meeting). McCarthy's new label was undoubtedly a galvanizing factor. When McCarthy won the A. M. Turing Award, in 1971, the Association for Computing Machinery (ACM) noted that "it is ironic that his most widely recognized contribution turned out to be in the field of marketing, specifically in choosing a brand name for the field."[9]

Yet already at Dartmouth, "AI" was a contested label, with conference participants split on approaches and goals. On the meeting's fiftieth anniversary, *AI Magazine*, the official organ of the Association for the Advancement of Artificial Intelligence, reflected on some of the original disagreements: "In some respects the 1956 summer research project fell short of expectations. . . . There was no agreement on a general theory of the field and in particular on a general theory of learning. The field of AI was launched not by agreement on methodology or choice of problems or general theory, but by the shared vision that computers can be made to perform intelligent tasks."[10]

Conference participants came from different backgrounds and with distinct agendas. Ray Solomonoff, for instance, was apparently determined to "convince everyone of machine learning," which then was far from synonymous with AI and was quite different from the approach of logicians like McCarthy.[11] AI's boundaries were also already murky. A bibliography on AI compiled in 1960 by economist Martin Shubik lists "AI" papers alongside publications in fields such as game theory and operations research, which were also concerned with "rational" decision making and computer simulation.[12] This proximity to economics already anticipates demands for AI to distinguish itself from other disciplines.

Despite these ambiguities, early practitioners seemed optimistic about creating human-level intelligence in a computer program. The optimism was captured in an infamous memo of the MIT Artificial Intelligence Lab, one of the first academic AI laboratories (cofounded by Minsky), written in July 1966. The memo, authored by Seymour Papert, describes plans to build—in the scope of one summer—an artificial vision system that could recognize objects.[13]

Practitioners had some reason for optimism: the term "Artificial Intelligence" charmed the Pentagon's elites, and they poured money into the field. In the 1960s AI "became the new buzzword of America's scientific bureaucracy." Noted AI practitioners at MIT such as McCarthy and Minsky received unrestricted funding from the Pentagon. Reflecting on his relationship with the Pentagon's research agency at the time, ARPA (later renamed DARPA, or Defense Advanced Research Projects Agency), Minsky said: "It was heaven. It was your philanthropic institute run by your students with no constraints and no committees."[14] Another influential figure in AI and former student of Minsky's, Patrick Winston, noted that the agency "has always been run by individual princes of science"—individuals like Minsky.[15] This alliance with the Pentagon gave the field its superficial coherence and force.

The attention to AI's princes came at the expense of other fields vying for the war machine's attention, notably cybernetics. Heinz von Foerster, a prominent cybernetician at the University of Illinois, recalled that the phrase "AI" simply captivated the Pentagon:

I talked with these people again and again, and I said, "Look, you misunderstand the *term* [Artificial Intelligence]." . . . They said, "No, no, no. We know exactly what we are funding here. It's *intelligence!*" . . . At the University of Illinois, we had a big program which was not called artificial intelligence. It was partly called cybernetics, partly cognitive studies, but I was told everywhere, "Look, Heinz, as long as you are not interested in intelligence we can't fund you."[16]

In a similar vein, Stafford Beer, a major proponent of cybernetics, complained that "artificial intelligence," as promulgated by Marvin Minsky and his colleagues, was "a con trick"—a way to raise funds from the Pentagon while in practice "simply [doing] the sort of things we [cyberneticians] were all doing anyway."[17]

Indeed, the Pentagon has steadily sponsored projects under the label "artificial intelligence" from the 1960s to the present (see figure 1.1).[18] In the early years just a couple of elite institutes received most of DARPA's funds. Until the early 1970s essentially all of DARPA's AI grants were given to the Massachusetts Institute of Technology and Stanford University.[19] For a while funding was still highly concentrated: between 1970 and 1980 MIT, Stanford, and Stanford Research Institute (SRI) received over 70 percent of the agency's AI funds. This helped cement the alliance between the Pentagon and the burgeoning field's elites who, as we will see in this chapter, were often eager to enlist in the Pentagon's missions.

Yet optimism and money were not enough to resolve the fundamental question of what AI actually was as a field or even a concept. The spirit of early documents suggests that AI may be defined as the pursuit of "human-level intelligence" in machines, but this won't do. Not all researchers shared that goal: some explicitly rejected it; others thought it impossible. If not human-level intelligence, then, what is the endeavor about? Is AI a kind of science, and if so, what justifies having it be a separate "field"? Is it instead a technological project concerned with automation

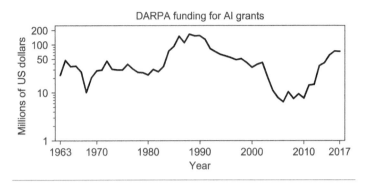

FIGURE 1.1 DARPA funding for grants categorized as "artificial intelligence" by the agency, 1963–2017. Amounts shown in 2017 U.S. dollars. Data obtained from DARPA via a Freedom of Information Act request. See Defense Advanced Research Projects Agency, "DARPA Artificial Intelligence Grants Records, 1963–2017 (Case No. 19-F-0077)," 2019.

and efficiency of existing industries? Or perhaps merely a fundraising strategy? These were the questions critics and even some AI practitioners would soon raise.

Accounts of AI usually deal with these questions by ordering AI's trajectory into periods based on the kinds of systems AI practitioners build (or by their relation to fields such as cognitive science or cybernetics).[20] In such narratives, AI begins in the "symbolic age."[21] In this period, practitioners argued that human knowledge could be captured in symbolic representations and rules, based on mathematical logic. Expert systems, developed in the 1970s, exemplify this idea. As the traditional histories go, this period was followed by a "connectionist" era, from the late 1980s to the early 1990s, in which neural networks dominated. In contrast to models of the "symbolic" period, neural network models try to capture statistical relationships between inputs and outputs fitted from data—they leave no place for the "knowledge engineer" of the symbolic era whose task was to translate what human experts knew into rules. By a dominant telling of AI's history, the present "age of AI" is a revival of connectionism where, thanks to better computers and larger data sets, AI's promise of delivering human-level intelligent machines could finally be realized.

Labels such as "symbolic," "logical," and "connectionist" are useful to understanding the narratives told about AI, but they are ultimately limiting. Such distinctions privilege technical aspects of computing systems over all others. Moreover, narratives that revolve around these distinctions obscure the diversity found in any given "period," for instance, "symbolic" and "nonsymbolic" systems have coexisted, and early computing systems combined logical and statistical elements.[22] Most important, these distinctions miss what seems to be a far more defining aspect of "AI": a remarkably plastic endeavor that was never held together by coherence of its ideas, methods, or problems, but precisely by what its nebulosity affords—an easy fit within imperial and militaristic projects.

As we will see, while AI's computing systems were changing substantially, its narratives and animating ideologies have been remarkably consistent.

A MILITARIZED, MANAGERIAL, SCIENTIFIC SELF

The conceptions of "intelligence" produced by AI practitioners reflect the military world in which they worked. As practitioners embraced their patrons' agenda, they extrapolated "general" models of the self from military needs. The field's early systems demonstrate this slippage between AI as tool for solving military, managerial, and scientific problems and as an attempt to understand the human self.

Perhaps the most celebrated early AI systems were developed by Allen Newell and Herbert Simon in the 1950s, who began working together at the RAND Corporation, a military think tank. The frameworks the pair would become famous for had the imprint of Newell's earlier work at RAND, which was in fact about people, not machines.

Newell and colleagues worked on "simulations" of an air defense control center responding to aerial attack. These were experiments with people who had to manage the control center under different scenarios staged by the experimenters. The subjects (either military personnel or volunteer college students) received information from radar and other sources about "enemy" planes and had to respond by controlling interceptor aircrafts and weapons (figure 1.2). Newell and colleagues designed different "task environments" for their subjects: scenarios that varied along features such as the number of attacking aircrafts, which presumably affected the difficulty of the task. The idea was that by studying the subjects' response in different task environments, one could understand how to better manage air defense centers.

Since people were carrying out this "simulation," the experimenters had to consider factors such as motivation. Newell and colleagues reported that they had to "motivate" their men (all subjects were men) and tap into their "intense motivation with the value of defending our country from enemy bombs": "These men, the three military crews and the college students, cherished the value of 'defense' as dearly as the rest of us, and perhaps more. But the bright and shining ideal can be tarnished by the vicissitudes of every-day life. We were not averse to refreshing the value. We told them how important the value was—not 'just the

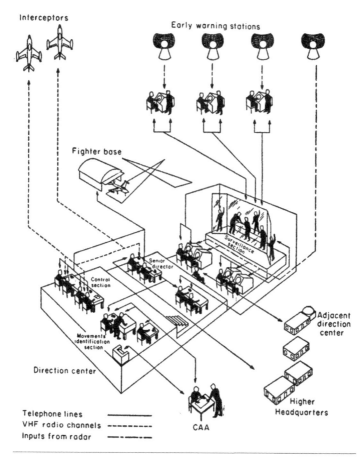

FIGURE 1.2 Figure from RAND report (1959) on the air defense center simulation.

facts, ma'am,' but with as much dramatic impact as we could muster."[23]

Newell and Simon moved from these messy simulations with people to more controlled ones with computers. Their basic idea—which aligns with Newell's air defense work—was that "man" is "an information processing system, at least when he is solving problems."[24] They build systems based on this idea, which they believed were quite the advance. In 1958 Simon famously declared, "There are now in the world machines that think, that learn, and that create"—and supposedly, "the range of problems they can handle will be coextensive with the range to which the human mind has been applied."[25]

Newell and Simon's most famous system, the General Problem Solver (GPS), exemplified their idea of "man" as "an information-processing system." As with the air defense experiments, "task environment" was a key concept. In GPS, a task environment is defined as the set of operators that agents may use and their possible outcomes, which were formalized using symbolic representations. Making GPS work was essentially about developing computing systems that can work with these symbolic representations.[26] (Note that Newell and Simon's work had little to do with the prediction and quantification that usually fall under the label "machine learning" today.[27])

Essentially, Newell and Simon took a framework developed around military tasks to exemplify universal "intelligence." And as Alison Adam has argued, they tried to validate this model of the self through experiments with all-male, likely all-white and economically privileged subjects—a milieu that could reflect the pair's understanding of "intelligence" as being primarily about abstract puzzle solving, whether in chess or in the control of an air defense center.[28]

But despite the professional success of Newell and Simon, GPS raised AI's identity problem that we encountered earlier. It remained unclear how this work distinguished AI from other disciplines that employ "rational decision making," notably economics. In fact, Simon's pronouncements about machines that "think" and "learn" were part of his address to the Operations

Research Society of America, an audience with many economists and statisticians. To this audience, he also presented his work as a tool for enacting managerial thinking: "We are now poised for a great advance that will bring the digital computer and the tools of mathematics and the behavioral sciences to bear on the very core of managerial activity—on the exercise of judgment and intuition; on the processes of making complex decisions."[29] Within Simon's address, there is already tension between AI as a quest to replicate human intelligence and as a technique for management.

A widely celebrated system that followed GPS, DENDRAL, would raise similar questions about whether AI was really "general" or a mere redressing of highly specialized calculations. DENDRAL's domain was chemistry. The motivation for the system grew in part out of the practical needs of National Aeronautics and Space Administration (NASA), which was sending vehicles to Mars with mass spectrometers onboard.[30] DENDRAL's goal was to help identify the chemical structures consistent with mass spectroscopy data. Using formal rules (elicited from chemists) that determine the spectra produced by different chemical groups, DENDRAL would search through the space of possible chemical structures and use heuristics to narrow down the possibilities. DENDRAL was considered the first of the so-called expert systems that would become synonymous with AI—at least for a while. Like GPS, then, DENDRAL was about effectively searching through a combinatorial space of symbolic representations.

Yet the narratives around the system were far grander. DENDRAL's developers also argued that AI systems would make the implicit knowledge of domain experts (like chemists) explicit, and that this process might illuminate the logic of science.[31] At one point, in fact, Edward Feigenbaum said AI's greatest contribution might be its "gain to human knowledge" by "making explicit the heuristic rules of a discipline."[32] DENDRAL was also described as "sorcerer's apprentice," a computer program that works "at the intellectual level of a chemistry Ph.D."[33] Here again, we have slippage from solving narrow problems to wild generalizations about human intellect.

Despite the praise, though, DENDRAL was not even considered AI by some practitioners early on. Feigenbaum, DENDRAL's codeveloper, reflected on the initial reactions:

> For a while [Feigenbaum recollects], we were regarded at arm's length by the rest of the AI world. I think they thought DENDRAL was something a little dirty to touch because it had to do with chemistry, though people were pretty generous about oohs and ahs because it was performing like a Ph.D. in chemistry. Still, DENDRAL seemed like a large collection of specialized facts about chemistry, with very little artificial intelligence in it.[34]

Such systems had to be constantly promoted in order to sustain the impression that AI is real and on the cusp of a breakthrough. One way to do that was to appeal to specialized hardware that, if delivered, would unleash the full power of the dominant computing paradigm (say, expert systems).[35]

Another way to try to make AI seem coherent was to exclude alternatives to the favored computing paradigm. Neural network models of the time, such as Frank Rosenblatt's "Perceptron" model, didn't fit the mold of symbolic computation that people like Simon or Feigenbaum viewed as AI. The Perceptron did not operate on symbols. Its aim was to fit a quantitative statistical relationship between a set of inputs and desired outputs. The Perceptron's mode of reasoning looked more statistical than logical. In putting together the book *Computers and Thought* (1963), an influential compilation of AI papers, Feigenbaum and his coeditors decided to exclude such neural network research because "those kinds of projects were somehow different" and considered "too speculative."[36] Reflecting on this choice later, Feigenbaum acknowledged that "AI is hard to define anyway" and that "most of the time it ends up being viewed as those things which the AI people are doing." AI was indescribable.

AI CONTESTED AND RECONFIGURED

Despite an alliance with the Pentagon that secured steady funding, AI's nebulosity and doubts about its practical utility led to attacks on the field. In response to criticisms, AI practitioners and their allies reconfigured their endeavor in order to show how each of its wings serves military needs.

One biting critique came from the philosopher Hubert Dreyfus. RAND hired Dreyfus for the summer of 1965 to write a report on philosophical issues relating to AI (though his overseers would later regret their decision and delay publication of his report).[37] In his report, Dreyfus compared AI to "Alchemy" and derided the field's proclivity for hype. He also offered several critiques of the epistemic foundations of the field, which he later developed into the book *What Computers Can't Do* (1972). Prominent AI practitioners viewed Dreyfus with some contempt, and the bitter responses he drew revealed AI's fragility.[38] But Dreyfus was also easy to dismiss as an "outsider" who lacked technical, scientific authority.

An attack that was harder to ignore came in 1973 from the prominent mathematician Sir James Lighthill, who was commissioned by the UK Science Research Council to evaluate the merits of AI.[39] The report he produced not only was critical of the field's apparent lack of progress but also questioned AI's coherence. The critique drew great attention; the BBC even hosted a television debate with Lighthill and prominent AI practitioners, including John McCarthy.

Some of Lighthill's arguments picked on the nebulous aspect of the endeavor. If what researchers mean by "AI" is simply automation of narrowly defined tasks, based on expert domain knowledge, Lighthill argued, then the endeavor has been "moderately successful." But, he asked, if that's the essence of it—not the pursuit of "general" intelligence—then how is AI different from other forms of computer-assisted automation? Lighthill claimed British computer companies were already pursuing the narrower goal of automation without calling it "AI," so why insist on a new label and discipline?

Lighthill's criticism was not well-received. Some AI practitioners have since argued that his report led to cuts in AI funding, and they acknowledged that they had to relabel projects that were previously branded as "AI."[40] At this point in the 1970s, U.S. military agencies were also arguably less enamored with AI. The early goal of instantiating human-level intelligence in machines did not require special justification; the utility to empire was obvious. But absent that, some doubted whether AI deserved the dedicated funding it was receiving from DARPA.

Practitioners then had to justify AI's utility to the agency: DARPA had requested a "road map" that would summarize AI's past accomplishments and set milestones for its future. In documents like the road map, AI practitioners carve the field into tracks (such as vision, natural language processing, and symbolic reasoning) and explain how each could advance patrons' aims. But this activity raises difficulties. For one, dividing AI into areas is challenging; it foregrounds the endeavor's murky and contested boundaries. Furthermore, DARPA expected researchers to commit to tangible goals and schedules, which can expose gaps between AI's image and its reality. Furthermore, the document was to be evaluated by George Heilmeier, a director at DARPA whom many practitioners perceived as hostile to AI.[41]

Discussions of road map drafts among the coauthors reflect these frustrations. In his critique of one draft, Allen Newell lamented that "what we are, in and of ourselves, is not particularly pleasing to him [Heilmeier], and that our characterizations of our field do not fill him with scientific ecstasy." He added: "All transformations of scientific fields by rhetoric alone, whether we are trying to create a sow's ear from a silk purse or vice versa, are equally impossible."[42]

It was not impossible, as it turned out, to reframe AI in terms the Pentagon found appealing. As veteran AI researcher Nils Nilsson pointed out, DARPA's "command-and-control" category was "sufficiently vague" to encompass much of AI, however carved up.[43] Moreover, AI's subfields were from the start organized around a militaristic frame: vision research to detect "enemy" ships and spot resources of interest from satellite images, speech recognition for surveillance and voice-controlled air craft control, robotics to develop autonomous weaponry, and so on. Indeed, already in the 1960s, AI's various research strands were articulated using military tasks such as "tactical commander's management aide" and "missile range picture analysis" (figure 1.3).[44] This militaristic frame was accompanied by a capitalist view of nature as a place for "resource extraction." Early AI systems, such as the Prospector, for example (developed at SRI), were meant to mimic expert knowledge of "economic geology" in order to more efficiently identify mineral extraction sites.[45]

POTENTIAL APPLICATIONS OF ARTIFICIAL INTELLIGENCE

Row	Task (1)	Significance DoD (2)	Non-DoD (3)	Difficulty Ill Defined (4)	Technical Risk (5)	Time Scale (6)	Program Requirements Level of Effort (7)	Confidence (8)
A	Aircraft records analysis	5	6	7	7	7	5	4
B	Economic/political models	4	8	2	4	3	4	10
C	Interactive scene analysis for cartography	7	3	2	2	2	3	8
D	Maintenance aids (near term)	8	7	4	3	4	4	8
E	Maintenance sensor-requirements analysis	7	5	7	5	6	5	4
F	Manipulators for dangerous tasks	3	6	3	2	2	4	8
G	Mapping and modeling of geographic areas	7	5	5	6	7	4	7
H	Missile range picture analysis	4	2	1	6	4	5	7
I	Political modeling	7	5	7	9	9	6	8
J	Remotely piloted vehicles	6	5	7	8	9	9	5
K	Resource exploration	7	9	2	3	5	5	9
L	Ship recognition	3	1	4	7	6	3	3
M	Tactical commander's management aide	9	9	5	4	5	8	3

FIGURE 1.3 Table from SRI report on AI and its applications, presented to DARPA in 1975. Tasks that AI could perform or help with are ranked according to their significance to the U.S. Department of Defense (DoD) or society (non-DoD), technical feasibility, level of effort required, and other considerations (1 is low, 10 is high).

Thus AI practitioners could rather easily situate their nebulous endeavor within an imperialist frame. Attempts to alternatively ground AI in an epistemic doctrine or practical goal always come to an impasse, even in the hands of ardent supporters. An SRI report in 1976, for example, defined "AI" as the craft of making computers "smarter" but then noted the circularity: "No one has offered satisfactory definitions of either 'intelligence' or 'smarter.'"[46] More than anything else, AI's systems are united by how they are narrated and justified.

AI AS THE MANIFEST DESTINY OF COMPUTING

What some AI practitioners perceived as a funding crisis in the mid-1970s did not last long. AI soon received more attention from the media and investors. DARPA's "Strategic Computing Initiative," established in 1983, allocated major funds for AI research. In 1984 the U.S. Department of Defense funded 71 percent of MIT's Computer Science department and 62 percent of its Artificial Intelligence laboratories.[47] By the end of that decade, as Paul Edwards has observed, "phrases like 'expert systems,' 'artificial intelligence,' and 'smart' and even 'brilliant weapons' were part of the everyday."[48] The militarized frame gave AI its apparent coherence and force, while AI practitioners promoted their endeavor through imperialist narratives with strong racial and gendered elements.

These justifications were needed because what AI meant had remained unclear. A survey sent to practitioners in the early 1980s resulted in 143 definitions of the term.[49] This continued to be a stone in the practitioner's shoe. When the Association for the Advancement of Artificial Intelligence (AAAI) formed in 1980, its president, Allen Newell, addressed AI's lack of definition in his first message to the society. The address is fraught with tension, as Newell deals with clearly controversial issues while simultaneously telling his audience there is nothing to see here. He begins by likening AAAI's formation to a "birth," which "according to some" is "always traumatic," "a shock to come from the womb to the world"—a problematic choice of words in a field dominated by men that was learning to cater to the Pentagon's violent agenda. But for Newell, AAAI's "birth" was not violent but "almost wholly benign," a welcome development: "In a world where not much is benign at the moment, such an event is devoutly to be cherished."[50]

At the very least, however, Newell acknowledges "AI" is not a benign label. AAAI's charter, he notes, merely lists the term as the subject but leaves "the semantics behind these terms . . . to us, the society to determine"—which "seems pretty undefined" and suggests "artificial intelligence is to be what we make of it."

Practitioners in this period continued to make AI into the tool that could advance U.S. hegemony. The very motivation for AAAI was essentially nationalistic, as was the framing around AI's impending breakthroughs. A *New York Times Magazine* piece in 1980 expressed optimism about having "machines that can think"—that can "understand" language, learn from experience, and even feel emotion—for such intelligent machines could scour databases to "amass knowledge about worldwide terrorist activities" and answer questions about "how terrorists in the Middle East, for example, are different from those in Italy or El Salvador." These machines, according to the piece, could also serve as personal assistants with the equivalent of a college education. Academics helped fuel these narratives: an MIT professor told the magazine there are "excellent chances" of having artificial intelligence by the end of the twentieth century.[51]

Even as AI was fraught with internal disagreements, government and military officials viewed it as a source of technological might. AI practitioners cultivated this impression by framing their work as essential to American empire while employing racialized, gendered, and patriarchal tropes.

The American reaction to Japan's state-sponsored AI project is a telling example. In the early 1980s Japan's Ministry of International Trade and Industry had announced its "Fifth Generation Project," a plan to revamp the economy using "AI"—a term that at the time was largely synonymous with expert systems. The plan included building specialized hardware for running computing systems of the sort Feigenbaum and colleagues were building.

Edward Feigenbaum, naturally invested in the U.S. expert systems industry, teamed up with the writer Pamela McCorduck to formulate a counterplan to Japan's project. In their book *The Fifth Generation* (1983), they portrayed Japan's plan as a grave threat to U.S. hegemony: "The American computer industry has been innovative, vital, and successful. It is, in a way, the ideal industry. It creates value by transforming the brainpower of the knowledge workers, with little consumption of energy and raw materials. Today we dominate the world's ideas and markets in this most important of all modern technologies. But what about tomorrow?"[52]

In weaving their own imperialist narrative, Feigenbaum and McCorduck paint Japan as the one with imperial aspirations: "The Japanese have seen gold on distant hills and have begun to move out." Japan's plan, more ambitious than mere takeover of the computer industry, was reportedly to "establish a 'knowledge industry' in which knowledge itself will be a salable commodity like food and oil. Knowledge itself is to become the new wealth of nations." While Feigenbaum and McCorduck say Japan's plan is too bold to be delivered on schedule, they urge it be taken seriously. Otherwise, Americans would regret even more bitterly their previous defeats by the Japanese electronics industry ("Have you ever seen an American VCR that isn't Japanese on the inside?"). If the United States does not act, they warn, "we may consign our nation to the role of the first great postindustrial agrarian society."[53]

Presenting the Japanese project in this way—an imminent threat that would result in either unimaginable loss or great American ascendancy—was a calculated move. When the book was being pitched to publishers, McCorduck suggested the following framing in a letter to Feigenbaum:

> We want to be darlings of the intelligentsia. How do we do that? We become Diderot, offering to involve—nay, insisting upon involving—every intelligent expert on every topic. We offer a hellish vision of what will happen if this opportunity isn't snatched away from the Japanese, but we also offer a celestial vision of what can happen if we meet the challenge. To wit, everybody gets into the act. We can echo Voltaire: "This vast and immortal work seems to reproach mankind's brief lifespan."[54]

To stage their drama, McCorduck and Feigenbaum employed racialized and gendered imagery. *The Fifth Generation*'s cover features a figure that embodies their Orientalist conception of Japan as imperial enemy (figure 1.4). The figure is fashioned after the Statue of Liberty, but the face of Libertas is replaced with a face wearing the traditional makeup and hairstyle of a geisha. While the rest of the book cover is flat, the geisha's face and neck are printed in embossed form, further emphasizing her foreignness in the body of Libertas. The figure's right arm still carries a torch, but the arm is robotic, not human. In this image, the Japanese enemy not only has encroached on American liberty but has done so by colonizing the body of the free, white, Western woman. In this way, Feigenbaum and McCorduck reproduce the patriarchal arc of white supremacist narratives in which the white woman stands for white purity and a masculine force—in

FIGURE 1.4 Cover of Edward A. Feigenbaum and Pamela
McCorduck's book *The Fifth Generation: Artificial Intelligence
and Japan's Computer Challenge to the World* (1983).

this case, the state's elite technocrats—must defend her from attack by a racialized enemy.[55]

For all their efforts, however, Feigenbaum and McCorduck's book revealed more about the wants and fragilities of the American AI industry than about Japan's plans. Acutely aware that skepticism of Japan's initiative could apply equally to the AI industry at home, the authors worked to deflect this criticism. They argued that the adversary's advantage lies, in part, in not being hampered by questions concerning the nature of AI. The Japanese, they said, do not waste time on "those arid little debates so beloved by Western intellectuals, debates centered on the question of whether a machine really can be said to think."[56] The pair's proposed way forward was self-serving: to thwart the "Japanese threat," one would need to stop asking questions about AI's foundations and instead invest in hardware specialized for the computing systems that Feigenbaum and colleagues were developing.[57]

Feigenbaum and McCorduck's propaganda campaign was largely successful in stirring panic among U.S. politicians.[58] As Alex Roland noted, while the American computing community did not necessarily take Feigenbaum seriously (some "derided Feigenbaum as 'chicken little'"), the political establishment mostly did. Feigenbaum testified to Congress about the Fifth Generation and "infected the legislators with his sense of alarm." Feigenbaum's language in his testimony is telling. He told Congress, "The era of reasoning machine is inevitable. . . . It is the manifest destiny of computing."[59]

Partly due to Feigenbaum and McCorduck's efforts, DARPA's budget for AI grew. The Microelectronics and Computer Technology Corporation (MCC) was also formed in 1983, an alliance between the government and computing industry firms offered as a way emulate Japan's heavy state-sponsorship model "without getting bogged down in the socialist mire of direct government intervention in the marketplace."[60] (Only three years later, however, the MCC would somewhat backtrack from the initial goal of implementing artificial intelligence on an "elusive" specialized computer.[61]) Also in 1983, George Keyworth, President Ronald Reagan's science advisor, wrote that the administration is committed to "maintaining U.S. supremacy" in AI and supercomputing, which is considered vital for "national security."[62] AI managed to remain both murky and somehow essential for American hegemony.

Leading figures within AI fostered this impression by participating in military projects, such as the Reagan administration's Strategic Defensive Initiative (SDI) (the so-called Star Wars project). In an infamous television address in 1983, Reagan laid the vision for SDI, asking, "What if free people could live secure in the knowledge that their security did not rest upon the threat of instant U.S. retaliation to deter a Soviet attack, that we could intercept and destroy strategic ballistic missiles before they reached our own soil or that of our allies?" AI, and software generally, was supposedly integral to this goal: the *New York Times* reported in 1986 that SDI's success depends on "the prodigious difficulty of developing computer software to manage the course of a battle."[63] Prominent AI practitioners such as Simon and McCarthy were also consulted about the prospects of SDI, and though they were not of one mind, their debate centered on the technical feasibility of the system, not its broader purpose.

Into the late 1980s prominent AI practitioners continued to consult for the Pentagon and offer new narratives about AI's necessity for its agenda. In 1989 DARPA convened a panel of academics to review its "Semi-Automated Forces" (SAFOR) program, a platform for simulating the battlefield. According to agency briefings, the simulated scenarios are meant to capture an "uncertain and lethal environment which integrates the maximum use of violence with the maximum use of intellect." The simulated battlefield is constructed from a Cold War mindset; "agents" in the program are modeled after "Soviet Regiments."[64]

In their report for DARPA, AI practitioners evaluated SAFOR using a mix of technical considerations (such as whether the agency chose the right programming language) and tactical ones (like whether the use of AI would achieve the military's aims in a cost-effective way). For example, Rodney Brooks, a prominent AI researcher from MIT, considered the advantages of scaling up the program so that soldiers may "experience some of the large scale aspects of battle that are not generated by, say, 300 tank simulators."[65] Brooks also considered the finances of the project, pointing out "that for significantly less than $20B it would be possible to replicate the current hardware to provide enough simulators that the whole U.S. Army could be involved in a battle simulation simultaneously." Overall, the panelists were enthused about DARPA's project. Douglas Lenat, known for his work on the "common sense" reasoning project Cyc, felt the endeavor was "only the second program . . . in almost two decades of such panel meetings, advising, and consulting, where my reaction has been 'I want to get more actively involved in this!' "[66]

DISSENT FROM EMPIRE

It's hard to deny that as a field, AI has catered to the needs of American empire. But some AI practitioners have come to question their field's subservience. For instance, Terry Winograd (at Stanford University) and Joseph Weizenbaum (at MIT), both influential figures within AI, have made it a point to refuse military funding.[67]

Weizenbaum's critique of militarism demonstrates our running theme of nebulosity: how AI's flexible character lets it bend, through collaboration between AI practitioners and patrons, to military aims. Weizenbaum delivered his critique in an article in 1985 for the magazine of Science for the People (SFTP), an antiwar and anticapitalist group formed in the 1960s (figure 1.5).[68] In the article, titled "Computers in Uniform: A Good Fit?," Weizenbaum explained that the military presents its aims in terms vague enough to cover every branch of AI, and practitioners then formulate all their projects to fit within the militaristic frame. As he pointed out, the three wings of DARPA's Strategic Computing program—the "battle management system," the "autonomous vehicle," and the "pilot's assistant"—were meant to capture "almost every branch of work in AI."[69]

Contrary to many of his colleagues, Weizenbaum rejected the idea that the military's vague rubric gives practitioners intellectual freedom to pursue whatever they like. (This was in fact one of the notions that SFTP worked hard to refute.) Rather, he argued, AI researchers sculpt their research so as to serve the militaristic agenda—so much so that students who want to pursue a different course wouldn't be able to find academic advisors.[70] AI is so beholden to its military masters, he wrote, that "what we get, of course, like little dogs sitting under the table feeding on the bones that our masters drop, very occasionally what we get is wristwatches and things of that kind. And, somehow, we think that this is a natural process." This dynamic, he continued, is "the fallout of gigantic efforts to make it possible to kill more and more people ever more efficiently."

Weizenbaum's critique is powerful, and his position as MIT professor and record of technical achievement within

COMPUTERS IN UNIFORM: A GOOD FIT?

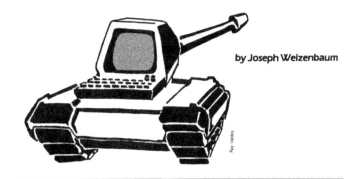

by Joseph Weizenbaum

FIGURE 1.5 Figure from Joseph Weizenbaum, "Computers in Uniform: A Good Fit?," *Science for the People* magazine, 1985. Illustration by Ray Valdes.

computing made it hard for his colleagues to completely ignore. Yet criticisms of militarism as such were rare and hardly well-received, as to be expected in a field bankrolled by the Pentagon. For one, the originator of the "AI" label, John McCarthy, rejected the notion that the U.S. Department of Defense could have nefarious ends in mind, such as surveillance. He claimed that "Weizenbaum's conjecture that the Defense Department supports speech recognition research in order to be able to snoop on telephone conversations is biased, baseless, false, and seems motivated by political malice." Furthermore, he added, the critiques of the Pentagon by the likes of Weizenbaum are harmful to the nation: "The failure of many scientists to defend the Defense Department against attacks they know are unjustified, is unjust in itself, and furthermore has harmed the country."[71] It was far more acceptable for practitioners to criticize "military applications" of AI (as opposed to militarism or imperialism), but here the objections were different. Practitioners questioned whether their computing systems would actually be useful to the military or whether computer-controlled weapons may pose a risk to the soldiers that wield them.[72] Others raised concerns regarding the "explainability" of AI systems: How would the military make sense of the actions taken by AI-driven weapons systems?

Despite the field's general subservience to the powers that be, in the late 1980s AI's nebulosity became a sore point again in mainstream discussions.

HAUNTED BY AMBIGUITIES

The alliance between AI and empire lent the endeavor temporary coherence. It helped make "AI" a commonsensical notion in circles committed to upholding American hegemony. Yet AI's ambiguous foundations continued to haunt it, threatening to call the field into question.

In the 1980s AI's nebulosity surfaced in the mainstream—an episode quickly labeled "AI winter." A newspaper article in 1988 described the hesitation on the part of software companies to invoke "AI" because of the "bad press" the label was getting.[73] Some investors, frustrated by the apparent failure to commercialize expert systems, blamed it on the term. One entrepreneur who had raised millions for an expert system company said the rush over AI was a "mass delusion" fueled by an ill-defined label: "In the 17th century, people said 'tulips' and the world went nuts. AI was a more virulent case because it was more difficult to define."[74]

Contrary to standard accounts of "AI winter," the activities that fell under "AI" did not cease in the face of this doubt. Even reports from the midst of so-called winter indicate that some companies simply "folded their AI operations into another division."[75] Moreover, expert systems, then advertised as the hallmark of "AI," were still being widely promoted for their commercial value. Financial firms like American Express were touted as some of the most successful users of these systems. Expert systems were apparently used for credit scoring, insurance underwriting, and portfolio management, among other tasks. Still, even within finance AI was being called into question. In 1988 a finance professor claimed the utility of expert systems for finance was greatly exaggerated. She asked, "What kinds of financial tasks would you entrust to a truly dumb (i.e., needs explicit instructions about everything), literal-minded, by-the-rules person, even one possessing flawless memory and endless patience?" The answer: tasks "where the consequence of an error is nil." Whatever expert systems can actually do, she concluded, could also be achieved "with much simpler traditional software."[76]

For practitioners, too, AI's nebulosity would sometimes be a problem. In the 1990s some practitioners wrote of "malaise" in the AI field and its "mistaken foundations."[77] Others wondered whether experts systems should even count as "AI." In an article titled "Is There Anything Special About AI?," computer scientist Roger Needham highlighted this change of heart: "Commercial AI is now big business, but AI itself is full of fundamental, unsolved problems; so what exactly is being marketed? Whether we wish to call it AI or expert systems, what are the scope and limitations of this technology?"[78] At this point, Japan's bid to build expert systems was also no longer considered a threat to U.S. hegemony. The *New York Times* reported in 1992 that Japan began giving its Fifth Generation Project software away for free because no one wanted to buy it (Feigen-baum was quoted as saying "no one is using the [Japanese-made] technology").[79]

AI's dominant computing engines, however, were about to get replaced.

PUTTING A NEW COMPUTING
ENGINE TO WORK

As we saw earlier, neural networks were not even considered "AI" by prominent practitioners in the early 1960s. These models, however, would come to exemplify the endeavor by the early 1990s. In terms of the distinctions that AI practitioners and cognitive scientists typically focus on, connectionist systems, based on neural networks, differ substantially from symbolic expert systems. Neural networks, of the sort that became popular in the late 1980s, do not rely on symbolic representations. Unlike in expert systems, in these connectionist systems there is no place for "knowledge engineers" that encode domain-specific knowledge. Instead, neural networks are trained to fit an input-output relationship based on a large set of examples, and the inferences they enable are statistical, not deductive.

Yet this new computing engine was plugged into old narratives about AI's importance to U.S. hegemony. The media reported the revival of the "quixotic science" of neural networks that could enable simulating the human mind on a computer.[80] And just as with symbolic approaches, neural networks were promoted by appeals to increased computing power.[81] In 1987 DARPA asked MIT's Lincoln Laboratory to assess the pros-pects of neural networks so that a "national" plan could be for-mulated. The report was positive, and DARPA soon began to invest in neural networks (though not always under the label "AI").[82]

Old imperialist narratives were rehashed around this new computing engine. After the Fifth Generation Project disbanded, the Japanese government announced a new decade-long project to build AI using massively parallel computation—and this time the focus was not on implementing logical reasoning with expert systems but on neural networks. The Japanese government offered foreign universities and agencies grants to participate, but the U.S. government declined. According to the White House, the Japanese state project had become "very practical, very commercializable," and the worry again was that Japan would "siphon off advanced American technology."[83]

Yet the incorporation of neural networks into the heart of the AI brand by no means signified a clean transition from a "symbolic" to a "connectionist" paradigm. As some of the field's more reflective practitioners have noted, a range of epistemic viewpoints can be absorbed into AI's militaristic frame. Philip Agre of MIT's AI laboratory has characterized AI as a "discursive practice": a way of telling stories that use concepts of intentionality and agency about computer programs.[84] Agre made efforts to "reform AI"—motivated by his critique of the field's prevailing epistemic premises (which I will return to in chapter 6)—but he thought these efforts had mostly failed: whenever he presented a computing system based on different epistemic assumptions, AI practitioners and their patrons at the Pentagon would quickly assimilate it into a pragmatic, militaristic frame.[85]

In the late 1980s the sense among practitioners that AI was in decline had produced new narratives about its importance—narratives that assimilate a wide range of computing systems and epistemic styles into a militarized frame.

IF IT'S GOOD FOR WAR, IT'S AI

One of AI's oft-repeated success stories, concerning its role in the Persian Gulf War of 1990–1991, shows that anything can count as "AI" provided it hooks into the requisite militaristic frame.

The Gulf War story revolved around systems that have little in common, technically, with the neural network models that were gaining media attention in the late 1980s. As the story goes, AI gave the military sophisticated planning and logistics capacities that helped the United States "win" the war, a claim repeated in triumphalist histories of the field. According to a U.S. Department of Commerce report in 1994, a planning tool (called DART) "solved the logistical nightmare of moving the U.S. military assets to the Saudi Desert" by helping to "schedule the transportation of all U.S. personnel and materials such as vehicles, food, and ammunition from Europe to Saudi Arabia."[86] This single application, according to Pentagon sources, has "more than offset all the money the Advanced Research Projects Agency had funneled into AI research in the last 30 years."

This narrative fits within a ubiquitous framing of the Gulf War as a "high-tech" computerized war (a framing that sidelines the indiscriminate bombardments that killed so many and destroyed civilian infrastructure).[87] This framing suggests that not only has war been radically transformed by computing, but everything around war, including its depiction, resembles a battlefield in which information-processing capacities and media savvy are as important as B-52 bombers.[88] Within this narrative, AI practitioners are simply one faction of war's technocrats vying for recognition.

But what do these narratives consider as "AI," and how is its significance articulated to invested powers? Daniel Crevier's history of the field, *AI: The Tumultuous History of the Quest for Artificial Intelligence* (1993), gives a paradigmatic answer.[89] The book is based on interviews with prominent practitioners, two of whom—Patrick Winston and Hans Moravec—reiterate AI's importance in the Gulf War.[90] In Moravec's telling, even e-mail, which he says was crucial for coordinating U.S. troops, grew out of "AI." The label's plasticity also shows when Moravec adds that U.S. military "planning and logistics also owed a lot to AI techniques. I mean simple things like: How do you pack a transport plane? How do you physically arrange the supplies? *That's a dynamic programming problem, which at one point was considered an AI problem. Also, scheduling is actually an expert-systems problem*. . . . when you face a complicated scheduling problem like the timing and coordination of Desert Storm, you need an expert system to solve it."[91]

The picture that emerges is of AI as a site where things that are useful to imperial aims are constructed. What the label picks out changes drastically, or is left undefined, but how it is served is remarkably stable: "AI" is that which can serve the American war machine, and what has served the war machine in the past can be "AI."

AI's circularity is also employed to naturalize the Pentagon's notion of an ever-expanding "battlespace," as Crevier's discussion shows. According to Crevier, Moravec lamented that even AI's most innocuous fruits can become weapons. Crevier concludes that "in spite of the desires of many in the AI research community, modern weaponry is constantly increasing its speed and savvy." By appealing to the supposed advances of AI, he goes on to naturalize the idea of autonomous war: "This evolution, in turn, imposes new, relentless constraints on field combatants, which make them dependent on information and advice provided by machines. The frenzy of modern battlefield activity often leaves the human link in the military control loop no choice but that of blind obedience to its electronic counselors."[92] There are several leaps in this argument. War is first presumed to be a computerized affair, one in which AI practitioners want credit for providing key tools. It is then taken as inevitable that more war technologies will be needed in order to keep up with this high-tech arena. The next leap is to presume war is nearly an autonomous game, with soldiers having to blindly depend on the computerized infrastructure that surrounds them. AI practitioners, by this logic, are victims of circumstance, having nearly anything they do get co-opted for military use. This circular reasoning becomes a way to argue for developing additional, "explainable" weapons in order to mitigate the opacity of computerized war. And computerized war, in turn, shapes how AI practitioners conceive of intelligence.

AI'S "KILLER APPLICATION"

As AI practitioners embrace the notion of computerized battlespace, military tasks continue to shape the field's models of self. This persistent slippage, between what is required to achieve military goals and what the human self must be like, is apparent in work on "cognitive architectures" from the 1980s. A cognitive architecture is an attempt to combine capacities that are generally investigated in isolation (such as vision and language processing) into a single agent. An influential line of work on cognitive architectures developed out of Newell's work on problem solving and culminated in the development of the Soar platform.[93]

Soar seeks to capture the mechanisms of general "human-level intelligence." It is meant to be the scaffold of computation

and representation that an intelligent agent would need to reason and act in the world—and do so in "explainable" ways. But
while Soar clearly embraces Newell and Simon's goal of realizing human intelligence in machines, cognitive architects have
argued that such intelligence is obscured when one examines
single tasks in isolation.[94] By their argument, building an agent
that performs object recognition separately from, say, language
processing will never produce general intelligence, which
requires integration of all these tasks. Hence these practitioners
looked for an application that could both justify AI's quest for a
"holistic" intelligent agent and demonstrate its practical utility.

What might such an application be? Soar's developers suggested that AI's "killer application" would be to use cognitive architectures like Soar to simulate "interactive computer
games."[95] "Killer" is not strictly metaphorical here: the proposed
application is to use Soar to simulate military operations in
enough detail so that the system can be used to train soldiers.
Soar would simulate the combatants, aircraft communications,
the battle terrain, and weather, among many other parameters.
It would also provide "explanations" for the simulation outcomes
in order to address worries about the opacity of computer-
controlled weapons. A version of Soar, TacAir-Soar, was built to
do this for the U.S. Air Force, which Soar's developers say dic-
tated the simulation: "All of the task requirements [for TacAir-
Soar] are set by existing military needs . . . and we were thus not
able to tailor or simplify the domain to suit our purposes."[96] This
articulation of the cognitive architectures program harkens back
to AI's 1960s promises to build "human-level" intelligence and
presents the simulated soldier as its ultimate manifestation.

But while Soar promises "general intelligence" like its ante-
cedent, GPS, there are also some important differences. Soar's
instantiations, such as TacAir-Soar, are as detailed as GPS was

abstract. To effectively serve the air force, great detail was needed; the battlefield had to feel "embodied" enough to convince soldiers in training. To achieve this, Soar had to abandon the symbolic purity of Newell and Simon's work and incorporate other approaches. This shows again how AI's systems morph to serve military needs and, in the process, take the military's aims as blueprints for what the self must be like.

In all these ways, Soar's trajectory mirrors that of "AI" broadly: a pursuit sculpted by empire's needs whose fruits aren't reducible to the epistemic distinctions that are typically applied to AI. But as we will see next, these distinctions are nonetheless used to sell AI's new iterations.

MIXING EPISTEMIC STYLES FOR EMPIRE AND PROFIT

As we have seen, when AI suffers setbacks, new computing engines, when situated in an imperial frame, can help bring it back into the limelight. The setbacks are typically overblown, though. The so-called AI winter, usually dated to the mid-1980s through early 1990s, is not reflected in funding levels for "AI" (at least from the Pentagon, see figure 1.1). If anything, it was the period following "winter" that was one of stagnation in the sense that Pentagon funding decreased and interest in AI did not seem to be sharply growing (though it was still mentioned regularly in the media). In this period, the need to mix epistemic styles—notably, to bring together "symbolic" and "probabilistic" approaches—became a theme of narratives about how AI could realize the imperial visions of its patrons.

In the 1990s probabilistic modeling and inference were becoming AI's dominant new computational engine and starting to displace logic-based approaches to reasoning within the field. These probabilistic frameworks, which crystalized in the 1980s, did not always develop under the umbrella of "AI" but also under headings such as "statistical pattern recognition," "data mining," or "information retrieval."[97] Regardless, these frameworks were being absorbed into AI's familiar narratives.

An article in *AI Magazine* titled "Is AI Going Mainstream at Last? A Look Inside Microsoft Research" (1993) exemplifies this turn. The piece omits AI's history of shifting in and out of the mainstream, claiming that "AI" merely had its "15 minutes of fame in the mid-80s," but that new developments in probabilistic modeling could put it back on the map. As always, there is slippage between AI as a way to understand the human self and as a tool for profit-making: the article suggests that probabilistic modeling could deliver an "electronic butler," thereby bringing AI into the mainstream.[98]

Such narratives often present probabilistic modeling in sharp opposition to logic-based approaches within AI, erasing the historically blurred lines between the two. This move is part of AI's propaganda, as it sets the stage for the claim that mixing these epistemic styles could fulfill imperial visions. A book by an AI practitioner written in 2015, for example, suggests that combining the disparate realms of symbols and probability is key to the development of what he calls "The Master Algorithm"—an algorithm that would learn the same way people do but then quickly surpass them. The power of blending these styles is conveyed through a heteropatriarchal metaphor: a literal "marriage" between the "Prince" of Logic (masculine and deterministic) and the "Princess" of probability (feminine and fuzzy).[99] According to the author, systems emerging from this union would have apparently "prevented a 9/11" and in the future would "help to dissipate the fog of war," power "the brains of military robots," and even boost the carceral state by turning policing into a "predictive" endeavor through application of techniques from "asymmetric warfare."[100] The Pentagon's dreams, all by mixing symbols and probabilities.

HOW EMPIRE SEES AI

AI Magazine's wish, in 1998, that AI would "go mainstream" was answered in less than two decades. By 2015 AI was everywhere, and how this happened is the topic of the next chapter. Before getting there, I want to briefly examine how AI is perceived and narrated in the 2010s, but not through the lens of AI practitioners, cognitive scientists, and others who are tuned to specific epistemic divisions. Rather, given the foundational role of the military in the field, I want to look at how others invested in American military power have come to understand AI.

In his book *Military Robots and Drones* (2013), military analyst Paul Springer devotes considerable space to AI and its military significance. While AI is seen as special—the apogee of military and tactical prowess, in a way—it is nonetheless presented as one technology out of several for achieving imperial aims. It is described as one of the "technological stars of the future" that could control drones and other automated weapons, outperform military experts (e.g., in reconnaissance operations), and even provide a way to read a person's thoughts by analyzing electroencephalogram signals. Springer surveys key AI laboratories, researchers, and companies and their connections to the military, essentially providing a field guide for interested military powers. The book contains biographical sketches of figures who, "even if they show no interest in creating military models," have "had a major effect on the creation of war machines."[101]

The list includes AI practitioners such as McCarthy, Simon, and Feigenbaum (indeed, several leading AI researchers have received civilian awards from the military).[102] These AI practitioners are listed alongside other figures considered essential for advancing militarized warfare, such as former U.S. secretary of defense Leon Panetta and President Barack Obama.

The discussion of drones, a focus of Springer's book, demonstrates how AI blends naturally into the established frame of automated warfare. Although AI commentators often discuss war instruments controlled by "intelligent" machines as a dystopian futuristic scenario, it has long been a reality, as military analysts such as Springer remind us. Drones have been employed by the U.S. military in Iraq, Afghanistan, and Yemen, among other places. As Springer notes, Obama's military strategy, like that of his predecessor George W. Bush, "has proven highly reliant on robotic platforms, including a sharp increase in the inventory and utilization of unmanned aircraft." The use of robotic weapons, says Springer, has been "a public relations boon to the [Obama] administration" since it allows "a demonstration of force and an erosion of Al Qaeda's leadership without increasing the strain on the military system."[103] Springer also describes the utility of automated weaponry for other states, such as Israel, the largest global exporter of drones. The Israeli military has used drones capable of fully autonomous flight for attacks in Sudan, Egypt, and Lebanon, and more routinely for surveillance, tear gas delivery, and other attacks in Gaza.[104] Israel also built automated "kill zones" alongside the Israeli fence enclosing Gaza. Many other states have been reported to use automated weaponry, including Russia and South Korea.[105]

Military analysts see AI as means to enhance this kind of warfare, which fits with 1950s visions of an "electronic battlefield." As AI resurged in mainstream circles, the label became a branding strategy for selling these kinds of weapons on global markets. Israeli drone maker Percepto, for instance, invokes "AI" for marketing, describing its products as based in "real-time machine vision and advanced AI technology." A representative of Israeli Aerospace Industries (IAI) has stated that "AI is at the heart of our operations," is "growing at a crazy pace," and is expected to be included "in most [of IAI's] systems within two years."[106] And although much of the discussion of automated warfare has centered on the notion of "autonomy," the extent to which such weapons are "fully" automated is immaterial—and typically impossible for observers (let alone the targets) of such weapons to discern. The salient point is that the "AI" label functions to promote an established weapons industry; an industry based on traditional military and economic might.

AI AS A NEBULOUS IMPERIAL TECHNOLOGY

In the 2010s, as in the past, AI figured prominently in imperialist discourses. In the summer of 2017 the Chinese government unveiled a plan to integrate AI into its military and civilian affairs, which provoked panic within the U.S. political and academic establishment. The Chinese plan led the U.S. government to consider limiting China's involvement with American companies.[107] In the same year, Russian president Vladimir Putin declared that whoever leads in AI "will become the ruler of the world." Following these developments, then U.S. defense secretary James Mattis called on the Pentagon to work more closely with Silicon Valley corporations in developing AI. By the following year the Pentagon had committed two billion dollars to building an AI center.[108]

AI is still framed as a power struggle among empires, such as the United States and China. *MIT Technology Review* published a "China special issue" in 2018 that evaluates the country's threat to U.S. hegemony. According to the magazine, China's dependence on foreign materials for making integrated circuits "could potentially cripple its AI ambitions." But "AI itself could change all of that. New types of chips are being invented to fully exploit advances in AI"—and China might be "reinventing microchips for the first time in ages." We have here another instantiation of the magical chip narrative we encountered with Japan's Fifth Generation Project in the 1980s. The current struggle over AI is taken to reflect, as it was then, a greater imperial struggle: the magazine warns that "China's chip ambitions have geopolitical implications," that such a chip could enable "new weapons systems," and that the chips are also "central to increasing trade tensions between the U.S. and China." If successful, China's hypothetical chip industry would make the nation "more economically competitive and independent" and thus pose a threat to U.S. "national strength and security."[109] Mainstream media generally equates AI "supremacy" with global hegemony, as a series of articles in the *Washington Post* show. One article refers to China and the United States as "two AI superpowers" at "battle for supremacy in the field."[110] Another piece states that "China's application of AI should be a Sputnik moment for the U.S."[111] Yet another article described China's national plan on AI as "the Chinese threat that an aircraft carrier can't stop" and suggested that beating China will require "a more nimble Pentagon."[112]

This rhetoric reflects what Edward Said has identified as the "cultural consensus" among U.S. intellectual elites in which "American leadership and exceptionalism is never absent."[113] In the nineteenth century, for example, American exceptionalism might have been justified by talk of "manifest destiny"—and as we have seen, AI practitioners echoed this rhetoric in the 1980s regarding Japan. But as Said observed, in times where overt colonial and imperial relations are less acceptable, "manifest destiny" is replaced by sanitized phrases like "world responsibility." The underlying logic, however, is the same: the United States must lead the world for the world's own good. AI is a convenient vehicle for this doctrine, usually in more sanitized form, as well as a site in which the relative gains made by warring empires can be assessed.

The idea that mastery of AI is an indication of national power extends beyond the United States and China. The British government, for example, formed a Council on AI in partnership with corporations, including Facebook, motivated by the premise that "a revolution in AI technology is already emerging. If we act now, we can lead it from the front. But if we 'wait and see' other countries will seize the advantage."[114] Likewise, the French government of Emmanuel Macron has invested two billion dollars in a national plan, and according to Macron, "if you want to manage your own choice of society, your choice of civilization, you have to be able to be an acting part of this AI revolution"—which means "having a say in designing and defining the rules of AI."[115] These discussions are even framed using concepts such as "balance of power," familiar from Cold War–era imperial discourse.[116]

The man perhaps most associated with American imperial strategy (and notions like balance of power) has also entered the ring of AI commentary. At age ninety-five, Henry Kissinger wrote a piece for the *Atlantic* titled "How the Enlightenment Ends" in which he called on the United States to make the study of AI a "major national project."[117] For Kissinger, the architect of bloody invasions, coups, and humanitarian disasters across the globe, AI represents something truly scary: the potential end of the Age of Reason. In Kissinger's framing—which is in fact the one promoted by the likes of Google—AI now exceeds humans in certain capacities, such as playing a game of Go, but does so in ways that are essentially uninterpretable. Kissinger wondered: Could this meaningless yet powerful force now govern the world? Kissinger even frames this possibility in the language of imperial conquest: "Was it possible that human history might go the way of the Incas, faced with a Spanish culture incomprehensible and even awe-inspiring to them? Were we at the edge of a new phase of human history?" In other words, might the world be swept by this "potentially dominating technology," relegating even powerful nations such as the United States to the fate of colonized people?

Kissinger's interest in AI is noteworthy insofar as it reveals how the concept aligns with the logic of American empire—a logic of governance that, since the Vietnam War, as historian Greg Grandin has argued, bears the imprint of Kissinger's worldview. And there is a palpable link between Kissinger's understanding of state power and his interest in AI. Kissinger, as Grandin observes, conceives of statecraft as an essentially aimless expression of power; an exercise of power for power's sake, unconstrained by greater values, goals, or pretense to meaning. Kissinger helped cast U.S. policy in that mold, and in doing so came to symbolize the circularity of American state power. "Kissinger himself has become the demonstrative effect," Grandin writes, "whatever substance there was eroded by the constant confusion of ends and means, the churn of power to create purpose and purpose defined as the ability to project power."[118]

It is easier to see in this light why Kissinger is captivated by a system like Google's AlphaGo, which learns to "dominate" humans at the game of Go by *action*—merely adapting to game wins and defeats—and making "strategically unprecedented moves," as Kissinger put it, apparently without any preset notion of meaning. In AI, Kissinger found a reflection of his own imperialist project: an endeavor molded by power, circular and empty.

In recent years AI reappeared in the mainstream and has continued to be shaped by American imperial interests. Like Kissinger, current think-tank intellectuals view AI as a broad force—not a mere weapon but rather a "general technology" akin to "electricity." While these experts hardly stop to scrutinize AI, their analysis is nonetheless partly correct. AI does function as a general technology; a tool that hooks into imperial narratives and modes of reasoning, without committing to any concrete instantiation or system. AI is a nebulous technology that is intuitively understood in the military's technocratic sphere.

Yet, in its recent reemergence, AI has spilled outside the world of military strategists and computing professionals and into discussions on matters such as racism and economic inequality. How did it get there?

2

IN THE SERVICE OF CAPITAL

I n the 2010s AI forcefully reemerged in the mainstream, rolling off the tongues of politicians, academics, policy experts, and journalists. Money flowed into a range of academic, corporate, and state-military initiatives on AI. How did it become so central again, and who stood to gain from this development?

I will argue that in this period, AI was rebranded to support a variety of capitalist visions and projects. AI's sudden reappearance temporarily diverted attention from systems of mass surveillance enabled by companies such as Google and Microsoft. The "AI" label refreshed these companies' neoliberal vision of world governance, which rests on centralized data collection. And in the hands of the flexible expert industry that these companies helped build, AI's nebulosity became a foil for neoliberal policies concerning labor, education, and science.

But unlike previous iterations, the rebranded AI became part of ostensibly progressive discourses, which surround a slew of corporate-academic initiatives. While these initiatives reference "ethics" or "social justice," they in fact sanction long-running projects of land accumulation and dispossession that universities and their corporate allies pursue. That is, AI's new progressive rebranding is not a real departure from the field's imperial roots but rather an adaptation to changing political sensibilities.

"AI" REAPPEARS, AN EXPERT INDUSTRY ASSEMBLES

Usage of the term "AI" spiked around the mid-2010s in both global and U.S. media (see figure 2.1). While AI drew great media attention several decades earlier, in the mid-1980s and early 1990s, interest then dwindled. In 2002 historian Philip Mirowski wrote that "AI has apparently lost the knack of blinding people with science, at least for now."[1] It was only around 2013 that usage rose sharply again, and within a few years "AI" seemed to be everywhere.

An expert industry quickly assembled around AI: universities launched centers and degree programs on AI and society, think tanks began writing AI policy papers, and the media started talking about AI nonstop. I use the term "industry" here to capture the flexible way in which many individuals, from distinct fields, organize around a new label. The experts show an entrepreneurial willingness to refit their endeavors based on emerging trends.[2] And so as new AI initiatives formed, existing institutes also changed focus. For instance, following a multi-million-dollar grant to study the "ethics and governance of AI," the Berkman Klein Center for Internet & Society at Harvard University reoriented itself, and scholars rebranded themselves as AI experts. The label's nebulosity facilitated this rapid uptake. Legal scholars specializing in copyright law, for example, would work on "AI and copyright"; artists, on "AI and art"; journalists, on "AI and journalism" or "AI and fake news"; defense intellectuals, on "AI and national security"; and so forth.

The expert industry embraced a purely technical narrative for AI's sudden importance. According to this narrative, because of increased computing power, larger data sets, and

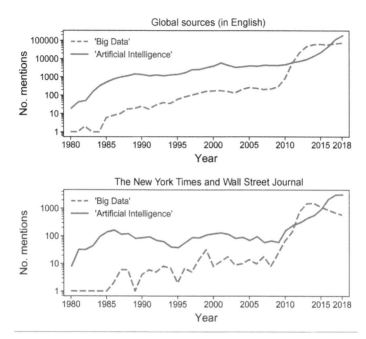

FIGURE 2.1 *Top*, number of mentions of the terms "big data" or "artificial intelligence" in global media sources (published in English), 1980–2018. *Bottom*, number of mentions in the *New York Times* and *Wall Street Journal*, used as proxies for U.S. mainstream media and business media. Note logarithmic *y*-axis scale. Source: Factiva.

algorithmic advances (typically related to neural networks), AI is finally realizing its promise to radically transform society—and therefore must be managed. This explanation is never fleshed out; it is simply assumed to be true and is in fact recycled from prior iterations of AI.[3] While such a technical story could never account for the social significance of AI, even in the narrowest terms this narrative fails to account for the label's recent uses. "AI" is applied to projects that use well-worn computing techniques and do not depend on either recent developments in parallel computing or particularly large data sets or neural networks.[4] It is used interchangeably with terms such as "machine learning," "big data," or even "algorithm." The term's nebulosity allowed virtually any decision made using a computer to be described as AI, depending on the context.

With the understanding that AI is a malleable technology of power, it is important to explore the political context around its dramatic rise.

A DIVERSION FROM
MASS SURVEILLANCE

In July 2013 Edward Snowden made public what would become known as the "Snowden revelations": detailed documentation about the systems of global mass surveillance operated by the National Security Agency (NSA). The general outline of the systems described in these documents was not news to journalists who have covered the American national security state. But the vastness of these systems shocked many citizens. Snowden's leaks also revealed the complicity of major platform companies in surveillance projects.[5] Microsoft installed a backdoor in its Skype messaging system for the NSA, while companies including Google, Facebook, Yahoo, Apple, and AOL allowed the agency to eavesdrop on their servers as part of the PRISM program.[6] While it is probably a stretch to say these findings radicalized a broad American public against mass surveillance, Snowden's disclosures did change mainstream political commentary and prompted worldwide protests.

The disclosures are relevant here because they contributed to the broad disillusionment with the platform companies that would soon follow. They made vivid the power of networked computing systems to collect vast amounts of personal data. They also demonstrated how these systems are antidemocratic and prone to co-option by governments. The global antisurveillance protests catalyzed by Snowden's disclosures foretold the downfall of Silicon Valley's "big data" doctrine: the idea that having more data collected by the likes of Google is universally beneficial. Scholars and media commentators began referring to Silicon Valley's agenda as "surveillance capitalism," arguing that Google's practices exemplify the term.[7] That platform companies were exploiting their users' data for profit and political gain became commonsense. The proliferation of narratives about "Russian interference" in the U.S. presidential election of 2016—which identified Facebook and Twitter as major culprits—only reinforced this notion.[8] Once viewed as somewhere between democratizing forces and benign entities, platform companies were now seen as potentially dangerous political actors.

But the term "artificial intelligence," with its nebulous air, refreshed the narratives about big data that Snowden's revelations began disrupting in 2013. "AI" is suggestive of futuristic machines that may do things better than people; it is a more cerebral term than "big data," which, following Snowden, conjures up the sense of centralized systems that collect data generated by us, the "users." The appeal to AI helped to mask how platform companies both enable and profit from mass surveillance and behavior modification.

Indeed, when AI catapulted into the mainstream in the early 2010s, it was often framed, as in earlier iterations, around building machines that surpass human cognition—but mostly kept apart from discussions of surveillance and the national security state. A *New York Times* report on Google's acquisition of the startup DeepMind—published in January 2014, less than a year after Snowden went public—emphasizes how DeepMind's "artificial intelligence technology" could further boost Google's "world domination of search." The article does not link search (or AI) to surveillance nor the Pentagon. It ends with a quote from DeepMind's cofounder about humanity's downfall in the face of AI: "If a super-intelligent machine (or any kind of super-intelligent agent) decided to get rid of us, I think it would do so pretty efficiently."[9]

This false separation of AI from mass surveillance could not last long, however, and the consequences of Snowden's disclosures for the rebranded AI were not lost on those cheering for the national security state. A *Washington Post* article in 2019 lamented the Pentagon's recent difficulties in recruiting engineers to work on AI, which is considered "essential for U.S. security." But happily, the author adds, "the Pentagon, after some false starts, is launching a creative effort to win the trust of suspicious software engineers who grew up in the shadow of Edward Snowden's revelations."[10]

But AI's reappearance did more than temporarily divert attention from a public confrontation with mass surveillance. As we will see, the major platform companies employed the term as fresh gloss for their usual political agenda.

REBRANDING AI TO ADVANCE GOVERNANCE BY THE NUMBERS

Corporations played a major role in staging AI's reappearance. They capitalized on AI to promote their vision of world governance—a vision that depends on mass surveillance. Consider the beginning of AI's recent boom, around the mid-2010s. By this time, "machine learning" and "big data" were popular catch-phrases. One could read popular commentary about the powers of "big data," collected and analyzed by platform companies, without encountering "AI."[11]

When the AI label resurfaced, it essentially stood for the same pursuits that were previously tagged by "big data." Businesses seized on this rhetorical flexibility. The Global Big Data Conference, a large-scale meeting of the corporate computing world established in 2013, was renamed within a few years the Global Artificial Intelligence Conference. Speakers at the 2018 conference were described as "AI pioneers," representing platform companies, consulting firms, banks, and pharmaceutical companies. According to the conference brochure, participants would learn "how to organize your AI team and toolset so you can increase productivity whilst democratizing the knowledge produced" and "construct an effective AI strategy."[12] "AI" here simply tags these companies' existing agendas.

The major platform companies facilitated the rebranding in part by launching new "AI" laboratories.[13] In the media, this has been portrayed as a battle for dominance in a burgeoning field, with headlines such as "Apple Lags Behind Google and Facebook on AI" or "Facebook's Race to Dominate AI."[14] These companies, however, merely hired academics who work on statistical data analysis to head the new laboratories. Many of these researchers would not have even identified as AI researchers prior to this move.[15] They worked in academic subfields related to statistical data analysis that companies like Google, Microsoft, and IBM were enmeshed with well before "AI" reappeared.[16] Tellingly, in 2018 Google changed the name of its entire research division from "Google Research" to "Google AI," while making clear that it will be continuing its usual activities.[17]

In short, "AI" signaled the continuation of centralized data collection, so that more aspects of life can be subject to quantifiable rule. Legal scholar Alain Supiot has called this vision "governance by the numbers."[18] Governance by the numbers works by first defining quantitative metrics and imposing them on different spheres of life, and then using these metrics to "program" behavior through rankings and benchmarks. The aspiration, as Supiot writes, is to reduce the "diversity of beings and things" so as to create "a total market, which seeks to encompass all of humankind and all the products of the planet."

The embrace of AI is a boon to governance by the numbers, since the systems that are newly celebrated as "AI" cannot work without clear metrics to optimize. The digital instantiation of governance by the numbers is obvious; it manifests in the ways platform companies build elaborate profiles of individuals and communities and use that information for profit and behavior modification. These companies have the data and computing power necessary to enact such quantified rule. And the appeal to AI helps carry their governance by the numbers into new arenas.

Science is one such arena. The long-standing effort to reorganize science as a neoliberal "marketplace of ideas" has paved the way for platform companies to intervene.[19] In this vision of governance by the numbers, scientific projects, articles, data sets, scientists, and institutions would be ranked in real time through a slew of market signals or metrics—fostering the illusion that scientific truth is universally quantifiable. Platform companies have been promoting this vision, and appeals to AI are part of the strategy.[20] For if supposedly superhuman AI systems can guide or replace scientists, then metrics that quantify "good" science will be needed—otherwise, what would AI systems "maximize"? Companies like Google are in the business of defining these metrics via platforms such as Google Scholar. Other platform companies are also using their computational capital to gain influence within science. The Chan-Zuckerberg Initiative, a for-profit company cofounded by Facebook's Mark Zuckerberg and his wife Priscilla Chan, recently acquired a startup company whose "AI" software supposedly "helps scientists read, understand and prioritize millions of scientific papers" by analyzing these metrics.[21]

As platform companies promote this vision of science, the metrics they collect are being held up as indicators of scientific worth. *MIT Technology Review*, for instance, claimed that Google was having an "annus mirabilis" and that its "surging investment in machine learning" launched the company "into the scientific stratosphere." The evidence for this was that Google researchers published over two hundred papers in 2016 alone, some in prestigious journals such as *Nature*.[22] Other analyses go beyond this to suggest that AI may even replace scientists. What comes through clearly in these discussions is the notion that scientific insight can be ranked and optimized; that AI may subsequently navigate science better than people; and that companies such as Google are poised to build such powerful AI.

AI's rebranding was an opportunity for companies to privatize more scientific research. Google and Microsoft have used the frenzy around AI to file patents on commonly used algorithmic techniques.[23] The label's nebulosity makes for broad patents: a MasterCard–owned company filed for a patent on a "Method for Providing Data Science, Artificial Intelligence and Machine Learning As-A-Service." AI made for hazy patents in the past, too: a patent in 1985, simply titled "Artificial Intelligence System," claimed "an artificial intelligence system for accepting a statement, understanding the statement and making a response to the statement based upon at least a partial understanding of the statement." This isn't far off from a 2017 patent on an "AI learning method and system" that "may transmit a question to users through a messaging service and may acquire learning data for the AI through reactions of the user to the transmitted question."[24] And as AI's rise recharges the chase after patents, the outcomes are interpreted as signals of scientific worth: one investment site noted that Microsoft is leading the current AI patent spree, having filed more than two hundred "AI-related" patents since 2009, while companies like Apple are "widely criticized for being slow" to file.[25]

In all these ways, AI's recent iteration has reinvigorated projects that were already in motion.[26]

THE AI EXPERT INDUSTRY'S CAPITALIST VISIONS

We have seen how AI's rebranding, facilitated by the major platform companies, helped serve a variety of corporate interests. Yet AI's appearance in so many arenas is not simply the result of powerful corporations working in isolation. It also required journalists, academics, and policy experts to take up the mantle of AI.

Riding the wave that they have helped to make, these burgeoning experts offer analyses of AI's social consequences in a growing collection of books and articles. In these works, the experts often use AI to advance neoliberal programs concerning labor, education, and other arenas.

This is perhaps clearest in discussions of AI and the economy. A theme of these discussions is that AI will make everyone better off by reducing the burdens of labor. The experts, however, generally foresee difficulties in the process. Automation by AI may lead to unemployment, for example, leaving people poor and marginalized. The transition to AI-driven society must therefore be managed, and AI experts have long recognized that this is a political problem, not a technical one. They present ways to navigate the transition that avoid wealth redistribution, taxation, or other policies that potentially threaten capital accumulation.

For example, in his book *Humans Need Not Apply: A Guide to Wealth and Work in the Age of Artificial Intelligence*, Jerry Kaplan discusses strategies for dealing with the job loss that he thinks AI will cause. Job loss is framed as an undesirable byproduct of technological progress, a loss that AI will more than compensate for according to Kaplan. He writes: "We don't need to take from the wealthy and give to the less fortunate," since the economy is "continually expanding. . . . So all we need to do is distribute the benefits of future growth more widely, and the problem will slowly melt away." How, then, to distribute the fruits of growth? Here, Kaplan borrows "free-market solutions" from economist Milton Friedman. Kaplan's plan includes cutting taxes for corporations using a new "objective" metric and restructuring Social Security, which he refers to as a "monolithic and opaque centralized system of investment" that limits individual choice.[27]

This understanding of a "post-AI" economy is echoed in a recent book by MIT physics professor Max Tegmark, *Life 3.0: Being Human in the Age of Artificial Intelligence*.[28] Tegmark explains how AI will transform virtually all aspects of life. Drawing on the work of neoliberal economists, he argues that an "AI-driven economy would not only eliminate stress and drudgery and produce an abundance of everything we want today" but even bring "wonderful new products and services that today's consumers haven't yet realized that they want." AI, he speculates, may give rise to superhuman artificial beings who'd depart our planet and settle across the galaxy. The futuristic tone is set aside, however, when it comes to labor issues. For one, Tegmark gives detailed advice on "career choice" for young people who want to avoid being replaced by intelligent machines: it is safer to become an entrepreneur, lawyer, doctor, or scientist (areas he considers not yet mastered by AI). He acknowledges that income inequality has been rising but adopts the usual explanation of neoliberal economists: technological progress inevitably rewards "the educated" who can compete in the market, and inequality is a byproduct. Tegmark notes that while some "on the left" attribute inequality to things like "globalization and/or economic policies such as tax cuts for the rich," the main cause is really "technology." And, like Kaplan, he thinks AI will more than compensate for the inequity.[29]

AI experts similarly repackage neoliberal positions in other arenas, such as education. Christof Koch, for instance, a noted neuroscientist, wrote in the *Wall Street Journal* that looming superintelligent AI will require people to augment their brains to stay relevant. While some may opt for "education" to keep afloat, Koch suggests that "training (and retraining) people takes time," and not everybody could switch from driving trucks (a vanishing profession, he presumes) to one of the jobs that AI experts consider more secure.[30] In his book *Superintelligence: Paths, Dangers, Strategies*, the philosopher Nick Bostrom likewise discounts education as "probably subject to diminishing returns," an ineffective means of acquiring the "superintelligence" demanded in the age of AI.[31]

Consistently, then, AI serves as pretext for run-of-the-mill neoliberal ideology. Visions of a purportedly transformative AI-driven world reduce to familiar tropes about individuals needing to adapt to a dynamic global market.

These capitalist visions rest on the idea that AI will provide an unmatched form of "slave" labor.[32] It would supposedly "free" people from their own labor, if only we let it. Although experts tend to refer to the "slave" in generic terms, or link it in passing to slavery in antiquity, the slave metaphor is always racial and gendered—especially when invoked by white professionals in North America. The persistent and unselfconscious appeals to slavery highlight the whiteness of the AI expert industry, and the racial capitalism that animates experts' visions. Several commentators, for example, have embraced the vision of so-called digital Athens in which AI will provide the "slave labor" that powered ancient Greek society.[33] Commentaries from the 1980s have likewise presented AI as a powerful "slave" that could end the need for human labor if the proper social policies are adopted.

The arc of such narratives is captured by noted AI practitioner Nils Nilsson's essay "Artificial Intelligence, Employment, and Income," part of a collection of essays published in 1986 on the impacts of AI. Nilsson begins with economist John Maynard Keynes's famous 1933 forecast that the working hours of the future will shrink owing to technological advances. Like other commentators in the collection, Nilsson sees AI as a powerful "mechanical slave" that could make Keynes's promise a reality.[34] Drawing on the work of well-known economist and AI practitioner Herbert Simon, Nilsson states that technology has always improved the human condition, and that AI will provide a labor-free source of "income," thus making everybody rich.[35] Getting in the way of this process, Nilsson says, would be "unfair to humanity," a hindrance to "our attempts to re-enter Paradise."[36]

Much of Nilsson's essay is devoted to thinking of ways to get people to accept this "slave" labor–driven world. Nilsson worries, for instance that people may dislike AI-induced unemployment or reject a human labor-free world. He therefore calls for short-term policies aimed at "alleviating the misery and poverty of the unemployed" but makes clear that state "welfare" programs or redistribution of wealth would be wrongheaded responses. Likewise, he urges that taxes on automation not be too high, lest they "destroy the incentive to automate." His essay is peppered with other policy prescriptions, such as work retraining is important, but "we must not assume that everyone who now holds a blue-collar or middle-management job can become a computer scientist."[37] Like recent commentators, Nilsson suggests funneling people toward jobs such as counseling that require the human touch machines currently lack. But his concern is that in the longer term, people simply wouldn't be able to get used to being "rich." He therefore urges that they be taught literature and the arts to fill the new leisure time. Such coping will be necessary, he concludes, for the transition to AI-driven society is inevitable: nations who lag in adopting AI will be punished by laws of the market.[38]

For decades, then, experts have promised that AI is on the brink of delivering capitalist utopia, which they narrate using racial metaphors. They use this promise to argue against threats to capitalism. Social movements, however, have drawn enough attention to injustices that operate across race, gender, and class lines to make these cheerful capitalist visions less tenable. The expert industry eventually had to adjust.

AI'S PROGRESSIVE VENEER AND
A WEB OF PARTNERSHIPS

Although AI formed in the depths of the military-industrial complex, the rebranded AI of the 2010s spills far outside that world. Present-day discourse includes not only voices from the military-industrial sphere that speak in futuristic imperial tones but also commentators who present themselves as critics of corporate power and advocates for social justice. These include academics from the social sciences, law, and other disciplines who have begun writing about AI in the 2010s. Their work is frequently framed around the "ethics" and "fairness" of AI and its impact on matters such as racial and gender discrimination.

With this progressive veneer, a web of AI partnerships grew across academic, corporate, and state sectors. All partners share the ideological commitment to AI as a coherent and powerful force that must be managed. They also view partnerships among so-called stakeholders—corporations, the military, universities, nonprofit organizations, and an amorphous "public"—as universally beneficial, a way to ensure AI is put to good use. A variety of initiatives that imbibe this model have emerged at elite universities, including Harvard, MIT, Stanford, New York University, and Carnegie Mellon.[39] These centers publish prolifically on AI's consequences for numerous social and political arenas.[40]

A prominent institute in this space is AI Now, founded in 2017 at NYU and backed by Microsoft, which describes its focus as "social and cultural issues arising from data-centric technological development." At first glance AI Now seems to offer a different discourse on AI compared with that of computing practitioners and entrepreneurs. The institute's leaders speak of racism and sexism and even labor issues; not typical emphases within Silicon Valley's corporate sphere. But while AI Now presents itself as an "independent" counter to major platform companies, it is nourished by those very corporations. Several of the institute's core members are either current or former employees of Google or Microsoft, and Google employees serve on the advisory board.[41] Other institutes in this space have similar corporate ties.[42]

AI Now was founded by former members of the Data & Society Center (also at NYU and backed by Microsoft), which had focused on social issues concerning "big data." In AI Now's

founding event, academic social scientists appeared alongside
representatives of Google, Facebook, and Intel, as well as White
House representatives. In such ceremonies, each sector plays a
part: academics make the endeavor look critical; major corporations give it money, power, technical bona fides; and the state
lends an air of policy cachet. The very creation a new center
around a new label—"AI" over "big data"—contributes to the
sense of a sharp break from the past. The suddenness and urgency
of what we have seen to be in part a corporate rebranding maneu-
ver is even inscribed into AI Now's name. By embracing AI as
a transformative force made possible by technical breakthroughs,
such centers are just rehearsing their sponsors' narrative.[43]

Funding structures facilitate this convergence between corporate patrons and their supposed academic critics. The "non-
profit industrial complex," as the INCITE! collective called it,
works to "manage and control dissent in order to make the world
safe for capitalism."[44] So when nonprofits, often backed by the
likes of Google and Microsoft, began offering multimillion-
dollar grants to study how AI will transform society—and
how partnerships with corporations can make that transformation "ethical"—academics were induced to accept the premise.
And while research that challenges the basic premise is unlikely
to win support, the institutes poised to receive these large
grants are already aligned with the program of managing dissent to protect capitalism.

As a result, both the large platform companies and the critics they bankroll are invested in AI's rebranding and its potential to benefit everyone. AI Now says, for example, that AI has
"extraordinary potential upsides, from reducing worldwide
energy consumption and addressing climate change," and now
"we still have an opportunity to influence the design and use of

these tools for good."[45] The web of partnerships would allegedly advance this unspecified "good."

But the reality that these partners create on the ground looks rather different.

PARTNERS IN DISPOSSESSION AND LAND ACCUMULATION

I have thus far focused on AI's rebranding and the changing discourse around it. My argument is that the expert industry uses AI to advance a variety of capitalist visions and projects, and that the web of partnerships created around AI caters to corporate interests.

But while these new partnerships are described with fuzzy abstractions, like doing "good," they in fact assist concrete developments. The rebranded AI's initiatives sanction tangible projects of dispossession and conversion of land into capital, projects that universities and their new partners in AI have long pursued.

To bring these projects into focus, it is helpful to trace the web of partnerships behind the major AI initiatives. MIT's Schwarzman College of Computing, launched in September 2019, is an instructive case. The new college was named after Stephen Schwarzman, the billionaire CEO of the Blackstone Group, a company that MIT has since described as a "leading global asset manager." Prior to the college's announcement, MIT had already formed numerous corporate partnerships around AI, including a joint laboratory with IBM, but the Schwarzman College is the largest of these yet. MIT had raised one billion dollars for the college, out of which Schwarzman had committed 350 million.

Schwarzman says he invested in MIT in order to build "ethical AI" that will work to everyone's benefit (he also gave 150 million pounds to the University of Oxford to do the same). Schwarzman's discourse on AI aligns with that of his hosts, and in spring of 2018 MIT celebrated the new college, and new patron, in a lavish gathering that included venture capitalists, diplomats, and national security elites.

As Schwarzman was being honored by MIT, his Blackstone Group was continuing to displace people across the world from their homes. In North and South America, Europe, and Asia, Blackstone has acquired buildings and converted them into rental units, which tenants have demonstrated are often uninhabitable. As the company increases rent prices, it ruthlessly evicts those who cannot pay, and in the United States, Blackstone has also been fighting against rent control. The United Nations' housing advisor has flagged Blackstone as a major contributor to a global housing crisis in which tenants increasingly find themselves at the mercy of "faceless corporations."[46] Blackstone has also extended its reach into the Amazon rainforest. Blackstone-owned firms develop ports and roads, thereby fueling the hostile takeover of lands by agribusiness that damages indigenous land and sovereignty.[47]

Blackstone's practices fit within a long history of dispossession sanctioned by state violence and international government alliances. In Brazil, the election of Jair Bolsonaro led to intensified deforestation and land grabs in the Amazon, which profits Blackstone. U.S. president Donald Trump has strongly allied with Bolsonaro, as both men promise their nations a strikingly similar return to a bygone era of whiteness. Bolsonaro has praised Brazil's military dictatorship—a period marked by violent invasion of white ranchers into the Amazon—and, like Trump, has promised to make his nation "great again." Bolsonaro has also been embraced by American financial elites: in New York, hedge-fund managers held a gala for him, sponsored in part by Blackstone. Bolsonaro has also dismissed climate change as a "Marxist conspiracy" and expressed regret that Brazil's military dictatorship was not able to kill all its socialist opponents. The agenda of Brazil's new president was aptly labeled "Bolsonaro's Southern Strategy."[48]

In this context, it seems fitting that MIT chose Henry Kissinger, a man involved with Richard Nixon's southern strategy and orchestrator of coups against South American socialist governments, to speak at the Schwarzman celebration. Kissinger, who is also Schwarzman's partner in various global policy initiatives, was supposedly invited by the university for his thoughtful analysis of the future of AI.

Not everyone at MIT embraced Kissinger's reinvention as AI expert, however. On campus, some protested Kissinger's invitation and the Schwarzman College generally.[49] This resistance tapped into ongoing campus discontent with the university and its alliances. One year earlier, MIT had hosted Crown Prince Mohammed bin Salman of Saudi Arabia as he was waging a devastating, U.S.-backed war on Yemen and reaffirmed partnerships with his government. Despite protest from the community, particularly following the Saudi government's brutal murder of *Washington Post* writer Jamal Khashoggi in October 2018, MIT chose to keep its ties. Like MIT's administration, Schwarzman is also allied with bin Salman (Blackstone Group manages the crown prince's assets). Some observers saw the Schwarzman College, and Kissinger's campus visit, as another example of the university's pursuit of money above all, its complicity with war crimes, and its imperviousness to criticism from the community.

One group of MIT students, faculty, staff, and alumni called for the Schwarzman College celebrations to be canceled or boycotted and urged holding a community-wide meeting to discuss the issues. The administration proceeded as planned, but on the day Kissinger spoke some three hundred protesters assembled on the steps of the MIT student center (figure 2.2). Nearly fifty years earlier, in 1969, Noam Chomsky had famously spoken from these steps to a crowd protesting the Vietnam War, explaining how places like MIT induce students into being "the pragmatic planners of American empire." "The inducements," Chomsky said, "are very real; their rewards in power, and affluence, and prestige and authority are quite significant."[50]

In a way, MIT's Schwarzman College shows how little has changed in the machinations of American empire. Empire's would-be planners are still being offered great inducements (money, prestige, new buildings, and faculty positions), this time under the banner of "ethical AI." And although many who protested the college framed their opposition on liberal grounds—that hosting Kissinger is inconsistent with the university's values and mission to make a better world—others spoke of MIT's long-standing roles in imperialism and racist oppression. One group of protesters eventually delivered to the MIT president's office a large inflatable missile with the word "complicit" on it.

The link between Blackstone's practices of global displacement and the housing situation in Boston was not lost on some protesters, either. The lack of affordable housing around Boston is due in no small part to the influx of biotech firms and other corporations who are drawn to, courted by, and sometimes lease land from universities like MIT. At the campus protest, it was pointed out that MIT's lowest-paid workers are hit hardest by these programs of gentrification and displacement. They're pushed to live farther away from campus while being denied

FIGURE 2.2 Protest on MIT campus against the university's
Schwarzman College of Computing, February 28, 2019.

benefits available to employees higher up on the university's
hierarchy.

Universities' contributions to displacement and gentrification
are neither coincidental nor new. They continue a long history
of North American universities—particularly the major ones
who now facilitate AI's rebranding—acting as "land-grabbing,
land-transmogrifying, land-capitalizing machines."[51] From the
University of California to MIT, the very formation of many
American universities was enabled by land grants based on
expropriated indigenous land. Since then, universities have
become full-fledged real estate agents that continue to accrue
lands and displace those who stand in the way. According to a
group advocating for affordable housing in Massachusetts, local
universities such as MIT "operate as for-profit real-estate developers that are looking to maximize profits . . . their profits lead

to gentrification and displacement of long-term residents, especially people of color."[52]

The universities' pursuit of land, like Blackstone's, is global. Thus Harvard, MIT's partner in charting the "ethics and governance of AI" and the world's richest university, owns not only hotels in the Boston area (where workers, predominantly migrant women, face abusive conditions) and vineyards in California and Washington state (where Harvard's practices jeopardize access to water) but also timber plantations in New Zealand (Harvard's so-called Timber Empire) and farmlands in South Africa, South America, Russia, and Ukraine.[53] By one estimate, Harvard has spent about one billion dollars on farmlands. On university-owned farms in South Africa, black farmers have been denied access to their land and burial sites. In Brazil, Harvard is estimated to own 300,000 hectares of land in the Cerrado region, neighboring the Amazon, which has been gradually destroyed to make room for agribusiness. Harvard-owned subsidiaries in the region have acquired lands from *grileiros*, land grabbers who violently displace indigenous communities and convert their land into farms that are sold to interested buyers (like Harvard) using fraudulent land titles. What follows has been devastating for local communities. Some Harvard-owned farms, for instance, have poisoned locals' drinking water and crops. As one resident of Piauí observed, the farm "use[s] pesticides such as Roundup. It destroys all of our crops. . . . They spray that poison from their airplanes and it contaminates everything. A bunch of pests appear, like the whitefly which we can't kill, and they destroy everything."[54]

Harvard is not unique in these practices; other rich universities (both public and private) have also acquired farmlands around the world, though the specifics are unknown. Even Harvard's pursuits, which have come under scrutiny, remain mostly obscured by what one activist called the university's "nebulous farmland network" and the "opaque corporate structure" around it.[55] So nebulous and opaque, in fact, that when a member of Harvard's own Board of Overseers resigned in protest—citing the university's "land purchases that may not respect indigenous rights" and "water holdings that threaten the human right to water"—she also noted that the investments defy proper evaluation.[56]

Nebulosity and opacity link the academy's effort to rebrand AI, on the one side, and their pursuit of land-as-capital, on the other. Like mechanisms of land accumulation, initiatives around AI are based on opaque and secretive corporate structures. These initiatives' abstract promises (like building an "ethical AI" that does "good") mask tangible projects that rely on concrete technologies—opaque financial instruments, intermediary partners and offshore investments—that universities and their partners have mastered. Initiatives of the rebranded AI serve to mask these global relations and their place in a broader history of imperialism and colonialism, or at best, to render these irrelevant. According to a liberal viewpoint common in the academy, "dirty" money is better spent on "good," universities' initiatives are presumed to be universally good, and the dealings of universities and their partners in the world should be viewed as peripheral.

The rebranded AI's initiatives are yet another example of why these dealings aren't peripheral. These initiatives show how technologies, projects, and personnel flow between academia, its corporate partners, and allied governments—a flow that works to impose political uniformity on the university's activities. Hence when Stanford launched its center for Human-Centered Intelligence in 2019, the university appointed Stephen Schwarzman to the center's advisory board; and at Stanford's own

exclusive celebratory symposium, Henry Kissinger was in atten-
dance. Like other initiatives to rebrand AI, this one was a thoroughly corporatized affair, with Google and consulting firms
like McKinsey providing funds, playing major advisory roles,
and sending their employees to become fellows at the university.

Here too, technologies of dispossession worked through a
web of partnerships. To give just a few examples: Schwarzman,
benefactor to both Stanford and MIT and an ally of Moham-
mad bin Salman, runs Blackstone Group, which manages bin
Salman's assets through opaque corporate schemes, the same
schemes that Blackstone and universities use to convert land into
capital and displace its inhabitants. Through opaque agreements,
both Stanford and MIT have partnered with bin Salman's government and with companies like Google that oversee these elite
universities' AI quests. McKinsey, the consulting firm promising to apply "AI for social good" and key partner in Stanford's
new AI center, has helped the Saudi government sell itself as
progressive in Western media—so much so that the Saudi government ministry has been referred to as "McKinsey ministry."
McKinsey was hired by a colonial governing board (created by
the U.S. Congress) to manage Puerto Rico's financial crisis,
even though the firm profits from the island's debt, just as several U.S. universities (including Harvard) do via endowment
investments.[57] Together, then, management experts, governments, and universities employ the same financial instruments
to jointly form AI initiatives and engage in colonial violence.

I have outlined how AI has given new wind to established pursuits of capital. This service was enabled by the prolific AI expert
industry and its cross-sector initiatives. Amid these nebulous-
sounding AI initiatives, projects of dispossession and land
accumulation are taking place. The rebranded AI's progressive

rhetoric, and the subject's association with abstract questions about the human mind, served to distract from these tangible pursuits.

But what is the basis of AI's supposedly transformative power that experts keep referencing? In part, the basis is a set of persistent myths about computation and cognition, like the notion that machines are surpassing the capacities of human thought. The next chapter explores these epistemic forgeries.

II

SELF AND THE SOCIAL ORDER

3

EPISTEMIC FORGERIES AND GHOSTS IN THE MACHINE

People are trapped in history and history is trapped in them.
—James Baldwin

n his book *Forgeries of Memory and Meaning*, Cedric Robinson examined how the representations of black people in Western culture helped construct whiteness. These representations and the myths accompanying them became, in Robinson's words, "Inventions of the Negro" and were always changing to suit imperial interests and meet antiracist challenges.[1] They were constructed with diverse instruments: from theater, film, fiction, painting, and even cooking to racial science.[2] This last pillar, racial science, played an important role because, according to Robinson, it forged a "scientific" basis for relations of power between whites and nonwhites—categories that racial science attempts to ground. Social configurations that did not already reflect these scientifically ordained differences in capacities and interests between, say, white and black people would have to be changed, while those that do would gain additional legitimacy. This is how racist scientists saw the situation, long past what is considered the heyday of racial science between the mid-nineteenth and early twentieth century. Francis Crick, a Nobel laureate celebrated for his work on the structure of DNA, declared in 1971 that "more than half of the difference between the average IQ of American whites and Negroes is due to genetic reasons," and this "will not be eliminated by any foreseeable change in the environment."[3] Racial science was thus always understood to have far-reaching political implications.

As Robinson argued, these representations of human beings, whether in science or the arts, employ "forgeries, "fictionalizations," and "counterfeits of history" in order to "racialize" cultures in service of political ends. Building on Robinson, we can say that to construct a body of knowledge that appears so solid that it can prescribe an entire social order, one needs epistemic forgeries. In racial science and across Western science more broadly, one pervasive epistemic forgery is the notion that scientific knowledge is "transcendent" of the political world—even though, as Robinson writes, "the most powerful economic, political, and cultural impulses of a social structure impose themselves as codes and desires on the conduct, organization, and imagination of scientists."[4]

Like the overtly biological racial sciences, AI has also threatened to prescribe the social order. According the expert commentary we have seen, machines with transcendent "human-level intelligence" would not only put certain people out of work but also require a total reorganization of society. These far-reaching conclusions, like those of racial science, also depend on epistemic forgeries.

Epistemic forgeries are the fictions about knowledge and human thought that help AI function as a technology of power. This chapter outlines three closely linked epistemic forgeries that recur within AI's history. The first is AI practitioners' presumption that their systems represent "a view from nowhere"—a universal "intelligence" unmarked by social context and politics. The second is that AI systems have either matched or exceeded the capacities of human thought. This epistemic forgery has come to the fore in recent years, and it draws on deep-seated notions in Western culture about hierarchies of intelligence. The third epistemic forgery suggests that these computational systems arrive at truth, or knowledge, "on their own," AI practitioners being merely the ones who set off the necessary conditions for computational processes to properly unfold.

The three epistemic forgeries work in tandem to produce fear and uncertainty about an impending social transformation ushered in by machine intelligence. AI's force, as an ideology and vehicle for political visions, partly depends on the extent to which such forgeries are believed authentic.

THE FIRST FORGERY: A VIEW FROM NOWHERE

Western science is not unique in claiming universality. Just as scientists often present their body of knowledge as universal, so too literary scholars offer certain works of literature as universal. And the universality of both canons, scientific and literary, has been challenged.

In her lecture "Unspeakable Things Unspoken" (1988), Toni Morrison examined the American literary canon's relation to the presence and experiences of African Americans. Morrison urged for a reframing of the debate on the canon's universality. The primary question concerning the canon, she argued, shouldn't be, "Why am I, as an Afro-American, absent from it?," but rather, "What intellectual feats had to be performed by the author or his critic to erase me from a society seething with my presence,

and what effects has that performance had on the work? What
are the strategies of escape from knowledge?" Morrison proposes
a literary analysis that surveys the damages—the escape from
knowledge—caused by the aspiration to universality. She asks,
"Is the text sabotaged by its own proclamations of 'universality'?
Are there ghosts in the machine? Unsummoned presences that
can distort the workings of the machine and can also *make* it
work?"[5]

There is, clearly, a world of difference between works of literature and computing systems. But not unlike literary texts,
computational systems and the discourse around them can be
analyzed for "ghosts" in Morrison's sense. The metaphor of
ghosts in the machine suits our exploration of the first epistemic forgery: that AI systems encode and illuminate a "universal" intelligence.

If we adopt Morrison's framing, the aim would not be to simply negate the universality of AI's pursuits by pointing out that
the interests and experiences of those outside AI's elite white
sphere are not reflected in AI systems (though that is true and
important). Rather, it would be to first understand the ways in
which the social context of the field's architects is imprinted in
AI's computing systems, their uses, and surrounding narratives.
And second, to see how this social context haunts the endeavor,
creeping in to spoil forgeries like the claim to universality.

We can begin our search for ghosts by looking at how AI's
influential figures imagined the future. Joseph C. R. Licklider
is one of those figures, and his visions had a lasting impact on
computing. Formerly an MIT professor and researcher at MIT's
Lincoln Laboratory, Licklider became head of ARPA's Information Processing Techniques Office (IPTO) in 1962, which gave
him power to allocate funds to academics.[6] IPTO sought "command and control" capabilities, a frame AI practitioners could

easily work within, and Licklider is seen as largely responsible for the Pentagon's extensive funding for AI. Under Licklider, IPTO funded several prominent AI groups, including those headed by John McCarthy, Marvin Minsky, Herbert Simon, and Allen Newell. But Licklider was far more than a bureaucrat in charge of funds. He also wrote several highly influential articles on computing and its future and is credited as the inspiration to numerous computing projects. Robert W. Taylor, who served as IPTO head after Licklider (and later founded Xerox PARC's Computer Science research laboratory), said Licklider had "laid the foundation for graduate education in the newly created field of computer science. All users of interactive computing and every company that employs computer people owe him a great debt."[7]

One of Licklider's influential articles, coauthored with Taylor, was "The Computer as a Communication Device" (1968). Consistent with Licklider's earlier work advocating "Man-Computer Symbiosis"[8]—which presented the computer as an aid, rather than adversary, to people—Licklider and Taylor argued that computers will be communication aids, as opposed to devices for what they call "informational housekeeping" (tasks such as tracking account balances). The article is both prescient and troubling. Licklider and Taylor describe "on-line interactive communities" that "will be communities not of common location, but of *common interest.*"[9]

Yet it quickly becomes apparent for whom these networks operate. Licklider and Taylor tell the reader, "Your computer will know who is prestigious in your eyes and buffer you from a demanding world." It is clear from their examples that the target user is an established professional, making business trips and sending telegrams. The online network will enhance and expand that imagined user's professional activities.[10] Even this scenario of the professional, though, was civilian dressing for deeply militarized activities. The hypothetical user in "The Computer as a Communication Device" perhaps resembled Licklider himself, who was busy pitching new visions of command and control to the Central Intelligence Agency and National Security Agency, while also overseeing ARPA's Behavioral Sciences Program, which was engaged in secretive "counterinsurgency" research abroad.[11]

But perhaps the most striking part of "The Computer as a Communication Device" is not the idea of an online network spanning great distances but the claim that the presence of computers will transform in-person interactions. Face-to-face conversation, in Licklider and Taylor's view, would be enhanced by having a computer serve as intermediary. The computer would help "men" communicate and compare their "mental models."

As in other texts of this genre and period, the references to "Man" ostensibly stand for all humankind. Looking at the article's figure on "mental models," however, we get a more specific sense of "Man" (figure 3.1). According to Licklider and Taylor, the "most important models are those that reside in men's minds. In richness, plasticity, facility, and economy, the mental model has no peer." What would such "mental models" look like, and who will be doing the communicating? The article answers this with a cartoon showing two men wearing suits. In the mental model of the man on the left, there is a bikini-clad woman, and in that of the man on the right, a bicycle. As the cartoon shows, computer-aided communication transforms these mental models. In one man's transformed mental model, the woman is gone, and the bikini pieces hang on the bicycle, and in the other's mental model, the woman is hunched over a pair of bicycle wheels, her body appearing to serve as the bicycle's frame. This makes clear what Licklider and Taylor envisioned as futuristic

When mental models are dissimilar, the achievement of
communication might be signaled by changes in the structure
of one of the models, or both of them.

FIGURE 3.1 A figure on "mental models," reproduced from Joseph C. R.
Licklider and Robert W. Taylor's "The Computer as a Communication
Device" (1968). Courtesy of the Computer History Museum.

communication by "Man." In this understanding of communication, women serve as (literally) the sexual objects of men's
mental gymnastics.

The challenge facing the developers of AI's early celebrated
systems, funded by Licklider's IPTO, is how to masquerade this
white, masculine, and militarized perspective as universal.

We have already seen one such attempt with Allen Newell
and Herbert Simon's GPS, originally presented as a "general"
approach to intelligence. While GPS tries hard to abstract away
time, place, and the body, it was hardly "contextless," as Alison
Adam showed. As she has argued, Newell and Simon took the
narrow range of activities valorized in their own social milieu—
logical puzzles and games such as chess—and "extrapolated from
such a bounded problem solving situation to make an important claim about the nature of general problem solving." Newell

and Simon offered experimental validation for their system, but as Adam inferred, these were done with subjects that were overwhelmingly male and likely "white and middle-class," given the "considerable financial resources needed to attend a relatively elite US university." Newell and Simon's conclusions, as she says, are ultimately "based on the behavior of a few, technically educated, young, male and probably middle-class, probably white, college students working on a set of rather unnatural tasks in a U.S. university."[12] And the systems that followed Newell and Simon's, including those that are presented as radical departures from the pair's "symbolic" tradition, have also been similarly committed to forging a view from nowhere.

It would not be accurate, however, to conclude that Newell and Simon had nothing to say about "culture" or their own stance. They did, and this is where the haunting begins, and the fictitious basis of the view from nowhere becomes apparent.

In their book *Human Problem Solving* (1972), Newell and Simon explained that their project is "concerned with the performance of intelligent adults in our own culture," which they attempt to situate by describing what their framework excludes:

The study [*Human Problem Solving*] is concerned with the integrated activities that constitute problem solving. It is not centrally concerned with perception, motor skill, or what are called personality variables. The study is concerned primarily with performance, only a little with learning, and not at all with development or differences related to age. . . . Similarly, long-term integrated activities extending over periods of days or years receive no attention. These restrictions on the scope of our study delineate a central focus, not a set of boundaries.[13]

Newell and Simon add that these decisions were the product of both "opportunism" and "philosophic conviction."

The pair presented a figure showing how various forms of human variation, including "cultural" variation, factor in their framework (figure 3.2). Here we see again the political imagination and racialized hierarchies that animate this work. In the figure, genetic variation is depicted by a one-dimensional "phylogenetic scale" in which "Man" is at the top and "Primates" are below (followed by "Monkeys"). There is also temporal variation, which is where Newell and Simon place differences in task "performance"; this is also where they see "learning" and "development" fitting in. Then we get to the cultural. There are what they consider as intercultural differences, such as those between the "U.S.," "French," and "Chinese" cultures, as well intracultural ones, such as those between a "Student," "Worker," and "Hippie." The hierarchical and ranked connotations of the graphic are apparent. The downward movement of a scale from superiority to inferiority—as seen in the "phylogenetic scale" with "Man" at the top—is also present within the figure's "culture variation" box (U.S. at the top, followed by French, and then Chinese) and the "individual variation" box (student on top, followed by worker, and then hippie).

Newell and Simon's figure exemplifies AI's persistent quest to order the world into ranked cultures, populations, and individuals. The pair's "philosophic conviction" may simply be that it is white men in suits who shall order the world in this way.[14] Their "universal" understanding of intelligence apparently gives them the license to do so.

But the figure also shows how social context haunts their work, as it would haunt AI's later iterations. In this instance, even the ardent advocates of a symbolic, declarative, and mathematical problem-solving approach to "intelligence" concede that some aspects of thought might lie beyond their system. Or do they? The figure can be taken to mean that what is missing may be filled in without fundamental revision to the framework. Yet

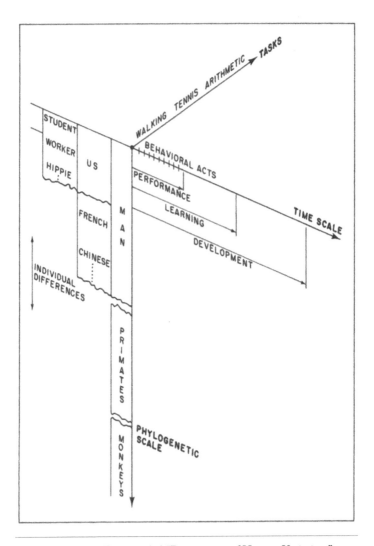

FIGURE 3.2 Figure titled "Dimensions of Human Variation," reprinted with permission from Allen Newell and Herbert A. Simon's *Human Problem Solving* (1972). Copyright Allen Newell Estate and the University of Chicago.

once Newell and Simon say something about "culture," they reveal their situated perspective and provide a glimpse into the endless range of human activities that need to be ignored in order to see "Man" as an "information-processing system" operating from nowhere.

The haunting continued, as GPS's aspirations were never realized. AI practitioners would later backtrack and acknowledge that GPS was not really "general" (an AI textbook from 1992 states, "We Lied about the G").[15] But they then had to find ways to discount the social elements. As Adam has observed, GPS's failure came to be "seen as more of an implementation problem . . . and the empirical research on which its design is founded, is regarded as less problematic than its excessively clumsy implementation." The basic premises of GPS have continued to shape AI.

Yet since AI's engines change quickly, GPS and related systems critiqued by Adam (like Soar or Cyc) would be unknown to many who consider themselves AI practitioners since the mid-2010s. The view of AI as a "knowledge engineering" endeavor, which produces large systems containing thousands of logical rules, is far removed from what the label "AI" conjures in recent years. The more recently celebrated systems nonetheless construct similar fictions, and in these systems, too, we can find ghosts.

THE SECOND FORGERY: SURPASSING HUMAN THOUGHT

Since its rise in the 2010s, as in its prior heydays, AI is presented as a cohesive and transformative force, key to military and economic hegemony. In part, these narratives rest on an epistemic forgery: the notion that AI systems have matched, or exceeded, the capacities of human thought (a claim that itself presupposes the existence of a "universal" intelligence). This forgery has persisted long past Newell and Simon's GPS. A characteristically triumphalist AI history from 1993 even concludes that "the main battles of the twenty-first century" will not be "fought over issues such as the environment, overpopulation or poverty," but rather "about how we cope with the creations of our human ingenuity; and the issue, whether we or they—our silicon challengers—control the future of the earth."[16]

In the rebranded AI, this forgery was given new wind by commentaries that suggest human-level machine intelligence is either looming or already here. Experts and the media routinely report on "AI systems" outdoing people in a range of activities, such as recognizing images, detecting emotions, or playing video games.[17] Quite often, however, the notion that people will be replaced by superhuman AI is put forward without reference to any specific systems. Instead, commentators offer vague sketches of an AI-driven future. For instance, outlets such as CNN run stories about robots soon "replacing" journalists without any evidence for why this might be the case.[18] Likewise, the prestigious Nieman Foundation for Journalism at Harvard University predicted that, by the end of 2017, "robots will analyze complex editorial content of all lengths, and provide feedback to the humans sitting behind the keyboard."[19] One columnist for the *Guardian* declared in 2019 that "AI can write just like me" and urged readers to "brace for the robot apocalypse."[20] There are similar reports about AI radically altering the practice of science. These narratives are tied to the forgery of universality: an article in the *Atlantic* magazine, for example, suggests that science is "in decline," partly because the random nature of individual scientists' "previous experiences" plays too large a role in scientific discovery—but that "outsourcing to A.I. could change that."[21]

The viability of AI systems exceeding human thought is also conveyed through dystopian scenarios. The *Guardian* reported that Silicon Valley billionaires are "prepping for the apocalypse" by buying secure hideouts in New Zealand, the "apocalypse" being a situation of "systematic collapse" that may include nuclear war or "rampaging AI."[22] Similarly, Silicon Valley mogul Elon Musk has stated to considerable fanfare that current work on AI is "summoning the demon" and that AI is "our biggest existential threat."[23] These narratives are testament to the unstated consensus among experts that AI possesses transformative powers; this is why fantastical commentaries can pass without even referencing specific instantiations of AI or its history. And even the most critical observers of the major platform companies have been swept up by the propaganda about AI's superhuman capacities. Glenn Greenwald, a journalist who played a key role in reporting on Edward Snowden's disclosures, claimed that every time we use Google search, we feed the company's "real business"—which, "unseen to us," is actually "to analyze how the human brain functions, so that it can replace and then improve upon brain functioning in order to create artificial intelligence that's more potent than the human brain."[24]

Mainstream commentary does sometimes contain caveats about AI's superhuman potential, but they are modest. Some surveys of AI practitioners, for one, suggest that they disagree about the timeline and viability of superhuman AI. Practitioners certainly disagree about these issues, but the disagreement is rather minimal. A survey cited by the prolific AI commentator and physicist Max Tegmark shows that practitioners believe there is at least a 50 percent chance or higher that "AI" will "probably reach overall human ability by 2040–50" and that it is "very likely" (90 percent chance) to do so by 2075. Survey participants also estimate that once human-level AI arrives, there is a 10 percent chance "superintelligence" will be reached within two years, and a 75 percent chance it will be achieved within thirty. Tegmark concludes that "among professional AI researchers," dismissals of human-level AI "have become minority views because of recent breakthroughs" and there is "strong expectation" that human-level AI will be achieved within a century.[25] The very preoccupation with these predictions contributes to the sense that human-level AI is viable or near.

What would such human-level AI look like, according to experts, were it to arrive? The vision tends to be set by the day's most attention-grabbing systems. Currently, these are computing systems that use neural networks, sometimes in combination with reinforcement learning, a set of frameworks in which computational agents are trained to learn by reinforcement signals (described in more detail below). These systems carry many narratives of AI's triumph over human thought. In some respects, these exemplars of AI from the 2010s are radically different from the celebrated AI systems of the 1960s. The more recent systems are based on data-hungry statistical computation that has little in common with AI's "knowledge engineering" stream (associated with Newell, Simon, or Feigenbaum). Yet all these systems are premised on the epistemic forgeries of universality and the defeat of human thought. But because the computing engines are so different, these forgeries take on different forms.

To see how the forgeries manifest, consider some of the most celebrated systems. One is DeepMind's system for playing Atari computer games, which reportedly outperforms human players. Another celebrated system is AlphaGo, also developed by Google's DeepMind, which has beaten human champions at the game of Go.[26] These systems exemplify the aspiration to a radical empiricism. The Atari-playing system, for instance, receives as input images of the game and learns to play based on reinforcement signals (i.e., how many points it scored in the game). Both the Atari and Go playing systems are presented as free of any human knowledge. The Go-playing system, according to DeepMind, has apparently "learned completely from scratch" and is "completely tabula rasa," which allows the system to "untie from the specifics [of games]." Much more than merely outperforming human players, the system is said to have "understood all the Go knowledge that's been accumulated by humans over thousands of years of playing," which the system was able to reflect on and subsequently "discover much of this knowledge for itself."[27]

The "tabula rasa" rhetoric masks the fact that all these systems have an inductive bias that dictates what patterns they can detect from data and how. Even from a traditional cognitivist perspective, it is possible to critique these systems for having an inductive bias that diverges wildly from people's behavior in the same contexts.

Indeed, cognitive scientists have challenged the claims made about deep learning–based systems. One study evaluated Deep-Mind's systems and offered several important objections.[28] For one, the Atari-playing system received the equivalent of roughly thirty-eight days' worth of play time. This extensive training allowed the system to obtain high scores, especially in games that do not require longer-term planning. However, a person who gets only two hours of play time can beat the deep learning system in games that do require longer-term planning.

More important, such systems do not acquire the same knowledge about games that people do. The systems are imprinted with particulars of the training data that prevent the sort of generalization people find effortless. The trained deep networks are "rather inflexible to changes in its inputs and goals. Changing the color or appearance of objects or changing the goals of the network would have devastating consequences on performance if the network is not retrained."[29] For instance, a game-playing system trained with the goal of maximizing its score gets "locked" into this objective. People, by contrast, can flexibly adopt different goals and styles of play: if asked to play with a different goal, such as losing as quickly as possible, or reaching the next level in the game but just barely, many people have little difficulty doing so.

The AlphaGo system suffers from similar limitations. It is highly tuned to the configuration of the Go game on which it was trained. If the board size were to change, for example, there would be little reason to expect AlphaGo to work without retraining. AlphaGo also reveals that these deep learning systems are not as radically empiricist as advertised. The rules of Go are built into AlphaGo, a fact that is typically glossed over. This is hard-coded, symbolic knowledge, not the blank slate that was trumpeted. Nonetheless, the idea of a radically empiricist and general system (which in actuality is confined to narrow domains) is taken to mean DeepMind's approach is ready for grand quests. The company presented AlphaGo not simply as an achievement in computer game playing, but as a way "to discover what it means to do science."[30] The system was presented as a major step toward fulfilling DeepMind's mission: to "solve intelligence" and "use that to solve everything" (see figure 3.3).

These narratives extrapolate from abstract mathematical problems to general intelligence, in the same way Newell and Simon have in the past. Then as now, AI practitioners claim to have uncovered a recipe, even if only in sketch form, for universal intelligence. In the controlled domain of games, the forgery of universality might pass. But when the recipe is applied to broader arenas, the historical context of human life, cast aside by practitioners, begins to creep in.

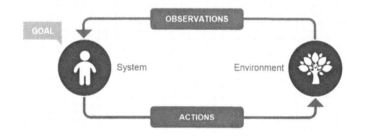

FIGURE 3.3 *Top*, mission statement of Google's DeepMind; *bottom*, framework for achieving it.

SEEING LIKE A DEEP NETWORK

Since seeing cannot be so easily severed from the seeing subject, artificial vision is a place where the epistemic forgery of universality loses much of its force. The rebranded AI presents a narrative in which humans are outperformed on a variety of visual tasks—such as classifying images—by deep network–based vision systems. But what does the world of images look like from the perspective of a deep network? How does a deep network "see"?

The answer depends not only on the structure of the deep networks, clearly, but also on the data set of images that are used for training. Deep network–based vision systems are often used for classification (assigning a label to an image from a predefined set of labels) or captioning (assigning a phrase or sentence to an image), which requires training on a large corpus of images.

The training images typically lack salient historical context. While they are generally real photographs, they play the role of pseudo-Platonic ideals: a "generic" child riding a bicycle, dog chasing a ball, surfer riding a wave, and so forth (see figure 3.4). These images serve as self-evident exemplars of objects and situations that end up in databases such as Microsoft's COCO (Common Objects in Context), where they are classified into categories.[31] Such databases themselves promote the illusion of universality, according to which photographed objects and scenes can be placed into indisputable categories. Yet, as Brian Wallis observed, the "very literalness of photographs produces an uncontrollable multiplication of meanings in even the most banal images."[32]

To interpret even the most banal of images, a background understanding is needed that is missing in artificial vision systems presented as tabula rasa perceivers. This is why, to these systems, an image of people escaping a flood may look like "people on a beach," and a crashing airplane like "an airplane on a tarmac" (figure 3.5). As some cognitive scientists have argued, an understanding of physical scenes, and of human emotions and intentions (easily seen in the faces of those photographed), is missing. But while this critique is revealing, it does not call for abandoning universality. The cognitive scientists who raised this objection imply that the deficiencies can be fixed by supplementing the associationist deep network with hierarchical knowledge of objects and their relations (encoded using symbolic

FIGURE 3.4 Performance of Google's Show and Tell. Reproduced from company paper; see text.

formalisms, for instance). That is, teaching the deep network to "really see" situations. This view doesn't challenge the premise of an artificial system that "sees" without having a body or a history, then, but merely suggests different computational building blocks for building one.

There have been other critiques of existing artificial vision systems on similarly narrow, but still informative grounds. For instance, computer scientists showed that the perceptual space of deep network–based image classification systems differs wildly from that of people. Such systems are trained on the generic image data sets (mentioned above) and assign labels to images, usually with a confidence score. With a simple procedure, it is possible to get these systems to assign high-confidence labels to images that look like noise or abstract patterns.[33] The procedure starts with a pool of random images and iteratively mutates them—randomly perturbing each image's pixels—and then

a woman riding a horse on a dirt road an airplane is parked on the tarmac at an airport a group of people standing on top of a beach

FIGURE 3.5 Captions generated by a deep network model. Reproduced with permission; see text.

selects only those images that are most confidently classified as the label of interest. After many iterations, this procedure produces random-looking images that are confidently classified by the system as, say, an "armadillo." This shows how these systems are tuned to local visual features in a way that is at odds with human eyes. This bizarre inductive bias prompts another objection to the idea that computing systems can "out-see" people. Artificial vision systems do not have a body—which is arguably where the relational and physical notions that these systems fail to detect originate. Indeed, bodies have been traditionally ignored within much of AI and cognitive science (a point that will be revisited in chapter 6).

Yet a more fundamental gap between human thought and artificial vision systems concerns the historical context of human life. Political and social contexts, which are generally of no interest to AI practitioners, shape how people see their world.

The historical power dynamics among people can be read in photographs, although AI systems are blind to such dynamics. The blind spots can be exposed by probing vision systems in a different way from that intended by their developers. To illustrate this, I have used Google's deep learning–based image captioning system called "Show and Tell"—representative of the systems that have been claimed to outperform people in the visual arena—to analyze a series of images.[34] Show and Tell was trained on thousands of photographs and can produce a label for an image it has not processed before. When Google showcases the system, it uses banal, generic-looking images that get assigned impressive, or at least reasonable, captions. The images I used, by contrast, were not generic nor banal; they were specifically chosen to demonstrate how historical context shapes the interpretation of scenes.

Consider a photograph of Palestinians arriving at a checkpoint operated by Israeli soldiers (figure 3.6, left). A Palestinian man lifts his shirt to show the soldier, who is motioning to him from the top of a small hill, that he is unarmed. Google's deep network gave the image the caption "A group of people standing on top of a snow covered slope." For a statistical pattern recognizer, the light dirt might look like snow—but the sun, the clothing, and the relationship among those photographed make that an absurd description. Similarly, a 1960 photograph of Ruby Bridges, a six-year-old African American girl being accompanied to a desegregated school by U.S. marshals, is registered as "A group of men standing next to each other" (figure 3.6, middle).

There are many more complex relations among the photographed that are missed. Consider the scene of an Israeli soldier holding down a young Palestinian boy while the boy's family try to remove the soldier (figure 3.6, right).[35] Google's deep network produces the caption "People sitting on top of a bench together" (the "bench" perhaps being the boy). The motives and intentions of the individuals are entirely lost.

It isn't possible to make sense of group scenes without history, either. For instance, Google's system registers an image of Palestinians praying in protest outside the mosque, with the

a group of people standing on top of a snow covered slope
a group of men standing next to each other
a group of people sitting on top of a bench together

FIGURE 3.6 Captions generated by Google's Show and Tell deep network. Image credits: *left*, Ammar Awad/Reuters; *middle*, U.S. Department of Justice; *right*, Reuters.

Dome of the Rock in the background, as "A crowd of people standing around a parking lot filled with kites," probably because of the colorful shirts of the men in prostration (figure 3.7, left). Similarly, a 1960 photograph from South Africa's apartheid regime, in which black men line up to receive passbooks from a panel of all-white officials, is captioned as "A black and white photograph of a group of people" (figure 3.7, right).

When one looks at photographs, the history of gender oppression cannot be ignored, either. An ad from the 1960s where a woman is used as ashtray support for a man smoking a cigar is captioned as "A black and white photo of a woman wearing a tie" (figure 3.8, left). Another image—in which a woman carrying a stack of towels is a fleeting background figure and a man watches television on the couch—can instantly evoke the gendered division of household labor yet is registered by the deep network as "A woman sitting on the couch with a laptop" (figure 3.8, right).

A counterargument to these examples might be that with a larger training data set, the same computational system might be able to "understand" even these images. That would presume,

a crowd of people standing around a
parking lot filled with kites

a black and white photo of a
group of people

FIGURE 3.7 Captions generated by Google's Show and Tell deep
network. Image credits: *left*, Ahmad Gharabli / AFP; *right*, unknown.

however, that a mapping from images to labels is enough; that
the "information" is there, inside a large corpus, and it is only a
matter of finding the right model to decode it. But more training on labeled images will not prepare the system for something
like Ruby Bridges's photograph. This image is not an instance
of a "type" of visual configuration that can be extracted from an
arsenal of captioned images. The space of photographs cannot
be meaningfully parceled into ever finer categories, such as "six-
year-old African American girls being protected from violence
on the first day of school in the United States of the 1960s."

The failures of deep learning–based vision systems reinforce
the fact that motivations and goals are essential to grasping
scenes, as cognitive scientists have argued. But they also show
that scenes unfold in a historical context that shapes their interpretation. Computing systems, by design, excise this historical
context—and are haunted by it.

Historical context also haunts the design of these systems. All
these systems depend on the substantial human labor needed to
assemble and curate training data, which is hidden from view;
this being another way in which the appearance of universality

a black and white photo of a
woman wearing a tie

a woman sitting on a couch with a laptop

FIGURE 3.8 Captions generated by Google's deep network Show and Tell. *Left*, a sexist ad for cigars from the 1960s; *right*, an image used to depict unequal division of household work between men and women. Image credits: *left*, Cigar Institute of America; *right*, CORBIS.

is staged. Google's Show and Tell, as we saw, was trained on hundreds of thousands of captioned images—but who provided the captions? Some image data sets that were used for training the system, such as Microsoft's COCO, were captioned by workers on Amazon's Mechanical Turk platform (AMT).[36] Google researchers also used AMT workers in evaluating the image-captioning system by having them score the model-generated captions. From the universal-intelligence perspective, what matters is that the captions were produced or validated by *some* human. The identity of the viewer isn't considered relevant, although it plainly shapes how images are seen: a photograph of a checkpoint in occupied Palestinian territories may well be perceived differently by a viewer in Ramallah compared with a viewer in London. And while AMT does in fact allow the employer to select workers based on country, Amazon has recently limited the worker pool to the United States.[37]

As Lilly Irani has argued, the predominantly U.S.-based employers on the platform prefer U.S. workers because, among other things, "they are likelier to be culturally fluent in the kinds of linguistic and categorization tasks" that are delegated to AMT.[38] The restriction shows how social context does matter. But despite the probable restriction of workers to the United States, the developers of the Show and Tell system reported just 65 percent agreement among AMT workers regarding the validity of computationally generated captions.[39] Universality was being spoiled again. In cases of disagreement, the developers averaged the scores, which blurs contextual differences and services the illusory view from nowhere.

Building systems that aspire to a false universality can be profitable, even as the forgery fails. In the settings that interest corporations, small gains on narrow tasks can be lucrative, and glossing over context pays off. As Microsoft researchers have argued, in systems that predict user clicks on digital ads, for example, "even 0.1% of [average] accuracy improvement would yield greater earnings in the hundreds of millions of dollars."[40]

THE THIRD FORGERY: SETTING THE CONDITIONS FOR MACHINES

The pretense of universal machine intelligence, which exceeds human capacities, is politically useful but unsustainable. The promise of human-level intelligence always proves too grand and computers recalcitrant in realizing it.

But the fiction of an AI that rivals human cognition is accompanied by a more elusive epistemic forgery. This is the third epistemic forgery, which posits that "truth" can be elicited by launching a computational process that operates independently of people, and whose inner workings cannot be understood by them. By this forgery, the process, once set in motion, is beyond anyone's control, yet its outcomes are superior to what any human collective can achieve through deliberation. This forgery leaves only two roles for people: first, the experts have to set the conditions for said computational process to unfold, and second, everyone else must do their best to adapt to the results, while acknowledging that the procedure's logic will remain forever indecipherable. This forgery not only elevates experts—as they will wield this fantastical force—but also serves to absolve society's most powerful from responsibility for social arrangements.

In some ways, this epistemic forgery is old and familiar. Stanley Kubrick's film *Dr. Strangelove Or: How I Learned To Stop Worrying And Love The Bomb* (1964) cleverly conveys the trickery. As an all-out nuclear war with the Soviets looms, the U.S. president is weighing Dr. Strangelove's plan to save a limited number of Americans ("a nucleus of human specimens") in deep mineshafts. Mr. President recognizes the moral dilemma this plan poses: "Well I . . . I would hate to have to decide . . . who stays up and . . . who goes down." Dr. Strangelove offers a way out: "Well, that would not be necessary Mr. President. It could easily be accomplished with a computer." But Dr. Strangelove's next lines undercut the notion, as he struggles to restrain his right arm (apparently having a mind of its own) from launching into a Nazi salute: "A computer could be set and programmed to accept factors from youth, health, sexual fertility, intelligence, and a cross section of necessary skills. Of course it would be absolutely vital that our top government and military men be included to foster and impart the required principles of leadership and tradition." Dr. Strangelove goes on to justify other arrangements for the hypothetical bunker, notably a ten-to-one ratio of women to men, with the women chosen for possessing "highly stimulating" sexual characteristics (which the men of the war room agree is "an astonishingly good idea").

The scene distills the absurdity of seeing computing as standing apart from people and institutions. But since the 1960s this fiction has taken on more elaborate forms, and it now manifests in AI's celebrated systems. The intellectual basis of this forgery comes from neoliberal economic theory and behaviorist psychology, two fields that have historically overlapped with AI. It is worth exploring how theorists in these fields articulated the epistemic myth because, as we will see, the rebranded AI's narratives draw on both fields.

The opaque yet all-powerful computing device that is central to neoliberal economic theory is "The Market" (presented as a singular entity)—an information-processing device that "knows" more than any human individual or group could possibly know.[41] This epistemology was articulated by Friedrich Hayek, who leveled it as an argument against centrally planned economies (which he saw as defining of socialism). According to Hayek, any individual's knowledge is local and incomplete, yet all this knowledge must be factored into the organization of society. Yet Hayek claims that an individual's knowledge cannot be articulated; it can only be elicited through behavior, that is, by the response to market signals. Hayek therefore challenged the notion that people could use what they think they know to "order" society.[42]

This was not just an abstract debate: this understanding of knowledge was marshaled to absolve society's elites of accountability. Hayek argued that while workers could be persuaded that wealthy capitalists rig the economy to promote exploitative labor, this is in fact impossible, since the set of facts that govern the markets "*is no more available to capitalists for manipulating the whole than it is to the managers that the socialists would like to replace them. Such objective facts simply do not exist and are unavailable to anyone.*"[43] Put differently, society's richest do not shape the market but, just like the poor, are under its control. No one can be held responsible for this natural force. All society can do, apparently, is make room for it to grow.

This view appeals to the major corporations promoting AI because they are in the business of creating ever-expanding markets. Yet this neoliberal epistemology runs deeper: it is also used to narrate how AI systems built by these companies work. And as in all neoliberal doctrines, this epistemic thesis is used to discount people's knowledge and human collective action, and to absolve powerful institutions of responsibility for social arrangements.

The rebranded AI's narratives rehash these ideas. *Wired* magazine suggests that AI systems now possess "alien knowledge," enabled by "post-paucity computing," which is incomprehensible to the "puny human brain."[44] These systems outdo us in ways we cannot follow, and so we must yield to them just as we must yield to the market.

This perspective is vividly demonstrated in a *New York Times* piece by Steven Strogatz, noted mathematics professor at Cornell University and media commentator, on the powers of AI. The piece centers on Google's Alpha systems. Strogatz describes the future when Google would deliver its ultimate system, "AlphaInfinity": "We would sit at its feet and listen intently. We would not understand why the oracle was always right, but we could check its calculations and predictions against experiments and observations, and confirm its revelations."[45]

In the realm of science, Strogatz writes, people would merely be reduced to "spectators, gaping in wonder and confusion." Eventually, though, "our lack of insight would no longer bother us" because "AlphaInfinity could cure all our diseases, solve all our scientific problems and make all our other intellectual trains run on time." Strogatz concludes with a sketch of the future: "We did pretty well without much insight for the first 300,000 years or so of our existence as Homo sapiens. And we'll have no shortage of memory: we will recall with pride the golden era of human insight, this glorious interlude, a few thousand years long, between our uncomprehending past and our incomprehensible future." Readers of the *New York Times* would find this view familiar, as it is a redressing of standard neoliberal doctrine.

This perspective on AI inherits neoliberal doctrine's primary contradiction. The contradiction arises when a centralized elite sets the conditions for a magical computational process (whether the market or a computing system) and decides when it works or needs fixing, but also claims that this process is beyond human control. The corporations building AI's celebrated systems likewise espouse decentralized democracy over hierarchical control, but corporate elites dictate what counts as data and how it is used; the mythical flat, democratic market doesn't exist.

Staging our third epistemic forgery entails navigating this contradiction. How is it done? Usually by downplaying the role of the elite class, as well as by drawing on models of the self that discount people's knowledge.

The newly celebrated AI systems do this by appealing to behaviorist psychology, whose proponents have also offered ways to present social arrangements created by an elite class as natural. DeepMind's core principle, for instance, is a behaviorist one: that "intelligent" behavior can be programmed via the right regimen of rewards and punishments (figure 3.3).[46] The success of DeepMind's systems is attributed not only to deep networks but also to reinforcement learning.[47] Reinforcement learning imbibes the behaviorist principle that intelligence arises by individual agents being disciplined by the environment.

This understanding of the self discounts people's knowledge. We can see this through the work of behaviorism's famous champion, B. F. Skinner. Like Hayek, Skinner was suspicious of explicit knowledge and believed individuals can be objectively assessed only through their "behavior." According to Skinner, rather than paying attention to people's "feelings, their states of mind, their intentions, purposes and plans" in order to change behavior, one should tune the environment.[48]

Behaviorism, then, promises to be the science of controlling individuals' behavior and, by extension, whole societies. Skinner recognized that this aspiration invites an obvious challenge: Wouldn't the elite who have this "scientific" expertise be in a position to manipulate the rest of us?[49] Skinner's response is that the elites of behaviorist science are not the "exploiting elite"; they cannot be, because "their task is not to control people but to bring people under the control of more effective physical and social environments. They operate upon the environment, not upon people."[50] Skinner's argument mirrors the neoliberal framework in which capitalist owners do not control the market but merely set the conditions for it to operate. Analogously, for Skinner, the elite do not directly control the lives of individuals but simply tune the environment in which people operate.

The rebranded AI's narratives fuse these neoliberal and behaviorist myths. The major corporations that dominate these narratives both create totalizing markets (through platforms that modify behavior) and then serve up a model of the self in which responding to such reinforcement or market signals is the core of what it means to be "intelligent."[51] This shows how the design of AI's computing systems is informed by a specific conception of social order, and how the celebration of these computing systems reaffirms that social order.

REJECTING THE FORGERIES

The mirage of a superhuman yet indecipherable computational process serves multiple functions in narratives about AI. This illusion not only elevates the idea of a view from nowhere by treating such a computational process as a natural force; it also deflects scrutiny from institutional power by steering our gaze toward inert algorithmic boxes.

AI practitioners and their patrons have long fixated on the innards of computing systems, seeing computers as entities that can "make decisions"—thus reinforcing the forgeries described in this chapter. This view raised worries about "explainability" (the military, for one, wanted to explain computerized battlefield decisions). Following AI's rebranding in the 2010s, explainability again became the clarion call for many experts who see it as a solution to AI's opacity.[52]

Decades ago, however, some reflective AI practitioners offered alternative views of computing systems that reject the epistemic forgeries and the misplaced notions of explainability they suggest. Some practitioners recognized that computer programs have little life except as instantiations on actual physical computing systems, which exist in a dynamic social context. This means that "explanations" of a computing system's behavior could never be confined to the neat and abstract space of algorithms.

The computer scientist Joseph Weizenbaum, for instance, argued that ordinary computer programs are effectively "theoryless." These programs can be quite large and are often developed by multiple people. There is no algorithm one could write down that fully encapsulates how such a program works in practice.[53] If such an abstraction were available, computing systems would not be as difficult to run, maintain, and debug as they are. Computing practitioners in the corporate world have long recognized this messy reality as it interfered with attempts to hurry teams of programmers to meet the demands of profit.[54]

For these reasons, Weizenbaum offered a different metaphor for computing systems. Rather than seeing a computing system as a realization of theory, which would mean it can be "explained" in algorithmic terms, he argued for seeing it as an intricate bureaucracy. In this bureaucracy, different subsystems, glued together somewhat haphazardly as a product of circumstance, generate outcomes that are subject to disputes over "jurisdiction." This is why programmers, he argued, often "cannot even know the path of decision making" that unfolds in their own programs, "let alone what intermediate or final results" will be produced.[55] Implicit in this argument is the simple observation that every computing system exists in a social envelope. Contrary to the epistemic forgeries we have reviewed, people decide what counts as data, when the software's output is correct, when it needs revision, and so on. Furthermore, all these decisions are shaped, sometimes in unpredictable ways, by the physical constraints of the computing medium. Computing systems are therefore generally not reducible to algorithms nor to the source code of the software they run.

These observations rarely concern the contemporary AI expert industry, even though the computing systems with which these experts are occupied are fraught with the same difficulties. Thus when these commentators claim that, say, systems using neural networks are indecipherable because of their large number of parameters, they are favoring mathematical abstraction over the situated social reality of computing systems. In practice, one does not deal with an abstract neural network but rather its instantiation as software, which is subject to bugs, changes, updates, and hardware constraints. Things that are considered peripheral to the abstract description of a neural network—such as the decision of when to stop training the model or the versions of different pieces of software used to perform numerical calculations—factor into the "decipherability" of the actual system.[56] That is why it is a stretch, one with political significance, to presume that computing systems that use neural networks are somehow uniquely "indecipherable."[57]

This appeal to abstract indecipherability can be a way to mask institutional power. Consider the narratives we saw earlier about the indecipherability of neural network–based systems, which emphasize those systems' incomprehensibility to people, including their very developers. There is a modicum of truth to this: after a neural network is trained on some data, no easily interpretable rule necessarily emerges that explains its behavior. And all such systems are instantiated physical computing systems, which makes Weizenbaum's points applicable. However, a blanket acceptance of indecipherability is also a gift to institutional power. After all, if AI systems outdo people and hence must be used—everywhere from the court system and policing to hiring decisions—yet are indecipherable, then who or what can be held accountable? This deflection is common within AI commentary; for example, in the title of a *Washington Post* piece in 2018: "A.I. Is More Powerful than Ever. How Do We Hold It Accountable?"[58]

The concern with this misguided question traps us in a loop over these conundrums: Has AI exceeded all human capacities or just some? If it has exceeded them, and therefore must be used, is it decipherable? Could those who build opaque AI systems give us tools to explain, and potentially "de-bias," the decisions made by their systems? And since experts say that making systems more transparent would supposedly make them less effective, how will such cost-benefit tradeoffs be managed?[59]

Here, the AI expert industry attempts to solve problems resulting from its own epistemic forgeries, which only produces dead-ends. Thirty years ago, when analyzing their day's expert industry's discourse on computers in the workplace, Ruth Perry and Lisa Greber captured these dead-ends: "We humans are seen as ships before the storm of technology, lifted or buffeted by forces beyond our control; in the wake of the storm we adapt, choosing the least unpleasant from a limited set of options."[60] The epistemic forgeries presented in this chapter, and the expert industry that reproduces them, are part of that same storm.

We have seen that different streams within AI have shared a commitment to epistemic forgeries—to seeing computation as a natural force, standing outside politics, that surpasses people's capacities and remains indecipherable to them. While these forgeries manifested differently at different periods, in general, the historical context of human life was buried.

In the next chapter I explore how these epistemic forgeries work to naturalize capitalist systems of racial and gendered oppression—at a time when the successes of social movements have forced AI's expert industry to frame itself around social justice.

4

ADAPTATION, NOT ABOLITION

Critical AI Experts and Carceral-Positive Logic

With all our boasted reforms, our great social changes, and our far-reaching discoveries, human beings continue to be sent to the worst of hells, wherein they are outraged, degraded, and tortured, that society may be "protected" from the phantoms of its own making.

—Emma Goldman

S ystems of white supremacy do not sit still; they change in the face of resistance. After the dismantling of chattel slavery in the United States, white supremacy was reinforced by the convict lease system and Jim Crow laws. Following gains made by social movements in the 1960s, white supremacy was reinstated by institutions and policies affecting housing, banking, health, education, and more, as well as through a growing system of mass incarceration. These developments were accompanied by discourses of equal rights, color-blindness, and multiculturalism.[1] Such progressive veneers helped mask the reconfigured rule of white supremacy.

AI doesn't sit still, either. As we have seen, AI forcefully reemerged in the 2010s, with an expert industry assembling around it. Like their predecessors, these experts presented AI as key to maintaining U.S. global hegemony and used AI as a foil to argue against policies that threaten capital accumulation. Yet AI's rebranding in the 2010s also gave rise to AI experts, in academia and not-for-profit organizations, that reference social justice. These experts focus on AI's links to issues such as racism and economic inequality. And while these experts work with and for the largest platform companies, they position themselves as critics of these corporations. This chapter focuses on this ostensibly progressive wing of AI's expert industry, which I will call "critical AI experts."

Like others in the expert industry, the critical experts say AI is completely reshaping society. By claiming to be the progressive guardians of this nebulous force, they create space for themselves to oversee, shape, and write policy for an unlimited number of social and political arenas. Critical AI experts use their position to reinforce white supremacy with a progressive face— doing so by serving the usual epistemic forgeries with language appropriated from radical social movements. Their work shows how AI can be adapted to changing social conditions while still serving the aims we encountered earlier.

This chapter examines AI's adaptation through discussions of mass incarceration in the United States. Mass incarceration is a system predicated on white supremacy, shaped by global capital and the imperial aims of the state—the nexus of the agendas AI has served. Yet through years of activist struggles, the discourse on this system has shifted. Mass incarceration can thus illuminate the commitments of critical AI experts, the limitations of their critique, and the adaptability of AI as a technology of power.

As historian Robin D. G. Kelley has argued, social struggles can "generate new knowledge, new theories, new questions," and the "most radical ideas often grow out of a concrete intellectual engagement with the problems of aggrieved populations confronting systems of oppression."[2] Activists resisting mass incarceration continually produce such knowledge, and in recent decades they have had to confront the links between computing and incarceration. There has been the emergence of "predictive policing," which is presented as a data-driven way to keep communities safe, as well the rise of so-called algorithmic sentencing, which according to the *New York Times* is "seen as a way to dispense justice in a more efficient way that relies more on numerical evidence than personal judgments."[3] All this made computing a major issue in the struggle against mass incarceration.

When activists examine the roles of computing in mass incarceration, as we will see in this chapter, their analyses grow outward. They look at how the "inner" layer of computing systems is sustained by "outer" violent institutions, which they place in a historical context. Activists pay attention to the political forces, global and local, public and private, that sustain the carceral system; they are not blinded by "AI."

Critical experts, by contrast, peer inward into the computing box. Committed to the fiction that AI makes decisions, they urge for an AI that is "ethical" and less "biased," as encapsulated by calls for "algorithmic accountability" (or "algorithmic justice"). At best, the call for algorithmic accountability could be viewed as recognition that the internal structure of data-hungry computing systems encodes politics. But algorithmic accountability can also be a sleight of hand, an epistemic forgery. The oft-repeated notion that "algorithms exercise their power over us"[4] obscures the fact that algorithms alone don't do things in the world; people do. Algorithmic accountability places a veil over institutions that enact violent decisions and create the conditions for the decisions to be made in the first place. This burial works to naturalize incarceration.

The critical AI experts' discourse thus embodies what I will refer to as carceral-positive logic: a mode of reasoning that, using progressive-sounding rhetoric and technological sensibilities, both justifies and calls to expand the carceral system, while masking structures of institutional violence and their history. Like other "-positive" discourses, carceral-positive logic is meant to make us feel good, or better, about its subject (incarceration, in this case). This is done by appropriating the language of social justice movements, which distinguishes carceral-positive logic from crudely procarceral stances that use coded phrases like "law and order."

The categories used in this chapter, such as "activist" versus "academic expert," are admittedly somewhat artificial. While activism and academic work aren't mutually exclusive, in this chapter there is a real difference between activists fighting against the oppression of their own communities who, as part of that struggle, must confront the computing arms of the carceral state, and academics at prestigious universities who, bankrolled by the likes of Google or Microsoft, speak of social justice activism. The latter have the world's loudest megaphone. They pen pieces for the largest media outlets; their reports are featured in venues like the *Wall Street Journal*; they participate in exclusive gatherings of CEOs and political elites. The community organizers considered in this chapter, by contrast, do not swim in these circles—they are oppressed by them. The struggles over mass incarceration bring out these distinct epistemologies and commitments.

I examine these conflicting epistemologies and commitments by comparing how activists and critical AI experts analyze two facets of mass incarceration: the deportation of migrants and predictive policing.

ACTIVISTS TACKLE INCARCERATION AND COMPUTING

Social movements have scrutinized the U.S. carceral state for years, including its brutal treatment of migrants. In recent years, these injustices have entered media discussions in a major way. Following the Trump administration's so-called zero-tolerance immigration policy, American corporate media began covering the practices of separating families and detaining children in camps carried out by the Immigration and Customs Enforcement Agency (ICE). Although U.S. border police had separated families for decades before ICE was formed, images of caged migrant children now circulate widely, and even some establishment politicians have called for abolishing ICE.[5]

ICE was formed as part of the expansion of the national security state under President George W. Bush. In 2002–2003 the Department of Homeland Security (DHS) and its subagency ICE were founded as new organs of incarceration, deportation, and surveillance under the banner of a global "War on Terror." ICE continued to grow under the administration of President Barack Obama. In 2018 alone, nearly twenty years after its creation, ICE held over forty thousand people in detention, and the agency continues to demand more resources.

ICE's operation depends critically on data sharing among local, state, and federal agencies—a use of computing that has long worried anticarceral activists. Activist groups working for migrant justice, such as the group Mijente, have protested Amazon, Microsoft, and Salesforce for servicing ICE and other wings of DHS (figure 4.1).[6] Activists at Mijente recognize that unglamorous computing practices powerfully shape who gets rounded up and deported: sharing names, fingerprints, or biometric data is more than enough to affect people's lives. This "interoperability" of databases across agencies is key, for one, to enhancing the links between ICE and local prisons. According to a former ICE secretary, interoperability enables "a virtual ICE presence at every local jail." Data collected in jails is then propagated: through ICE, the Federal Bureau of Investigation (FBI) passes fingerprint to DHS, where they are cross-referenced with immigration databases.[7]

Yet these are familiar uses of computing that do not fall under the fundable rubric of "AI" that the AI expert industry is after. And activists haven't framed these issues around "AI," nor around phrases such as "algorithmic accountability" or "algorithmic bias" invoked by critical AI experts. Instead, activists have focused on how technical systems fit into the political system that fuels deportations and detentions, as outlined in Mijente's report *Who's Behind ICE?*. The report highlights the role of "cloud computing" in enabling data interoperability across agencies. But as the report argues, cloud computing has been more than a data

FIGURE 4.1 *Left*: Protester hangs a sign outside Microsoft offices in San Francisco, California, that reads "Detaining children for profit: brought to you by Microsoft" (July 2018). Photograph by Fight for the Future. *Right*: Activists with Mijente protesting outside Amazon headquarters in Seattle, Washington (October 2018). Some protesters are holding masks imprinted with Amazon founder Jeff Bezos's face. Photograph by NWDC Resistance.

storage and processing service; it was also a way for Silicon Valley companies to more closely align with the national security state. Lobbying groups in Washington, backed by companies like Amazon and Microsoft, helped ensure that the government would adopt those companies' cloud computing services. As the report notes, a "revolving door" between Silicon Valley companies and government was created. Companies such as Amazon, Microsoft, Google, IBM, and the CIA-backed surveillance firm Palantir then went on to build critical cloud infrastructure for DHS. These companies, as the report summarizes, "do the government's bidding" by enabling systems that "target and punish *en masse* those it deems 'undesirable'—immigrants, people of color, the incarcerated and formerly incarcerated, activists, and others."[8]

Critical AI experts, enmeshed in the corporate world, are far more constrained in their criticisms. There is some protest in these halls, to be sure; employees at Google and Microsoft have called on their bosses at various points to end contracts with ICE, the Pentagon, or the army.[9] But it is less tenable for the experts we have encountered to question the capitalist and imperial agenda that binds their patrons to the national security state—especially as corporate leaders reaffirm their commitments (following employee protests, for example, the president of Microsoft said the company "is proud" to work with the Pentagon).[10]

But the divergence between activists and critical AI experts runs deeper. Activists at groups such as Mijente recognize that they are struggling against long-standing institutional violence. They therefore see past the superficial divides between policing and immigration control. Jacinta González, an activist with Mijente, said that while many people speak of the "intersection" between criminal justice and immigration enforcement, Mijente sees them as part of the "same system that is constantly expanding." For González, ICE is "just a police force dedicated to immigration." Whenever policing activity increases, she adds, so does immigration enforcement. Data interoperability across agencies, enabled by cloud computing, further erodes any separation. Treating these forces separately, then, only obscures that ICE is part of an expanding mass incarceration system.[11] And as Mijente's report argues, this system's expansion is shaped by international politics. Interoperability, for instance, allows governments to more efficiently control migrant flows. Sharing of criminal history and biometric data between the U.S. and Mexican governments not only helps control migration into the United States but also serves the Mexican government's need to police migrants heading north from Central America (a flow the U.S. government is also bent on limiting).

Critical AI experts' analyses, by contrast, elide these violent structures. Experts instead home in on computing systems with the view that by intervening at local points, these systems can be reformed. The discourse on computing and predictive policing, which I will turn to next, makes this clear.

CRITICAL AI EXPERTS
NATURALIZE POLICING

The successes of social movements, like the Movement for Black Lives, have made it impossible for established political and media circles to ignore the injustices of policing and the court system. Policing and criminal sentencing became major topics for AI experts who presume that, as part of its general transformation, AI is reshaping policing and the legal system.

Critical AI experts argue, however, that the computing systems used in policing and the court system are racially biased. Indeed, software used in several U.S. states systematically assigns higher "risk assessment" scores for African Americans, which then factor into judges' sentencing decisions. According to critical AI experts, the path forward is to understand which populations are being discriminated against by the software and to work to reduce that bias. As Kimberlé Crenshaw has argued, however, when discussions of incarceration are framed around "at-risk" populations, the result is "subtle erasure of the structural and institutional dimensions of social justice politics."[12]

Critical AI experts erase institutional violence by packaging epistemic forgeries from the computing world with a progressive-sounding discourse on social justice. The result is a carceral-positive logic that ultimately naturalizes policing and calls for the expansion of the prison-industrial complex.

The work of Data & Society and AI Now, two major centers in the critical AI space, exemplifies carceral-positive logic. As with the rest of the AI expert industry, the stance of these experts is profoundly shaped by their patrons. The centers, both backed by Microsoft and affiliated with New York University, are aligned not only with private power but also with state power. AI Now was formed through a collaboration among researchers (some working at Data & Society and Microsoft), the White House, and the National Economic Council. Data & Society, on the other hand, is sponsored by several U.S. Justice Department–backed initiatives devoted to reforming the police's image. One sponsor is the Center for Police Equity (CPE) whose mission is "empowering law enforcement agencies with useful data and tools to continuously improve and strengthen relationships with the communities they serve." According to the *New York Times*, the CPE's agenda is plainly "to improve the morale of the police and

the community's perception of officers."[13] The CPE advocates for
increasing the diversity of the police force, which it says is neces-
sitated by recent years' "tragic events" of "officer-involved shootings and attacks on law enforcement officers." Apart from CPE's
deceptive equating of the murders of (mostly) people of color by
police ("officer-involved shootings" in their language) and "attacks
on law enforcement officers," the focus on diversity distracts from
the structural violence embedded in policing.[14] The underlying
premise here is that policing is a force for public protection.

As sociologist Alex Vitale has argued, however, the history
of policing undercuts this idea.[15] American policing originates
in colonialism, slavery, and protection of the interests of the
wealthy. Some police departments began as private militias
hired to break workers' strikes; others, as fugitive slave patrols
or armed forces accompanying white settlers into new territories in the nineteenth century. These goals never ceased to animate policing, even as its forms have changed. When slavery
was abolished, for instance, police forces were used to suppress
black voters and enforce vagrancy laws and other elements of
Jim Crow law. War abroad has also continued to mold domestic policing, as a "militarized vision of policing" was adopted
during the Cold War, bent on suppressing social movements
through counterintelligence.[16] For all these reasons, Vitale
argues it is more accurate to view policing "as a system for managing and even producing inequality by suppressing social
movements and tightly managing the behavior of poor and non-
white people: those on the losing end of economic and political
arrangements."[17]

Liberal policing reforms (like the call for diversity) mask the
injustices police are tasked with managing. As Vitale points out,
police departments are in fact nearly as "diverse," by self-reported
race categories, as the national population. The disparity between

the police and policed communities—obvious in scenes from Ferguson, Missouri, following the killing of Michael Brown, or from Baltimore following the murder of Freddie Gray—usually stems from the extreme segregation of communities of color. This segregation is the product of structural racism and decades-long policies such as redlining; problems that diversifying the police force cannot fix. Likewise, community-based policing measures ignore the fact that policed communities and the police aren't equals; that the police target and surveil certain populations by design. This is why police departments often view community-based policing as a form of intelligence gathering, as Vitale notes.

Crucially, these liberal reforms do not change the institutional incentive to criminalize, which operates along the lines of race, gender, class, and legal status. Already in the 1930s, George Padmore commented on the profitability of criminalizing non-whites in his comparative study of racial capitalism. Writing about the Jim Crow South, Padmore noted that the police became a force for rounding up black people based on labor demands, with the result being that "whole communities of able-bodied blacks are commonly apprehended. All kinds of frame-up charges are made against them." It paid off in multiple ways: "the judges and the police get the court fees, and the landlords cheap labour."[18] Present-day police departments are still committed to generating revenue for municipalities through ticketing, arrests, patrols, and other mechanisms guided by categories of race, gender, class, and legal status. Liberal reforms such as community-based policing will not dismantle this structure.

Yet when critical AI experts tackle policing, they cloak the liberal policing reforms promoted by their patrons in the language of computation and data. This is exemplified by the discourse on "predictive policing," a set of surveillance techniques police departments and the FBI use to identify high crime areas (so-called hot spots) and individuals viewed as likely to commit crimes. Predictive policing is generally sold as a more efficient way to distribute police personnel and resources. For AI experts, predictive policing meets a certain epistemic aesthetic. As the term "predictive" implies, this form of policing depends not only on large amounts of data but also on statistical analysis, which, as we have seen, has been rebranded as "AI." Furthermore, when policing is presumed to be about public safety, the emphasis on prediction evokes dystopian futures in which the police target people and communities falsely considered crime-prone because of the bias in their data sets. Moreover, it makes criminalization, social reform, and incarceration the purview of technical experts.

AI Now's work on predictive policing exemplifies this turn. AI Now represents the more progressive wing of corporate-backed AI commentary, and it cultivates a critical image. In discussing policing, for instance, the institute has approvingly cited Black Lives Matter and the Marxist cultural theorist and activist Stuart Hall. And unlike many of its corporate sponsors and partners, AI Now doesn't outright promise to eliminate all bias from computing systems.[19]

Through this progressive veneer, AI Now offers a critique of policing that nonetheless reaffirms and ultimately calls for the expansion of the carceral system. The institute's framing supports the premise that the police are about protection; that more resources should be allocated to data-driven liberal reforms; that police departments can be agents of change if put in dialogue with the proper "stakeholders" (notably policy-oriented academics and corporations) and oversight committees; and that the interests of entities that profit from the prison-industrial complex need to be taken into account.

AI Now's report on predictive policing—titled "Dirty Data, Bad Predictions: How Civil Rights Violations Impact Police Data, Predictive Policing Systems, and Justice" (2019)—demonstrates the wavering path to these conclusions.[20] The report, published by *New York University Law Review*, does not reference "AI," but the media presented it with headlines such as "Artificial Intelligence Is Now Used to Predict Crime. But Is It Biased?," capitalizing on the label to gain attention.[21] The report analyzes police departments who were already under federal investigation for their practices. AI Now describes these departments as having engaged in "racially fraught" and "sometimes unlawful practices" which constitute "dirty policing." Dirty policing produces what the report terms "dirty data" that reflect the "bias and misassumptions" of policing, which disproportionately affect people of color and the poor.

In a balancing act, the report manages to condemn police practices on seemingly general ground while upholding the promise of data-enabled policing reform. On the one hand, the "bias" in the data is described as "systemic" because it reflects policing practices; and this dirty data, already the product of dirty policing, could only yield more dirty policing. There is no simple technological fix to make data "unbiased," according to the authors, and any data generated by these problematic police departments might be tainted. The report also emphasizes the general lack of oversight of police departments.

Yet, on the other hand, "dirty policing," as the name suggests, is still presented as deviant. For example, the report criticizes the Chicago Police Department for its "fraught" and "unlawful" uses of the racial profiling "stop-and-frisk" policy, but not for employing stop-and-frisk in general. In a similar turn, the report criticizes the New Orleans Police Department for not having its Palantir-made predictive policing system "scrubbed for errors

and irregularities" that result from "dirty data," but not for having used a predictive policing system generally (nor for working
with Palantir). Furthermore, all the police departments surveyed
in the report were already under federal investigation for illegal
practices, creating the sense that the system can correct its own
flaws. The report in fact calls for enhanced federal oversight of
police departments as a key reform. Overall, the authors accept
the notion that policing is about "public safety."[22]

While making nods to radical perspectives, then, AI Now's
report amounts to a narrow critique of predictive policing as
currently practiced. The crux of this critique is that in light of
"suspect police practices," "data manipulation," and "lack of oversight and accountability measures regarding police data collection, analysis, and use," it appears that "any predictive policing
system trained on and actively using data from jurisdictions with
proven problematic conduct cannot be relied on to produce valid
results without extensive independent auditing or other accountability measures." The report's references to "skewed" predictive
policing systems, the invalid results they produce, and the dirty
data they are based on all suggest that unskewed, validated, and
"clean" data-fueled predictive policing is possible. What is being
challenged here is not policing itself, or police surveillance of
communities, or even predictive policing categorically. Rather,
the report simply challenges the ways in which those things are
currently implemented, especially in police jurisdictions officially
flagged as problematic by the government.

This framing poses a dilemma, however. If bias cannot simply be removed from data because it is "systemic," as the report
suggests, then what would reform look like, beyond enhanced
federal oversight? For this, AI Now outlined a policy framework in 2018—addressed to public agencies such as the police—
for implementing "algorithmic impact assessments." Through

analogy to the finance world, the framework calls for "data audits" by external experts ("interdisciplinary researchers" in the report's language, presumably groups like AI Now). In collaboration with other "stakeholders," these experts will audit the systems used by public agencies. Using reasoning that mimics community-based policing, the report urges agencies to "alert communities about the systems that may affect their lives" and for communities to have a "voice" in "conversations" on algorithmic matters between agencies, companies, and academic experts.[23]

AI Now's suggested framework presumes that private companies ("vendors" in the report's language) will continue to profit from computing systems sold to public agencies (such as police departments). It even suggests that private industry's "trade secrecy" is a "challenge" to successful public-private partnerships. According to the framework, agencies should therefore partner with companies that cooperate with the proposed auditing measures, and cooperation can be encouraged by increasing market competition among vendors. Finally, it is recommended that agencies expand their own capacities in dealing with "automated" systems in part to "ensure public trust." This position is echoed by other not-for-profits in the sphere of critical AI commentary, such as the American Civil Liberties Union (ACLU). At an AI policy conference hosted at MIT, which included participants from the American intelligence community and the White House, the ACLU's executive director stated that "AI has tremendous promise, but it really depends if the data scientists and law enforcement work together."[24]

These recommendations highlight the expansionist dimension of carceral-positive logic. Reforms such as data "curation," "maintenance," or "auditing" all entail allocating more resources for computing systems used in surveillance and policing and the infrastructure around them, and hence to those profiting from the prison-industrial complex. This viewpoint is reflected by other critical expert centers. Data & Society, for instance, has participated in a policy conference with the U.S. Department of Justice that recognized the "growing ecosystem of third-party intermediaries"—like "businesses, nonprofits, and news agencies"—that "are making use of open criminal justice data, investing time, money, and resources into processing data before use, prepping data through cleaning, standardizing and organizing, and linking and aggregating different data sets together." It was recommended that "to encourage such reuse, data should be machine-readable and structured for interoperability."[25] This is essentially a call for more data collection, as well as the very "interoperability" that anticarceral activists argued enables mass deportation and incarceration.

Through these prescriptions, critical experts normalize the prison-industrial complex. By casting mass incarceration in the bureaucratic terms of data audits and curation, they continue the long-standing portrayal of prison as an "abstract site," to use Angela Y. Davis's term. When prison is kept detached from the pain and misery it inflicts and the labor it extracts, as Davis argued, it can do the "ideological work" that "relieves us of the responsibility of seriously engaging with the problems of our society, especially those produced by racism and, increasingly, global capitalism."[26] For critical AI experts, prison merely gets more layers of abstraction through debates on data and its auditing protocols.[27]

Thus expert centers such as AI Now and Data & Society have accepted the prison-industrial complex as fact, much like they have accepted "AI" as a done deal; a technological force that has thrown itself on us. By their logic, there is no turning back. The way to cope is to expand: to develop more codes of "ethics" and mechanisms of accountability, forge more partnerships, and increase market competition.

Abolitionist activists looking at policing, by contrast, want this expansion to end. They offer an understanding of policing grounded in the institutional violence that critical AI experts have tried to bury.

"BEFORE THE BULLET HITS THE BODY": ACTIVISTS TACKLE POLICING

Activists confronting policing have produced an entirely different discourse and set of practices from that of experts. Work by the Stop LAPD [Los Angeles Police Department] Spying Coalition offers a study in contrast.

Stop LAPD Spying is a community-based organization that has little in common with the not-for-profit sphere inhabited by groups such as AI Now or Data & Society. Many of the coalition's organizers live in heavily policed communities and volunteer their time to the group. At the time of writing, the coalition does not have nonprofit status. Beyond writing reports, the coalition regularly intervenes in local municipal hearings on policing, confronting politicians and police department officials, as well as police officers patrolling the streets. One of the group's aims is to reclaim the discourse on policing, which is largely dominated by media-savvy nonprofit organizations and academics.[28] According to the coalition, most nonprofits, including the ACLU, tend to ignore the voices of those most affected by policing.

The coalition's report on predictive policing, titled "Before the Bullet Hits the Body: Dismantling Predictive Policing in Los Angeles" (2018), offers a radically different framing of policing from that of critical AI experts. The report opens by stating the coalition's position with respect to the policy world: "This report does not take a top down policy reform or recommendation approach, nor does the report seek more 'transparency' and 'oversight' of policing, an institution that remains inherently violent and flawed by design."[29] Instead, it is concerned with "exposing multiple tentacles of state violence," including the "creation of the 'other,' knowledge production and the deep complicity of academia, corporate profit and the deadly impact and trauma of programs such as Predictive Policing on our communities."

As with activists confronting deportations, the historical arc considered here is far longer than that of critical experts. The coalition's report views policing as part of the settler-colonialist vision of the "New World"—"a world where everything 'old' had to be demonized, criminalized, contained, invisibilized." Surveillance of marginalized groups, an integral part of policing, was necessary to enacting this vision and creating the forms of knowledge that support it. When the report turns to current police practices, it situates them in this longer context, from American policing's origins in slave patrols and colonialist expansion to suppression of social movements.

Considering this history, predictive policing's data-centric allure is quickly deflated. It is "yet another tool," the latest installment in a "long lineage" of mechanisms of social control from slave patrols to the war on drugs and terror. In the backdrop of a booming prison-industrial complex, predictive policing should be understood as a "for-profit commodity" that through "misuse of public monies" capitalizes on the criminalization of marginalized people.[30]

But the report recognizes the political appeal of narratives centered on computing and data. With predictive policing, "the veneer of science and technology, algorithms and data processing" imbue the state with "power, justification, and supposed right to predict, to pathologize, and criminalize whole communities, and to trace, track, monitor, contain and murder individuals. This is the trajectory before the bullet hits the body." The data-centric frame, as the report argues, obscures the fact that "the police state is an ever-expanding endeavor that is fundamentally flawed by design."

The focus on algorithms and data limits the discussion on policing, according to Hamid Khan of the coalition. It fosters the notion that "data is dirty"—which Khan says it obviously is, being the product of a process he describes as "racism in, racism out, or in computer language: garbage in, garbage out."[31] Algorithms and data can suck attention away from what the coalition seeks to challenge such as "the very premise of what is crime, who assigns criminality, who punishes, and who profits."[32] In other words, inquiries into "dirty data" do not question the institutional authority that can decide whether a specific data collection or analysis method can be used in the first place. According to Khan, an understanding of policing's intent is necessary for seeing the broader picture and countering the "constant glorification of policing—particularly in the white imagination."

However, the coalition's efforts to situate policing in its broader historical and epistemological context do not come at the expense of detailed engagement with the computing systems used by the police. For example, its report examines the mathematical model used by PredPol, a predictive policing system company founded by researchers at the University of California, Los Angeles. Apart from explicating the model's key equation, the report offers a brief intellectual history of these mathematical models and how they move across academic, military, and corporate worlds. The academics behind PredPol, some of them anthropologists, had originally developed models of human

foraging behaviors and only later applied them to predict counterinsurgency behavior in Iraq for the U.S. military. Through
the founding of PredPol, these models were eventually applied
to crime in Los Angeles and other urban areas.[33]

Like activists resisting deportations, the coalition sees such
institutional links as central to sustaining mass incarceration. Its
report, too, names the "revolving door" between government and
corporations that serves companies such as Palantir (involved in
both systems of deportations and predictive policing). And while
policy-oriented academics take the prison-industrial complex as
something to work with—referring to it an "ecosystem" and
companies participating in it as "vendors," as we've seen—the
coalition sees it as one in a long series of configurations by which
the state and corporations profit from criminalizing nonwhites,
poor people, and other marginalized groups.

Since the coalition's report grew out of work in heavily policed
communities, it looks to those communities for alternatives.[34]
The coalition surveyed communities in Los Angeles about their
views of predictive policing and policing generally. The survey
also asked community members to describe their needs and
imagine alternatives to the current state of policing. The most
frequent responses paint a rather different picture than the one
that calls for more interdisciplinary academic expertise, new
public-private partnerships, or increased federal oversight. Those
surveyed often spoke of needing more places for kids to play,
more cultural spaces, more resources, shelter, food, and respect,
and called for disarming the police and abolishing the police
state (figure 4.2). An obvious theme here was the need to invest
in communities—what liberal policing reforms, or different
mechanisms of data collection and audits, cannot provide.

In our interview, Khan reiterated the importance of being
grounded in communities, one of many things he thought was

speaking to each other demilitarization of police
protect the children more
everyone is a potential friend abolish the police state
living wage education treated with dignity
places to go to the bathroom
more cultural spaces no police no gangs
more resources
more community spaces no drugs serenity clothing
no crime shelter respect food safe while walking around
community working together support one another
a place to play for kids
not to condemn but uplift less police police without guns
less tagging protection
feeling comfortable in the community
happiness safe

FIGURE 4.2 A representation of responses to a survey of policed
communities in Los Angeles. Image from Stop LAPD Spying
Coalition, "Before the Bullet Hits the Body—Dismantling
Predictive Policing in Los Angeles."

missing from the prevailing discourse on policing. He noted that
academics often hijack the conversation, marginalizing the most
relevant communities' voices, and framing things in ways that
serve state power.[35] For Khan, AI Now's report on predictive
policing was a prime example: "There's nothing new that is being
said [in AI Now's report]. . . . One would expect people who
have the resources and funding would not keep playing the same
old broken record. Of course it's dirty data. But then after all is
said and done, they sensationalize something [predictive polic-
ing] and come back and say, how can we have cleaner data? That's
bullshit, because you can't."[36]

The sensationalist discourse on predictive policing has led to debate within the Stop LAPD Spying Coalition about the best label for its work. Although the group views itself as part of an abolitionist tradition and sees abolition as an organizing principle for its work, Khan noted how "the term 'abolition' is all of a sudden becoming part of a double speak" where "people speak about 'abolition,' but they engage in notions like 'dirty data.'"[37] The relentless co-option of terms frustrates coalition members, because it means their work is grouped with organizations they view as antithetical to their own. Indeed, in much academic writing and media discussions, the work of Stop LAPD Spying Coalition is presented in the same breath as that of AI Now—as if both are part of the same "abolitionist" struggle against the data-hungry carceral state.[38]

ABSORBING DISSENT IN A WEB OF PARTNERSHIPS

The threads examined here—the activists in Mijente fighting deportation and those in Stop LAPD Spying Coalition fighting incarceration, on the one side, and critical AI experts (from AI Now), on the other—collided in the summer of 2019. In June the University of California, Berkeley, hosted its annual Privacy Law Scholars Conference, cosponsored by Palantir and Microsoft.[39] Mijente launched a petition ahead of the event, calling on the university to cut ties with Palantir for its role in servicing ICE and the carceral state. According to Mijente, "That a conference focused on privacy is sponsored by a firm whose profits derive from the mass accumulation of personal data for sale to law enforcement agencies is patently absurd."[40] But while Mijente's own report describes Microsoft's crucial role in enabling

ICE, the petition addresses only Palantir and does not mention the event's other sponsor, Microsoft. The codirector of the Microsoft-backed AI Now (at the time also a Google employee) cosigned a letter calling on the university to drop Palantir, while AI Now circulated Mijente's petition on social media. But Microsoft, somehow, had disappeared.

One month later, in July, Mijente co-organized a widely publicized conference in San Jose, California, titled "#TakeBack-Tech: A People's Summit for a Surveillance-Free Future." This gathering was described as an effort to cultivate the "broad movement" needed "to expose and derail the tech industry's efforts that are increasing surveillance and facilitating war, incarceration and criminalization, with no regard for civil or human rights."[41] One of the conference's specific goals was to reinvigorate efforts to "protect local communities" while also "targeting a broader set of companies" complicit in violence. In this conference, Stop LAPD Spying Coalition appeared in one session, and in another, the codirector of AI Now. The summit's evocative poster (figure 4.3) shows a purple figure, strengthened by a people's movement, taking down the gray cloud of the surveillance machine, decorated with the names of seven corporations complicit with the carceral state—including Facebook, Amazon, Palantir, and Salesforce—but not Google or Microsoft. And in October 2019 Mijente participated in a symposium hosted by AI Now, titled "The Growing Pushback Against Harmful AI." Not only did Microsoft recede into the background, but issues were now framed around "AI" and the need to avoid the "harmful" kind—a far cry from Mijente's report on the corporations fueling ICE's data backbone.

The apparent alliance between Mijente and AI Now demonstrates what Dylan Rodriguez has identified as the "*ongoing absorption* of organized dissent through the non-profit structure."[42]

FIGURE 4.3 Flyer for the #TakeBackTech summit, co-organized by Mijente, which took place in July 2019 in San Jose, California. Artwork by alejandro delacosta.

Corporations flex their muscles through nonprofit structures and, as a long history shows, end up co-opting or taming radical social movements.

In fact, through this nonprofit structure, corporations wield so much influence that the work of the experts they sponsor sometimes just reflects the corporate world's internal battles. For instance, while AI Now is indirectly partnered with Amazon, the company is not one of its main backers, and AI Now has offered some limited critiques of Amazon's treatment of its employees.[43] Compared with Google or Microsoft, Amazon has not been as aggressive in creating a research wing that includes social scientists or forming academic partnerships that can lend it a progressive image. At the same time, Amazon has rightly received negative press coverage for the abusive conditions its workers face, among other issues. All these factors have made Amazon a safer target for critique by AI experts.

But these are minutiae; Microsoft and Amazon are in the same business. In October 2019 Microsoft finally beat Amazon in a bid for the Pentagon's ten-billion-dollar cloud infrastructure contract, meaning that for the next decade, Microsoft will build the U.S. military's cloud-computing backbone.[44] At the same time, Microsoft has continued to invest in infrastructure for surveilling Palestinians in the West Bank on behalf of the Israeli military.[45] With strategic partnerships and clever branding, Microsoft manages to be on the front lines of both the battlefield and social justice.

Since the 2010s the discourse on AI has blended with discourses on social justice, which carceral-positive logic appropriates. But if there seemed to be a major difference between critical AI experts and unreconstructed entrepreneurs and CEOs, it was merely, to borrow from Jean Baudrillard, "a simulation of scandal for regenerative ends."[46] The regenerative end here is the expansion of computing systems and data collection—for governance by the numbers and enhancing the carceral eye—while installing more experts to maintain and justify such systems.

How does AI manage to move seamlessly between the worlds of military planners, corporations, and now progressive-sounding projects on social justice while still serving essentially the same capitalist and imperial agenda of white supremacy? The next chapter synthesizes what we have seen so far in the book to explain this feat.

5

ARTIFICIAL WHITENESS

*I am quite straight-faced as I ask soberly: "But what on earth is
whiteness that one should so desire it?" Then always, somehow,
some way, silently but clearly, I am given to understand that
whiteness is the ownership of the earth forever and ever, Amen!*
—W. E. B. Du Bois

I want to return to the question posed in the first chapter:
What is Artificial Intelligence? This question requires us to
account for AI's reappearances and shifts, and its place in
imperial and capitalist projects. The question also calls for an
explanation of AI's flexibility: its ability to move from the world
of Pentagon technocrats to that of self-styled "progressive" activists. This question also calls for an accounting of AI's models of
the self.

This chapter sketches the beginnings of an answer by explor-
ing "Artificial Intelligence"—as a concept, field, and set of
practices—through the ideology of whiteness, as discussed in an
American context by writers such as W. E. B. Du Bois and Toni
Morrison. My claim is that whiteness is the organizing logic of
AI, the frame that makes sense of its trajectory and political

functions, its epistemic forgeries and models of the self. Whiteness explains how experts become readily invested in AI and how they adapt it to meet social challenges, as well as the fragilities that result from this investment.

How is AI tethered to whiteness? In some ways, the "whiteness" in AI is overt. Having formed in the American military-industrial-academic complex of the 1950s, AI unsurprisingly bears the marks of that elite white world. This goes beyond the field's composition into its epistemologies. As a field, AI has consistently produced racialized, classed, and gendered models of the self. It has drawn on epistemic forgeries to pass as "universal" what in fact constitutes a white, elite, and masculinized perspective. And AI is often presented with overtly racial and gendered imagery, alongside colonialist narratives, as we will again see in this chapter.

But the whiteness in AI is also subtler than all that. AI has served the aims of whiteness by mimicking its ideological form. AI, like whiteness, has been hollow. From the start, it was a nebulous and contested concept. Through time, the label's boundaries have been repeatedly redrawn, and the field's venerated computational engines refitted. Yet these changes were steered by capitalist and imperial projects. As a product of an elite white world, then, AI became isomorphic to whiteness as an ideology: a quintessentially nebulous and dynamic endeavor, whose ebbs and flows are animated by capitalist and imperial aims. The practices by which AI's nebulosity was put in service of these aims are more defining of the endeavor than any technical characterization based on computing systems and their epistemic styles.

Thus AI lacked a coherent basis in the same way that racial categories (such as "whiteness") always have. But as with whiteness, AI's nebulous and shifting character has helped it serve tangible, destructive projects—from dispossession and land accumulation to mass incarceration. And as with whiteness, the premises of AI and its incoherent underpinnings are practically invisible to those who profit from it.

I argue in this chapter that AI therefore functions as a technology of whiteness. This amounts to two claims: that AI serves the aims of whiteness—and thus is a tool in the arsenal of a white supremacist social order—but that it also mirrors the nebulous and shifting form of whiteness as an ideology. One upshot of these claims is that in order to make sense of AI one shouldn't look for coherence in its internal logic or substance but rather recognize how the concept's emptiness confers AI with the malleability needed to service political projects that lie elsewhere. These seemingly external projects of empire and capital give AI its superficial coherence and make it into a technology of power.

As a technology of power with a nebulous core, AI can be adapted, like whiteness, to challenges from social movements. Since its rebranding in the 2010s, AI has been woven into progressive-sounding discourses on social justice that make room to discuss race, gender, and even racism. But as we will see again in this chapter, the progressive packaging doesn't preclude the reconfigured AI from serving white supremacy, sometimes in subtle ways.

RACIAL IMAGERY, CAPITALIST VISIONS, AND COLONIALIST NARRATIVES

AI commentary is suffused with racial imagery in ways that we have encountered already. There was, for instance, the racialized and feminized Japanese "enemy" constructed by Edward Feigenbaum and Pamela McCorduck in the 1980s, part of a campaign for an American counterplan to Japan's state-sponsored initiative, as we saw in chapter 1. And in this period, as before, AI was framed as a kind of powerful "slave" that could power the economy.

Racial imagery has continued to animate AI, and references to slave labor persist. In his recent book on AI, MIT professor Max Tegmark states that "the reason that the Athenian citizens of antiquity had lives of leisure where they could enjoy democracy, art and games was mainly that they had slaves to do much of the work." He asks, "Why not replace the slaves with AI-powered robots, creating a digital utopia that everyone can enjoy?"[1] The slave metaphor here is inescapably racial—in fact, there is no clearer testament to the whiteness of the AI expert industry than the gleeful appeal to slavery as the force that can save American society in the twenty-first century.

As Toni Morrison has argued, racial metaphors are generally mobilized to disguise "forces, events, classes, and expressions of social decay and economic division far more threatening to the body politic than biological 'race' ever was."[2] The artificial slave does exactly that. Accordingly, AI experts have used the slave metaphor to reinforce capitalist visions of society and argue against threats to capital accumulation. Richard Barbrook and Andy Cameron have observed that AI has long been presented as a way to make a productive Golem—"a strong and loyal slave whose skin is the color of the earth and whose innards are made of sand"—while burying the social and economic relations required for this vision. Whatever machines the experts dream of, Barbrook and Cameron write, "can never remove the necessity for humans to invent, build and maintain these machines in the first place." In other words, slave labor is not possible "without somebody being enslaved."[3]

Yet it would be misleading to conclude that the artificial slave is mere dressing for the "real" capitalist agenda. Racial fictions run deep. Their constant presence in AI puts the field in the same category as the overtly biological racial sciences, such as eugenics, which are notorious for their racialized and gendered models of the self.

Tegmark's account of AI, for one, is predicated on a totalizing racial hierarchy. His premise is that AI will constitute "third generation" of life ("Life 3.0")—the first being bacteria ("Life 1.0"), and the second humans ("Life 2.0").[4] Such hierarchies get explicitly racialized through colonialist narratives, told by AI practitioners, that celebrate the supposed triumph of AI over human thought. For example, noted AI practitioner Jürgen Schmidhuber says it is probably a matter of decades until "human-level" AI is realized, and from there, it will be only a small step to achieve "superhuman" AI that, in order to utilize the vast "resources" of space, will eventually "establish a network of senders and receivers all over the galaxy."[5] In Tegmark's telling, such AI-created supercivilizations will recapitulate colonialist dynamics upon encounter. He writes that while "Europeans were able to conquer Africa and the Americas because they had superior technology," one superintelligent civilization may not so easily "conquer" another. But since "assimilating your neighbors is a faster expansion strategy than settlement," one superhuman civilization may assimilate the other based on the "superiority" of its ideas, thereby "leaving the assimilated better off." Tegmark concludes that AI could eventually "make us the masters of our own destiny not only in our Solar System or the Milky Way Galaxy, but also in the cosmos."[6] Du Bois thought whiteness was about "the ownership of the earth," but AI's luminaries want the whole cosmos.

Narratives of colonialization and imperial conquest are also echoed by the corporations that dominate the discourse on AI. Sometimes these companies even rehash themes of nineteenth-century colonialist discourse. Google, for instance, motivated its plan to instill a greater presence in Africa with the question, "Why is Africa dark?" (In this case, "dark" referred to the lack of Google-made mobile phones in the region.) As with the rest of Google's operations since 2018, the initiative targeting the continent is framed around AI, and the company's flagship project was the creation of an "AI" laboratory in Accra, Ghana.[7] A piece in CNN, authored by Google consultant, praised the effort: "Africa probably has more secrets about humanity than anywhere else in the world, and it is those secrets that 'computer programming that learns and adapts' (which is how Google describes AI) can help to uncover." The author considers various reasons for why "Africa's global reputation has suffered," such as "hunger, famine disease, poverty, and foreign aid" and the "consistency of conflicts and lousy leadership."[8] But the history of colonialism, enslavement, white supremacist governments, and other forms of exploitation by Western powers is omitted—an erasure that alone reinstates an imperial narrative. As Jemima Pierre has argued, "postcolonial" nations such as Ghana, where people racialized as white are a small minority, are still shaped by the global reaches and history of white supremacy—and Google's AI lab in Accra is a case in point.[9] The presentation of the lab reiterates nineteenth-century European colonial tropes of "the darkest Africa" as a site of savagery, as well as subsequent views, equally imperialist, of Africa's "darkness" as bearing many secrets that could benefit global capital.

Themes of imperial conquest and colonization are by no means limited to AI commentary, of course; they recur within the world of computing. The discourse on "cyberspace" is laced with imagery of colonization, openings of "new frontiers," and tales of "manifest destiny."[10] Rhetoric of colonization and conquest can also be found in the field of "Artificial Life" (ALife), which practitioners often describe as a quest to find the computational essence of life and reproduction. (Unsurprisingly, "ALife" capitalizes on the success of "AI" through its name.[11]) Some ALife practitioners conceive of themselves and the computational "organisms" they create as colonizers of new territories.[12] ALife practitioner Rudy Rucker even declared that "the manifest destiny of mankind" is "to pass the torch of life and intelligence on to the computer."[13] Moreover, some ALife systems employ concepts such as "miscegenation" to effectively codify racial and sexual hierarchies in computational terms.[14]

But while racial and gendered imagery abounds in the computing world, within AI, there is also a less overt manifestation of whiteness: one having to do with the flexible nature of whiteness as an ideology.

THE SHIFTING NEBULOSITY OF WHITENESS

The racial imagery we have encountered in AI discourse tends to be unstable. The rhetoric used by Feigenbaum and McCorduck in the early 1980s to describe a feminized and racialized Japanese "enemy," for instance, would be less palatable today. And Feigenbaum's declaration to the U.S. Congress that his nation must lead the world in AI, for it is the "manifest destiny of computing," probably would not be the choice phrase for contemporary experts.[15] Likewise, Herbert Simon and Allen Newell's early 1970s hierarchical depiction of "culture"—where "student" is placed above "worker" and "hippie," and where U.S. culture sits above that of the "French" and "Chinese"—would at best seem out of touch.[16]

This type of change is characteristic of the racial sciences, whose offerings have always been a moving target. As Nell Irvin Painter has observed, theorists of race such as Johann F. Blumenbach had to "walk a tightrope of contradictions" as they produced incoherent accounts of racial difference.[17] And the theories rapidly changed. Blumenbach's late eighteenth-century definition of the "five races" is long expired, for example, as is the account of the "eight races" embraced by W. E. B. Du Bois in the nineteenth century.[18] By now, attempts to ground race using anthropometrics are similarly out of fashion in mainstream science.[19]

The instability of the racial sciences demonstrates the shaky epistemic footing of theories of racial difference. But the instability also shows how nebulous whiteness is in that it can draw on the changing and contradictory fruits of the racial sciences. And the racial sciences are merely one component of the "makeshift patchwork" (as Cedric Robinson termed it) that is used to perpetuate white supremacy in response to new challenges and social conditions.[20]

American history offers many glimpses into the makeshift patchwork, and with it, the nebulous character of whiteness. The Naturalization Law of 1790 admitted only "free white" persons into the colonies, but such unspecified whiteness had to be revised after the large influx of Irish and Eastern European migrants—who were considered a "lesser" shade of white than the English colonists. This eventually led to what Matthew Frye Jacobson has called "the fracturing of whiteness": a condition where "whiteness itself would become newly problematic and, in some quarters, lose its monolithic character."[21] Americans of Japanese origin who sought citizenship on grounds of being "white" were rejected for not being "Caucasian"; migrants from India who claimed citizenship because they were deemed "Caucasian" by anthropologists were rejected for not being "white." The appearance of Arab migrants, too, threw a wrench in attempts to ground whiteness.[22]

Changing social and economic conditions meant that the instruments and logics that determined whiteness also had to change. To grasp whiteness, then, is not a matter of looking for its essence in any particular theory of race, but rather seeing how its ideological flexibility works to serve political interests.

In the latter part of the seventeenth century the colony of Virginia's slave codes repeatedly redefined whiteness using a calculus of capitalist and imperial interests. As more Africans were kidnapped into slavery and the supply of European indentured labor decreased, these codes helped to sustain the system of African slave labor.[23] For example, these laws instated that blacks who convert to Christianity would remain enslaved—a deviation from English law at the time, which forbade enslavement of Christians. There were other peculiar deviations from English law.[24] By English convention, citizenship passed through the father, yet Virginia adopted a rule where children born to enslaved women remain in bondage. As the notion of American whiteness congealed, such rules implicitly answered the question of whether mixed children could be "white," but did so in a way that helped slaveholders expand their labor force by exploiting black women's reproductive labor (and while sanctioning the rape of enslaved women by white men). Yet these dictates of whiteness were inconsistent, as they often are, across race and gender lines: white women, by comparison, faced fines and potential jail time for giving birth to a "mulatto" child. A variety of relations between whites and blacks were similarly punished by law, partly to repress cross-racial rebellions.[25]

In settler-colonialist societies, additional considerations go into the contradictory making of whiteness. While the one-drop-of-blood rule made one "black" in the eyes of the law—as conducive to maintaining the supply of unfree labor—Native

Americans often had to meet a more stringent criterion based on "blood quantum" in order to count as "Indian" for the U.S. government.[26] This did not mean, of course, that Native Americans became fully "white" with respect to privilege and social standing, but rather that the settler-colonialist impulse to erase indigenous peoples, or violently assimilate them into white society, was the prevailing consideration—and that this was a distinct logic from that applied to enslaved Africans.[27]

These are some of the contingencies and contradictions that go into the making of whiteness. As Charles Mills has observed, racial categories are thus simultaneously "unreal," in that they lack the solid grounding in phenotypic features such as light skin, and "real," in that racial categories have "a massive effect on people's psychology, culture, socioeconomic opportunities, life chances, civil rights."[28]

The all too real consequences of whiteness come from its connection to concrete systems of power. From colonial America to the present, whiteness has been intertwined with capitalist conceptions of property inscribed into law. One's whiteness functions *as* property in American law, as Cheryl Harris has argued.[29] Harris's breathtaking explication of whiteness as property begins with the phenomenon of blacks "passing" as whites. She recounts the story of her own grandmother, who, owing to a combination of phenotype and circumstance, could "pass" as white in her workplace in Chicago in the 1930s. At the time, this gained Harris's grandmother access to an economic opportunity (though at incalculable psychological cost) denied to women perceived as black.

Passing shows the artificiality of whiteness. Yet it also demonstrates the tangible rewards conferred by being seen as "white," which historically include the right to vote, own property, work, and choose where to live and whom to marry. There are also less tangible, though still protected by law, elements to whiteness. These include the expectation of certain futures and the right to one's reputation as a white person: in court rulings from as late as the 1950s, calling a "white" person "black" was considered defamation; the reverse clearly not.[30] By protecting these rights and expectations, American law has reinstated whites' "property interest" in whiteness—an interest predicated on the right to exclude others.[31]

How American law deals with whiteness has changed in response to popular struggle, but as Harris notes, "property interest in whiteness has proven to be resilient and adaptive to new conditions." Calls for affirmative action, for example, have challenged the notion that societies built on white supremacy can be made just by simply removing the most overt forms of discrimination. These efforts were contested in court by whites who saw affirmative action as "reverse discrimination." As Harris has argued, by siding with white plaintiffs and rejecting affirmative action in key instances, the courts have effectively defended white privilege. For instance, in admission to graduate schools, courts have defended the expectation of whites to be privileged over nonwhites by identifying certain criteria of "merit," such as standardized test scores, as neutral while ignoring alternatives.[32] These moves cement the notion that the law must protect the expectation of whites, as a group, to dominate educational institutions. White supremacy can therefore be defended by adopting more abstract, ostensibly nonracialized, criteria of "merit."

Indeed, while the right to exclude persists in all of forms of white supremacy—from colonial America to affirmative action cases in the 1970s—the manifestations of this right and its justifications have changed. As many have recognized, then, whiteness as an ideology cannot be stably grounded in any specific racial account because whiteness is empty. "Whiteness,

alone," Toni Morrison wrote, "is mute, meaningless, unfathom-
able, pointless, frozen, veiled, curtained, dreaded, senseless,
implacable."[33] Whiteness gets its significance, and its changing
shape, only from the need to maintain relations of power. AI
reproduces this quality of whiteness.

MIMICKING WHITENESS IN FORM

We have seen how AI is a tool that serves the dominant aims of
white supremacy. In that sense, it is not unlike financial and legal
instruments, which are also used to reinforce white supremacy.
But there is more to the linkage between AI and whiteness: AI
can perform its service so well partly because it mimics the
structure of whiteness as an ideology.

Like the ideology of whiteness, AI has been a nebulous, moving target from its inception. From the moment the label "AI"
was coined, its boundaries were unstable. What counts as AI has
repeatedly changed, as we have seen, and attempts to ground AI
in technical terms, along a set of epistemic considerations or even
scientific goals, could never keep this endeavor together.

There is, however, strong continuity to different iterations of
"AI," but it does not lie in the axes that cognitive scientists, philosophers, and AI practitioners have typically focused on. Continuity arises, instead, from the ways in which AI is situated and
justified. As we saw in chapter 1, AI was continually remade to
be that which can serve empire. This resulted in narratives that
recur across different periods in striking detail. Whether it was
as part of imperial competition with Japan in the 1980s or with
China in the 2010s, the "magical chip" narrative—according
to which the latest hardware would enable AI's promised
breakthrough—has been steadily rehearsed. Likewise, the use

of AI as a pretext to advance capitalist visions of society and thwart alternatives has been a fixture of AI expert commentary (as we saw in chapter 2). In every iteration, we find the practice of situating AI within capitalist and imperialist agendas.

AI's iterations did vary significantly in epistemic terms, and these differences played into AI's political functions. Each iteration brought distinct models of the self, which came with somewhat different implications about what it means to know, as well as about the roles AI practitioners would play in society. In the dominant narratives of the 1960s and 1970s, for example, the self was an agent in pursuit of rational goals whose inner processing was captured by symbolic representations (exemplified by Newell and Simon's work). Later, when expert systems became the celebrated form of AI, the dominant epistemic myths still revolved around human intelligence and knowledge as a form of symbolic processing. Expert systems also came with a specific notion of "expertise." Knowledge was to be elicited from "domain experts" by yet another set of knowledge-encoding (or "knowledge representation") experts, while AI practitioners were in charge of building the platforms that knowledge-encoding experts use. AI practitioners were also expected to "train" the knowledge-encoding experts; to help knowledge encoders elicit knowledge from domain experts.

In the late 1980s and early 1990s, neural networks—which weren't even considered "AI" by early practitioners—became AI's centerpieces and brought rather different fictions about the self. The self of this period was a radically empiricist machine. Since knowledge was now to be learned from data, the knowledge-encoding experts of AI's prior iterations weren't necessary. AI practitioners themselves also had a different role now. Their primary task was no longer to design computing platforms for encoding rich knowledge but rather to set the conditions for

machines to "learn" it from data in tabula rasa fashion (a framing that shares much with neoliberal economic theory). At a
technical level, their task was largely to choose a computational
architecture, decide what counts as data, and train the architecture until it produced the behavior of interest. In this framing,
experts were merely creating the conditions for a computational
process that was supposedly independent of them—and even
surpassed human capacities.

Although different in all these ways, every iteration of AI
consistently brought models of the self that were racialized,
classed, and gendered, and predicated on the same major epistemic forgeries (like the aspiration to a "view from nowhere," as
we saw in chapter 3). The salient point, then, is that while different epistemic tenets and computing systems were repackaged
as "AI" and others pushed out, the endeavor has rather stably
served an imperial and capitalist agenda (as with the ideology
of whiteness).

But as with the ideology of whiteness, AI had to be adapted
to new social conditions and struggles against oppression. The
rebranding of AI in the 2010s, as we saw, helped to divert attention from a confrontation with mass surveillance and a backlash
against Silicon Valley's neoliberal visions of data-driven world
governance. In this period, "AI" became a new gloss for familiar computing systems and projects, such as building platforms
of behavior modification and control. Models of the self,
informed by these political projects, were being served: the self
as a connectionist machine, not unlike prior iterations of AI, but
also an explicitly behaviorist conception of "intelligence" as the
product of environmental rewards and punishments. The
rebranded AI's experts, like their predecessors in the 1980s,
offered narratives about how AI would enable a capitalist utopia
and presented mastery of AI as crucial to imperial hegemony.

But the rebranded AI also gave rise to "critical AI experts" that speak of social justice (which we will encounter again later in this chapter). In this recent shift, AI continues to serve the same agendas, but with a progressive veneer; an example of its adaptability. As with the ideology of whiteness, this adaptability is enabled by AI's plastic character and incoherence.

Put differently, who counts as "white" and how "nonwhites" stand in relation to "whites," historically, cannot be reduced to any given theory of the racial sciences, let alone simple phenotypic features, since whiteness bends to political and economic agendas that vary across contexts. Similarly, what has counted as "AI" historically cannot be reduced to any technical or epistemic account of computing systems divorced from the machinations of empire and capital. The latter mirrors the nebulous character of the former, and in both cases the nebulosity is used to advance the same tangible projects of empire and capital.

This gives AI the "unreal-yet-real" aspect that is characteristic of racial categories. AI is unreal because it is nebulous, unstable, lacking in solid grounding, and continually redefined by powerful interests in ways that seem arbitrary. Yet it is real in that it is part of concrete, destructive practices. As we have seen, the nebulous-sounding initiatives around AI in fact support global projects of dispossession and land accumulation.

THE WHITE VOICE OF AI EXPERTS

The unreal character of AI has also made it, like whiteness, prone to breakdowns—occasions where the incoherence surfaces. But in AI's case, these moments are often exaggerated. As one commentator observed during the 1980s, "AI refuses to die."[34] AI persists, in part, because it captures the aspirations of the still very white expert class that reconfigures it in the service of empire and capital. In the experts' professional milieu, AI can be invoked with little to no explanation because it shares the unstated premises of whiteness. That AI is nebulous to the point of emptiness is invisible, along with the premises of whiteness generally, to those who are invested in it.

Raymond Lawrence ("Boots") Riley's film *Sorry to Bother You* (2018) brings out some of these premises of whiteness and their intimate ties to capitalism. The film's protagonist, Cassius ("Cash") Green, who is black, finds work at a telemarketing center. An older black colleague offers Cash some friendly advice: if you want to sell things over the phone, use your "white voice." The colleague explains: "It's not about sounding all nasal. It's about sounding like you don't have a care. Like your bills are paid and you're happy about your future. . . . Breezy, like you don't need this money, like you never been fired, only laid off."[35]

The white voice, as the film brilliantly demonstrates, is a politically useful fiction, not an imitation of any white person's voice. As Cash's colleague says, "It's not what all White people sound like—there ain't no real White voice, but it's what they wish they sounded like. It's what they think they're supposed to sound like." The white voice merely stands for what whiteness as an ideology promises to those who think they can climb up the ladder of privilege. Robin D. G. Kelley notes that this voice rests on an expectation: "Like whiteness itself, the white voice is a chimera, masking a specific class position and conveying a sense of being genuinely *worry free*, with no bills to pay, money in the bank, not a care in the world. This is the *expectation* of whiteness—an expectation many white people never, in fact, realize."[36]

A white voice dominates the expert discourse on AI. This voice tries to instill order by appealing to the expectation of whiteness. It instructs that the latest technology may be harnessed either for "our" universal good or for ill, and thus "we" have a rational choice to make about our future—a potentially marvelous future in which "our" problems are fixed by technical means through consultation with the appropriate state, military, and corporate "stakeholders."

The white voice can be heard in statements such as these:

- "We have tried to promote an optimistic view of AI as an activity with positive economic and social impacts even for low-budget countries or groups."[37]
- "[AI has] extraordinary potential upsides, from reducing worldwide energy consumption and addressing climate change . . . we still have an opportunity to influence the design and use of these tools for good."[38]
- "[The] AI-driven economy would not only eliminate stress and drudgery and produce an abundance of everything we want today, but it would also supply a bounty of wonderful new products."[39]
- "AI can make our legal systems more fair and efficient if we can figure out how to make robojudges transparent and unbiased. . . . [These could] treat everyone equally, transparently applying the law in truly unbiased fashion."[40]
- "[AI] is changing the world before our eyes. Once the province of science fiction, we now carry systems powered by AI in our pockets and wear them on our wrists. Vehicles on the market can now drive themselves, diagnostic systems determine what is ailing us, and risk assessment algorithms increasingly decide whether we are jailed or set free after being charged with a crime."[41]
- "The promise of AI to improve our lives is enormous. . . . Automated hiring systems promise to evaluate job candidates

on the basis of their bona fide qualifications, rather than on qualities such as age or appearance that often lead human decision-makers astray."[42]

- "AI will underpin our future prosperity. . . . This is only the start; the potential of AI is undeniable. . . . AI [could] free up time and raise productivity."[43]

- "So what career advice *should* we give our kids? I'm encouraging mine to go into professions that machines are currently bad at, and therefore seem unlikely to get automated in the near future."[44]

- "AI may lift us into a new kind of existence, where our humanity will be not only preserved but also enhanced in ways we can hardly imagine."[45]

All these commentaries suggest that "AI" can bring a wonderful future whose direction everyone can shape, thus encapsulating the expectation of whiteness and the reassuring quality of the white voice. The white voice here also reveals the intended audience. It is mostly professional elites who would accept the notion that the latest techno-product could be put to "everyone's" future benefit by networked leaders from the corporate, academic, and military-state worlds. To speculate on the management of these AI-based futures is to speak in the white voice.

There is real investment in the continued dominance of the white voice. Through the web of partnerships and initiatives we encountered in chapter 2, the commentators quoted are invested in the idea of AI as a coherent and transformative force that they can manage and interpret. Funds, media attention, university curricula, academic publications, and policy reports all rest on this notion—hence the investment. The investment in AI can be seen as part of what George Lipsitz has called the "possessive investment" in whiteness.[46] Like Du Bois and Harris, Lipsitz noted that there are tangible rewards to individuals who cling to their whiteness, possessing it like property. Leaving "AI" unscrutinized as commentators across the spectrum do pays off, and the white voice continues to dominate.

The white voice within AI, as in other discourses, can be interrupted when whiteness itself is challenged. Many whites are unable to withstand such challenges, a condition Robin DiAngelo has termed "white fragility." White fragility is the anger, defensiveness, and frustration that "racial stress" triggers in whites; stress that can be induced by simply naming structures of white privilege that are meant to be invisible. Identifying whiteness is jarring because of the widespread assumption that being white means having an "unracialized identity or location." Whiteness, as DiAngelo pointed out, "is not recognized or named" because it is presumed to be "a universal reference point."[47] In the white voice of AI commentary, the pretense to universality is obvious, and the idea of "universal" intelligence has been one of AI's major epistemic forgeries. Yet interruptions of white universality are rare, whether in AI or elsewhere, because, as DiAngelo writes, many whites inhabit "racially insular" environments where interlocutors who could "racialize" white people's understandings and experiences are absent. The discourse on AI has likewise developed within such racially insular spheres, and so the white voice of AI expertise generally goes uninterrupted.

In cases where AI has been challenged, however, the critics were often met with contempt, demonstrating AI's white fragility. Even critiques of the concept of AI on narrow grounds provoked extreme defensiveness from practitioners and were sometimes recorded in AI's histories as moments of crisis. As we saw previously, when the mathematician James Lighthill—who thought "the general purpose robot is a mirage"—challenged

AI's coherence as a field, he was met with derision, and practitioners blamed later funding shortages for AI on his critique. More general critiques, such as those offered by the philosopher Hubert Dreyfus—which we will revisit in the next chapter—were met with even greater hostility. Dreyfus was said to be merely validating "his passionately held preconceptions," of engaging in an "infra dig" quest to "discredit" the AI community, and prominent practitioners have broadly accused critics of using "arguments of emotion" or having "animosity" toward the field of AI.[48]

But while these critiques evoked great hostility, they weren't grounded in the understanding of AI as a technology of whiteness. To challenge AI as a technology of whiteness means taking seriously how its nebulous and shifting character serves power. This entails not only challenging AI's models of the self and their epistemic forgeries but also the legitimacy of the expert industry that gives the pursuit of AI its destructive powers and superficial coherence. Challenging, in other words, the institutions that sustain the endeavor.

WHITENESS AND THE POLITICS OF REPRESENTATION

If AI is a nebulous and flexible technology of power that helps to sustain structures of white supremacy, doing so in more roundabout ways than direct privileging of "white" over "nonwhite," then responding to it with a politics of representation is inadequate. Yet following the rebranding of AI in the 2010s, much of the discourse has revolved around the diversity of AI's professional orbit. These appeals to a politics of representation do not disrupt the projects AI serves; in fact, they sometimes provide these projects with new ammunition.

The group Black in AI exemplifies the focus on representation. The group's aim is to "increase the presence of Black people in the field of Artificial Intelligence," and Black in AI draws on the imagery and language of the U.S. civil rights movement and the black radical tradition: the group's logo is a schematic raised fist, associated with Black Power and workers' movements (see figure 5.1).[49] In principle, Black in AI's attention to representation is important—a recognition that the field of computing, like the broader corporate and academic worlds, has been dominated by white men to the exclusion of others. The composition of a field, as feminist inquiries into science and technology have repeatedly shown, undoubtedly shapes its directions, its questions, and the sort of knowledge it produces.[50]

But it is also essential to consider what is missed by Black in AI's understanding of representation, which is shaped by the fact that the group is firmly ensconced in the corporate world. The group's meetings are sponsored by companies such as Facebook, Google, Uber, and Microsoft, and several of Black in AI's main organizers are employed by these companies. The group embraces the initiatives of these corporations, such as Google's creation of an AI lab in Accra. While the narrative of an American multinational corporation presenting itself as harbinger of technological salvation invites a counter grounded in anticolonial and anti-imperial movements, Black in AI does not provide it.

Black in AI shares its corporate sponsors' view that AI is a coherent and transformative that can be harnessed to everyone's benefit. In this frame, the important task is to increase the "diversity" of the corporate and public labor force, as Black in AI's cofounder argued in a piece for *Forbes* business magazine.[51]

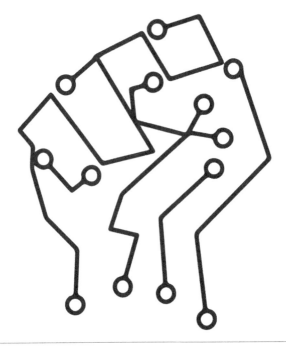

FIGURE 5.1 Logo for the group Black in AI. Credit: Black in AI.

The article appeared in a special issue on AI that was sponsored by Intel Corporation, alongside puff pieces that celebrate how AI can boost profits. The issue even included an article from Intel titled "5 Ways Technology Can Help Companies Create Better Narratives."[52] My point is that the focus on representation, as articulated here, works to do just that: help companies create better narratives.

A politics of representation also takes on more nuanced forms in the work of critical AI experts. The work of the MIT Media Lab, a major player in the critical AI space, shows how a quest for increased representation can end up reinforcing white supremacy in subtle ways.

The Media Lab was founded in the 1980s as a pioneering attempt to bridge the corporate and academic worlds.[53] Located at MIT, the lab is sponsored in large part by corporations (from Google and Microsoft to large pharmaceutical companies and weapons manufacturers), and in exchange these companies receive access to the lab's personnel and their products. The lab has cultivated its image as a progressive, diverse, and youthful hub, not only by drawing on the language of entrepreneurship and tech-utopianism, as it did in its early days, but also by appropriating the language of "disobedience" from social movements.[54] It is sold as a place where networked venture capitalists, entrepreneurs, technologists, and activists join in a struggle against oppression, a framing the lab has used for its recent AI initiatives.

Media Lab researcher Joy Buolamwini's work on facial recognition demonstrates how the politics of representation that emerges from this web of partnerships reproduces a logic of white supremacy. Through a combination of poetry, media interventions, and computational experiments, Buolamwini explored the logic of facial recognition software, which she takes to exemplify the racial and gender "bias" of AI. Buolamwini, who is black, describes how widely used software generally failed to identify her face in a photograph but could do so when she wore a white mask. In describing this experience, Buolamwini invokes Frantz Fanon's *Black Skin, White Masks* and his notion of the "white gaze," when she presents AI as constituting the "coded gaze."[55]

Buolamwini made these ideas vivid in a video poem titled "AI, Ain't I a Woman?"—a riff on a well-known transcription of Sojourner Truth's speech in 1851.[56] In the video, Buolamwini narrates the output of face recognition software (which she refers to as "AI") on a series of photographs of black women, including Sojourner Truth, Ida B. Wells, Oprah Winfrey, and Michelle Obama.[57]

The poem opens with the question, "Can artificial intelligence technology guess the gender of Oprah, Serena, and other iconic women?" Photographs of Wells and the cover of her *Southern Horrors* pamphlet later flash on the screen. The poem makes an appeal to the major platform corporations. As the logos of Amazon, Microsoft, IBM, Google, and Facebook appear, Buolamwini narrates: "Today we pose this question to new powers. . . . The Amazonians peek through windows blocking Deep Blues, as faces increment scars . . . collecting data chronicling our past, often forgetting to deal with gender, race, and class." Then the video cuts to a screenshot of IBM's facial recognition software, showing its 66 percent confidence score in detecting a "toupee" in a photograph of a young Michelle Obama. Buolamwini also shows how corporate facial recognition software detects the face in Ida B. Wells's iconic photograph but infers it is "Male" with high confidence (figure 5.2). All these results are taken to show the racial and gender "bias" of AI.

This understanding of bias is explored more systematically in "Gender Shades," a collaboration between Buolamwini and Microsoft's research center.[58] The premise of Gender Shades is that AI is a powerful force transforming society, and hence its biases must be studied.[59] Like the poem, the project asks whether facial recognition software can "guess the gender" of individuals based on their photograph. But the reference to gender should be interpreted cautiously here: the software only produces "Male" or "Female" labels, sometimes with a confidence score, and so cannot guess the "gender" in any substantive

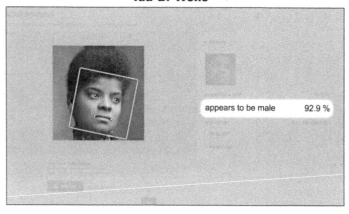

Ida B. Wells

appears to be male   92.9 %

FIGURE 5.2 Screenshot from Joy Buolamwini's video poem
"AI, Ain't I A Woman?"

sense—particularly if gender is understood as a dynamic state of being, not reducible to a photograph.[60] Nonetheless, the project's assumption is that male/female labels, alongside skin tone shade, can be used to probe the "intersectionality" of computing platforms. To do so, Buolamwini and colleagues compiled a series of photographed faces, which they ordered by continent, nation-state, male/female binary, and skin tone (figure 5.3). They then ranked the major facial recognition platforms based on how "correct" each was in assigning these predefined labels to photographs. The software's failures were interpreted as instances of underrepresentation of certain groups, notably black women—a "diversity" problem to be fixed, like that plaguing corporations. Indeed, Buolamwini has argued that having a more diverse workforce at corporations such as Google and Facebook can help deliver a transformative "ethical" AI.[61]

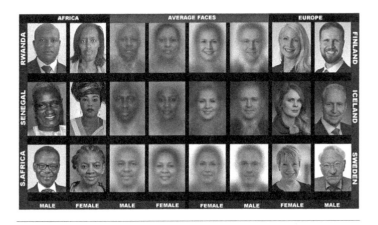

FIGURE 5.3 Data set of images used by Gender Shades project. Photographs of faces classified according to continent/nation-state, skin tone, and male/female binary.

Yet with this understanding of representation, Gender Shades offers something more dangerous. The project offers a quantitative metric of "diversity" that major enablers of the carceral state, such as Microsoft, can use to optimize their products for broader facial recognition. And this tangible offering also comes with a framing that makes it all look like a quest for social justice. Gender Shades and Buolamwini's commentaries therefore exemplify carceral-positive logic and the rebranded AI's adaptation to changing political sensibilities. By infusing the rhetoric of "bias" correction with imagery from the black radical tradition and civil rights movement, this line of work ultimately enhances the carceral eye, encouraging it to expand its scope; to objectify and classify more races, genders, and phenotypes, and their intersection with readily computable variables such as nationality (figure 5.3)—in short, to bring more of the world into the carceral eye's mineable digital catalog.[62]

In recent history there have been other calls to expand carceral techniques in the name of equal representation. Angela Y. Davis recounts the case of the state of Alabama's effort to reinstate chain gangs not just for men but also women prisoners, after incarcerated men filed a suit claiming that they were being discriminated against as men. As Davis explained, this paved the way for Sheriff Joe Arpaio of Arizona (often referred to as "America's toughest sheriff") to introduce chain gangs for incarcerated women in his state—referring to himself as an "equal opportunity incarcerator."[63] At the time, Arpaio declared that his prisons would be discrimination-free zones where women are treated just like men. Davis has also described arguments, made in the name of gender parity and even feminism, that women who flee should be shot at by the prison guards—just as men escapees are treated. Greater state violence against women should not, obviously, be the goal of feminism.

Buolamwini's calls are a world apart from these crudely procarceral arguments that call for direct carceral violence. Buolamwini's effort, by contrast, provides a progressive, even radical, cloak for the carceral eye's expansion—hence it is carceral-positive. And this carceral-positive stance gives the impression that platform companies such as Microsoft, Amazon, and Google are nearly on the same page as Frantz Fanon and Ida B. Wells (or may get there with some adjustments that are within reach).[64] This framing is not just a matter of theoretical debate; it plays into tangible projects. As the *New York Times* reported, Google has recently "sought out black homeless people" in Atlanta, Georgia, collecting images of their faces using mobile devices, in order to reduce the bias of the company's facial recognition systems with respect to nonwhites. In response to the newspaper's inquiry about these activities, Google executives stated: "Our goal in this case has been to ensure we have a fair and secure feature that works across different skin tones and face shapes."[65] Similarly, a Microsoft-backed company that provides the Israeli military with systems to surveil Palestinians in the West Bank, aided by facial recognition, has expressed their commitment to producing "technology [that] won't be biased based on gender or race. . . . We're very sensitive to such matters, so of all the companies in the world, Microsoft decided to go with us."[66] These companies are following a carceral-positive line of thinking.

Nabil Hassein has offered an alternative to this carceral-positive stance. Hassein takes it as given that "most if not all data collected by police [is] to serve their inherently racist mission." "It is equally clear," he continues, "that no technology under police control will be used to hold police accountable or to benefit Black folks or other oppressed people." On the point of representation more broadly, he writes: "Liberation of Black folks and all oppressed peoples will never be achieved by inclusion in systems controlled by a capitalist elite which benefits from the perpetuation of racism and related oppressions." In what Buolamwini diagnoses as a systemic bias to be corrected, Hassein sees an opportunity for subversion and respite, a chance "to gain some temporary advantages by partially obscuring ourselves from the eyes of the white supremacist state."[67]

Frantz Fanon had in fact articulated this very view in *Black Skin, White Masks*. On feeling dissected by the "white gaze," he wrote: "I slip into corners; all I want is to be anonymous, to be forgotten. Look, I'll agree to everything, on condition I go unnoticed!"[68] This instinct was not, of course, Fanon's final position. But whatever thread one chooses from Fanon's nuanced perspective in *Black Skin, White Masks*, it is incompatible with extending the carceral eye.

Whiteness has always been artificial, and in AI, whiteness as an ideology finds not only a useful technology but also another form of expression. AI advances the imperial and capitalist agenda of a social order based on white supremacy and does so by reproducing the nebulous and shifting character of whiteness. And AI, like whiteness, tries to pin down human nature, by constantly producing racialized, gendered, and classed models of the self that are imprinted with the political projects of white supremacy.

The frame of whiteness, as I have argued, helps account for AI's formation in the white military-industrial-academic complex of the 1950s, its subsequent reconfigurations, as well as its persistent epistemic forgeries. We can summarize the linkage between whiteness and AI as follows:

- Like whiteness, AI is nebulous, changing to meet new conditions and challenges, and therefore defies any essentialist characterization based on technical or scientific taxonomies. Like whiteness, AI cannot be understood without considering its imperial and capitalist origins. And like whiteness, AI is tied to racialized and gendered models of the self.

- Like whiteness, AI is hollow: its meaning derives largely from the imperial and capitalist projects that sustain it. As with whiteness, this emptiness confers AI with great malleability, allowing it to adapt to social change and continue to serve the same powerful interests. The computational domain offers layers of indirection and obfuscation, which help AI flexibly move beyond militaristic discourses into ones that invoke social justice or even black radical thought.[69]

- Attempts to expose the nebulous and incoherent basis of AI reveal the "white fragility" of those invested in it as a technology of power. These attempts have elicited the same hostile response as other efforts to name whiteness and structures of white supremacy (rather than viewing them as natural, meritorious, or byproducts of technological progress).

Ultimately, then, AI is a technology of power that serves whiteness in part by mimicking its structure. AI's trajectory provides an example of how whiteness can be reproduced in abstract domains, seemingly removed from the conventional spheres of power such as the law and economic policy.[70]

But if AI has been so intimately linked to whiteness, what, if anything, can be salvaged from it? This is the topic of the next chapter.

III

ALTERNATIVES

6

DISSENTING VISIONS

From Autopoietic Love to Embodied War

Attach a pacemaker to the heart of those machines you hate;
make it pump for your decolonizing enterprise; let it tick its own
countdown. Ask how, and how otherwise, of the colonizing
machines. Even when they are dangerous.

—la paperson

In previous chapters we saw that although AI's boundaries were contested and its computational engines always changing, the endeavor has consistently advanced imperial and capitalist visions. I have argued that AI is a technology of power that serves white supremacy and even reproduces the ideological form of whiteness. AI is nebulous and dynamic, with its reconfigurations steered by imperial and capitalist projects. AI practitioners have steadily produced racial, gendered, and classed models of the self that both reflect and recharge these projects.

This raises the question: Can something like what AI purports to be—an attempt to understand ourselves, our minds, and behavior in computational terms—be pursued differently? Might there be radical computational visions that shed AI's epistemic forgeries and oppose the imperial and capitalist interests that have sustained that endeavor? Since AI has been contested from the start, even by insiders, can we find alternatives in these critiques? Or is the endeavor, by virtue of its framing around computation, or its place in a scientific tradition intimately connected to state power and capital, so compromised that it will merely reproduce AI's flaws? These questions are not limited to AI. They can be asked about cognitive science, cybernetics, and biology—all lines of inquiry that have attempted to give a systematic account of the self.

One could question the scientific enterprise altogether, as some scientists and activists in fact have.[1] There are traditions that question the idea that scientific knowledge is produced only in universities or laboratories, and even challenge the very notion of the laboratory.[2] These challenges and the issues they raise are crucial, but my scope will be far narrower, and much more in the spirit of la paperson's call to probe "the heart of those machines you hate"—and to ask "how otherwise," even when the machines are dangerous.[3]

In this chapter I draw on critiques of AI, as well as dissenting visions of minds and bodies from cognitive science and biology, to explore the prospects of an alternative endeavor. These critical streams are worth examining because they frame thought and action in ways that emphasize those aspects that AI has traditionally ignored, such as the body and the situatedness of knowledge. These attempts usually fall under the banner of "embodied" or "situated" cognition, though these labels refer to a range of distinct approaches.[4] What they share, however, is a disavowal of AI's dominant epistemic premises.

The framing, feel, and language around embodied cognition certainly appear to be a radical departure from mainstream AI and cognitive science. Whereas many practitioners within AI and cognitive science emphasize centralized control and execution of plans in top-down fashion, embodied approaches talk of decentralization and emergence. Whereas cognitive orthodoxy looks to abstract declarative knowledge (the "knowing what"), the situated approach emphasizes practice and context (the "knowing how"). The aura is different in other ways, too. Many of the most influential works on embodied approaches acknowledge the social dimensions of their inquiry. Some even speak of love and collective living. These formulations deviate from the centralized "command-and-control" vision running through much of AI. For this reason, the embodied and situated streams were sometimes seen as hopeful alternatives by critics of AI.

Somewhat ironically, though, the embodied and situated streams are generally not situated within their own history and practices. The aura of embodiment elides the fact that these lines of inquiry were also shaped by imperial aims. Often these streams reproduced central elements of the orthodoxy that they were thought to overthrow, in the ways we will see in this chapter. But my aim is not simply to dismiss these attempts as naive or to promote the cynical attitude that the structures of empire and capital cannot be overcome. Rather, my purpose here is to take a closer look at what has been offered and how it has been practiced, in the hope of furthering attempts to sketch alternatives.

In her critique of AI's gendered epistemologies, Alison Adam raised the possibility that asking for a "feminist AI," as an alternative to existing AI, might be like asking for a feminist fighter plane.[5] This is to say that asking for "alternatives" to an endeavor such as AI is fraught with contradictions. Like Adam, I find the question of alternatives, posed in this chapter, vexing. The very way it is framed might simply lead to an impasse unless we revisit more fundamental premises. My discussion in this chapter can be read as an exploration of what these premises might be; what ought to be reconsidered or abandoned.

I will begin with one of the early and influential critiques of AI that draws on the tradition of philosophical phenomenology, since this tradition has influenced the embodied and situated streams within AI's orbit. The critique from phenomenology and its limitations will set the stage for our discussion of embodied and situated cognition.

A PHENOMENOLOGICAL CRITIQUE

As AI's critics have argued, the field has largely adopted the epistemology of the "analytic" philosophical tradition.[6] This epistemology—generally associated with Descartes, fairly or not—places boundaries between mind and body, and between the external world and the subject.[7] In this frame, subjects are primarily reflective, thinking agents: they observe and reason about an external world that they do not substantively shape. AI's challengers often borrowed from philosophers who have critiqued this analytic frame, such as Maurice Merleau-Ponty and Martin Heidegger. Merleau-Ponty, for instance, has argued that the sciences of the mind should move away from abstraction and be regrounded in the experience of being in the world. "Science manipulates things and gives up dwelling in them," he wrote, and therefore "confronts the actual world only from greater and greater distances." Scientific accounts of thought, he argued, employ increasingly opaque instruments and models in which to think is "to operate, to transform . . . phenomena produced by our machines rather than recorded by them." Merleau-Ponty thought that science instead needed to pay attention to the body and dispense with boundaries between world and subject, perception and action.[8]

The philosopher Hubert Dreyfus saw AI as a distillation of the "Cartesian" epistemology that Merleau-Ponty (and Heidegger) had critiqued.[9] Drawing on their work, he sketched one of the most well-known critiques of AI. Dreyfus's critique is rooted in the observation that any "intelligent" being in a position to discuss facts about the world must "already be in a situation." Human beings are always in the middle of things, facing a situation that demands action. The situation, Dreyfus says, is a product of our cultures and bodies. But the analytic epistemic frame, which valorizes abstract reasoning, fails to capture this basic condition of being. Dreyfus illustrates the point through a discussion of the most banal physical objects:

> No piece of equipment makes sense by itself. . . . What makes an object a *chair* is its function, and what makes possible its role as equipment for sitting is its place in a total practical context. This presupposes certain facts about human beings (fatigue, the ways the body bends), and a network of other culturally determined equipment (tables, floors, lamps), and skills (eating, writing, going to conferences, giving lectures, etc.). Chairs would not be equipment for sitting if our knees bent backwards like those of flamingos, or if we had no tables as in traditional Japan or the Australian bush.[10]

Even a chair, as Dreyfus argues, brings out the tradition and context that are normally taken for granted.

Dreyfus uses this phenomenological understanding to sketch a wide-ranging critique. He shoots many arrows at AI, from different and sometimes contradictory perspectives. At the core, he criticizes efforts to build "intelligent" systems based on formal, symbolic rules (such as Newell and Simon's GPS). According to Dreyfus, this is a senseless endeavor. To navigate an environment filled with objects, such as chairs, is simply part of being in the world. Reducing narrow swaths of this world to formal rules and categories as AI's "micro-worlds" or game-playing systems do, Dreyfus says, will not capture the rich background understanding that people take for granted. This line of reasoning gives Dreyfus's critique the feel of an in-principle case against AI.[11]

At other times, however, Dreyfus subscribes to a pragmatism that is not altogether different from that of AI practitioners. Here, we have the start of a theme that will emerge more fully later: a case where a critique of AI seemingly motivated by an opposing ideological perspective ends up reproducing much of AI's orthodoxy.

Like the practitioners he criticizes, Dreyfus subscribes to a distinction between the framework and its applications—and to the idea that frameworks "prove" themselves by leading to useful products. Alongside sweeping objections to the use of narrow domains, Dreyfus also posits milestones for AI, such as playing chess as well as grandmasters or driving a car. These challenges have made it easier to dismiss Dreyfus's critique with time, especially today when many seem to believe that roads dominated by driverless cars are around the corner. The embrace of pragmatic utility is a general weakness of Dreyfus's critique, as it is clearly possible to build systems premised on epistemic forgeries that still make for useful products.

Despite holding a privileged place for applications, however, Dreyfus's critique remains rather abstract. He fixates on AI's epistemology to the exclusion of the field's social context and politics.[12] Dreyfus is not altogether blind to these aspects; his critique is interspersed with observations about AI's social structure (recall his remark that AI is "the least self-critical field in the world"), but they are not developed. And while Dreyfus acknowledged that AI practitioners, driven by pragmatic aims, won't be swayed by his critique, he does not delve into the roots of their resistance.[13] Dreyfus does not, for one, analyze the ways in which the military-industrial complex has shaped AI's course.

Indeed, Dreyfus's own work developed in that militarized world. Recall that his first report on AI in the 1960s was written for the military consultancy RAND.[14] And in the 1970s and 1980s Dreyfus and his brother Stuart, an applied mathematician, were funded by the U.S. Air Force to develop a "situated" phenomenological line of thinking in the service of war. The Dreyfus brothers advocated for training pilots using a situated model, aided by flight simulators and other techniques, which they argued was far superior to pilots passively listening to instructors. As they wrote: "Every effort should be made to encourage the pilot's imaginative involvement," which their situated model apparently does, and having "training sessions in a cockpit . . . is a step in this direction."[15]

The ease with which this line of work serves military aims raises a deeper issue with the phenomenological perspective. In Dreyfus's phenomenological frame, individuals operate within a tradition or culture that appears fully formed, even static. But where does this preformed world come from? Who gets to define what is or isn't part of the phenomena to be explained? Situated pilot training illustrates the problem: Why are the pilots flying? Where are they going? How did the "emergency" situation they are in come about, and why is it crucial to study it? The phenomenologist has no time for that; the pilots are already in midflight. Taking the world as given in this way makes phenomenological inquiries amenable to justifying existing relations of power, a point I will return to later in this chapter.

Despite these efforts to demonstrate usefulness to the military, Dreyfus's program remained theoretical in that he had no alternative computer programs or mathematical frameworks to

offer, only arguments. And as he had anticipated, most AI practitioners did not take his critique seriously. Furthermore, the
AI community ridiculed him for positing concrete tasks that
computers could never perform (particularly after he was defeated
by a chess-playing computer program).[16] Some prominent figures
within AI derided phenomenology in general. As one of them
put it, "Phenomenology! That ball of fluff! That cotton candy!"[17]

Some AI practitioners, however, already critical of the dominant thinking in their field, took the phenomenological critique
seriously and tried follow its implications in practice. These practitioners were influenced not just by phenomenology but also by
heterodox conceptions of the relationship between organisms
and environments developed in biology and cybernetics—lines
of inquiry where a disembodied "analytic" epistemology has not
reigned supreme.[18]

PUTTING PHENOMENOLOGY
TO PRACTICE

Terry Winograd and Fernando Flores made a bold attempt to
reframe AI in their book *Understanding Computers and Cognition* (1986), a generic title that doesn't do justice to the unusual
nature of their project.[19] Weaving strands from phenomenology,
biology, linguistics, and their own experiences in building computing systems, Winograd and Flores developed a wide-ranging
critique of AI and cognitive science that had the technical
authority (and more inviting tone) Dreyfus lacked. They also
tried to lay a tangible alternative path for practitioners.

Winograd, a computer scientist at Stanford University, had
previously worked in the area of natural language processing.
His past work fit within mainstream AI (one of his computer

programs was even critiqued by Dreyfus). From the start, however, Winograd was uneasy with the assumptions made by his
peers.[20] He met Flores in California, where Flores would later
pursue a doctorate in philosophy with Dreyfus at the University
of California, Berkeley. Flores, an engineer by training, had
previously been minister of economics in Salvador Allende's
government in Chile, from 1970 up until the U.S.-backed coup
in 1973, after which he was jailed and later exiled. In his post in
the Allende government, Flores initiated a project (later dubbed
"Cybersyn") to build a system to manage Chile's economy using
cybernetic principles.[21] His thinking was influenced by the work
of British cyberneticist Stafford Beer, who accepted Flores's
invitation to come to Chile and help design the system.

Winograd and Flores's project was clearly shaped by Flores's
experience (their book is dedicated is to "the people of Chile")
and Winograd's discontents with mainstream AI. Their critique
is aimed at the "rationalistic tradition": the strongly held assumptions of AI, cognitive science, and philosophy of mind and language. But Winograd and Flores desire more than critique; they
are after "a better understanding of what it means to be human."
This isn't in order to find the "right answers" to any particular
question about being, but rather to ask "meaningful questions—
ones that evoke an openness to new ways of being," an openness
that Winograd and Flores hope will shape "our collective vision"
of computing.[22]

Contrary to mainstream AI and cognitive science, Winograd
and Flores privilege action over detached contemplation. They
recognize that "every action is an interpretation": our actions are
anchored in our interpretation of the situation we find ourselves
in, and act we must, as the world does not sit still while we contemplate. Winograd and Flores thereby get closer to dispensing
with the epistemic forgery of a view from nowhere that pervades

AI. In fact, they call for moving away from "Artificial Intelligence" altogether—suggesting it is a concept beyond repair—and toward human-computer interaction. Computers, in their view, should be aids to people, not substrates for simulating human intelligence or cognition.

Winograd and Flores's analysis of human-computer interaction combines phenomenology with insights from biology. They note that the phenomenological view, as articulated by philosophers such as Heidegger, started to make sense to them only through a biological lens. Flores especially was influenced by the work of Chilean biologists Humberto Maturana and Francisco Varela on the theory of autopoiesis, which offers an unconventional language for describing the relationship between organisms and environments. Flores had introduced Winograd to autopoiesis, and this concept became central to their alternative to mainstream AI and cognitive science.[23]

Autopoiesis is anchored in Maturana's maxim, "Anything that is said is said by an observer," or its later refinement, "Everything said is said by an observer to another observer."[24] It means there can be no experiences without a subject to feel them, and no science without a subject ("observer") who can reflect on the relation between subject and experience. This understanding grew out of Maturana's work on the neurophysiology of the frog visual system and his realization that, from the perspective of the organism, there is no difference between sensation and hallucination. If we picture ourselves inside the frog's nervous system as it is activated by stimuli, all we have is a "closed" (Maturana's term) system that continually produces neural activity. Maturana's argument is that it makes no sense to distinguish cases where the pattern of activity was induced by an "objective" external reality from hallucination. To the organism, the pattern of activity is all there is. Maturana therefore discards commonly held views about objectivity and puts the subject front and center. He argued that since living systems continually remake themselves—maintaining, for instance, the "closed" nervous system—they thereby structure their own experiences. He called this process of continual self-remaking "autopoiesis." Autopoiesis is how a living system maintains itself as a "unity": an entity that inhabits a boundary of its own making. The simplest unity is a single cell, which must re-create itself (by remaking its membrane, for instance) in order to stay intact.[25] Maturana and Varela thought that autopoiesis could be used to explain how the richness that we as "observers" might call language, cognition, and social behavior emerges.

Autopoiesis upends entrenched conceptions of cause and effect, and Maturana and Varela used this fact to argue against the view that organisms are "information-processing" machines. Consider a single cell's process of remaking itself. This process depends on protein synthesis, which in turn relies on nucleic acids (DNA and RNA) residing in the cell's nucleus. The received wisdom within molecular biology is that "information" about the identities of proteins is "encoded" in nucleic acids and later "decoded" by the cell. Once seen as an autopoietic unity, however, these simple notions of linear causality collapse. While a specific segment of DNA may be necessary to produce a given protein, the complex configuration of proteins inside the cell that keep the DNA intact (in a form that information-processing accounts would consider "readable") is also necessary. If there is "information" to be "decoded" in order to make a protein, then, it cannot lie exclusively in DNA sequence identity; it's also in the cell's internal environment. The distinction between "encoding" and "decoding" generally breaks down considering autopoiesis: for DNA to be "decoded," it needs to be intact, and so the activity of keeping it together—which is part of autopoiesis—couples "encoding" and "decoding." The point is that autopoiesis constrains all cellular activities, and this makes any division of cellular parts or processes into categories such as "encoding" and "decoding" problematic. Information processing, as a general metaphor for the cell's major activities, loses its coherence in the autopoietic framing.[26]

Rather than viewing organisms as information-processing machines, Maturana and Varela see the relationship between organism and environment as "a structural dance in the choreography of existence."[27] A key concept in their account is "structural coupling"—the relations between organism and environment that make autopoiesis possible. Observers looking at the history of structural coupling through laboratory experiments may cognize some aspects of it as "information processing." In cognitive science experiments, for instance, one might examine the history of an organism's behavior and describe the organism as "solving" a set of defined information-processing tasks. But the course of such a history, according to Maturana and Varela, is principally determined by the demands of autopoiesis. The structural coupling continues so long as the organism maintains its unity and this is what matters *to the organism*. The solving of tasks, then, makes little sense from an organism's "inside" perspective; it is better understood as a cognitive construction of the experimenter.

Winograd and Flores import the concept of structural coupling from biology into human-computer interaction. As they argue, the history of interactions between the computer and user can also be viewed as a structural dance, one in which, contrary to the information-processing framing, there is no particular "task" that the user (or computer) is trying to solve. Rather, what unfolds is an open-ended loop that can be stopped and restarted. When structured well, Winograd and Flores argue, that loop should allow users to fluidly navigate multiple worlds. The pair conclude their book with a discussion of "The Coordinator," a computer program meant to exemplify an effective structural coupling between people and computers. The Coordinator attempts to facilitate various workplace transactions between managers and their teams. In this domain, the company is the "unity" that must maintain itself while being coupled to various outside entities (customers, suppliers, and so forth).

Although Winograd and Flores's book began with a call to define new ways of being, The Coordinator was criticized for simply directing workers to be more "efficient" by managerial standards. The anthropologist Lucy Suchman has argued that The Coordinator merely reproduced, and possibly amplified, the power relations of the workforce: managers could assign employees tasks with defined schedules and supervise their work, but not the other way around.[28] Furthermore, while Winograd and Flores demonstrated clearly that predetermined categories (of the sort that pervade the rationalistic tradition of AI) fail to capture the pragmatics of language, The Coordinator uses similarly inflexible frames.

Winograd and Flores had anticipated some of this criticism. For them, "any opening of new possibilities closes others, and . . . this is especially true with the introduction of technology." Design, they argue, necessarily introduces "blindness," which is why "attention to the possibilities being eliminated must be in constant interplay with expectations for new possibilities being created." As for inflexible categories, they acknowledge that their computer programs parcel the world into rigid objects and properties. But they argue that it is in service of an analysis grounded in action, unlike in the rationalistic orientation where such representations are attempts to model external reality.

Still, it is indisputable that The Coordinator is designed from the perspective of managers and business owners. This is also a group that could plausibly view businesses as living things with reproductive needs, especially given the background of an American legal system that views corporations as persons. Indeed, The Coordinator became the basis for a company cofounded by Winograd and Flores that sold similar software and consulting services to businesses.[29] Flores eventually became a wealthy entrepreneur by selling his understanding of cognition, and later wrote with Dreyfus about how a phenomenological perspective can help companies thrive.[30] So while anchored in thoughtful critique, Winograd and Flores's project shows that it's not obvious how AI practitioners could build substantively different systems using the same old computational clay, while operating within the same institutional structures.[31]

Another AI practitioner, Philip Agre, was also inspired by the phenomenological critique to pursue a different kind of AI, and his work resulted in similar outcomes. Like Winograd and Flores, Agre, who worked at MIT's Artificial Intelligence laboratory, saw the stark difference between the rationalistic theory offered within AI and the realities of everyday life. Agre even suggested that AI's main virtue might be as a window into that difference.[32] But Agre understood (like Dreyfus) that practitioners are unmoved by abstract critique; they want to build computing systems. He therefore decided to build a computing system rooted in phenomenological analysis. He started keeping a diary of his everyday activities, such as cleaning the dishes and cooking, which revealed the great intricacies of all these tasks. Eventually, Agre settled on building a robot that makes breakfast. Yet, when forced to make progress on building an actual system, he found old rationalistic assumptions creeping back in. The richness of being, made vivid by phenomenological reflection, was unwieldy; programming required simplifications. Embodiment, too, when taken seriously, posed an enormous challenge. Just to describe the intricacies of the human hands that make breakfast led Agre to endless diversions into physiology and anatomy, only to find aspects of physics and physiology that are far too complex for computational simulation. When these details were abstracted away for the sake of progress, he found himself making the same rationalistic assumptions he had hoped to abandon.[33]

It turned out that for Agre, as for Winograd and Flores, phenomenology was far more suited for reinforcing existing social configurations than enabling new ones. While Agre's breakfast-making program didn't pan out, he later used phenomenological insights to offer career-building advice and explain how individuals can leverage social networks to advance professional goals. As he put it, the advice was meant to show people how "to become channels for the messages that history is urging on us."[34] By the phenomenological view, history's main message is to see oneself as an entrepreneur, maneuvering social networks to advance self-interests.

AUTOPOIETIC LOVE

At this point, it is worth revisiting Maturana and Varela's work, since they sought to explain the world that phenomenologists took as given. The hope for Maturana and Varela's account is that it would help make sense of the relationships between organisms, environments, and cultures without cementing already existing relations of power, as phenomenology has so far done.

Maturana and Varela see autopoiesis as the defining activity of living things, but for them, self-remaking is only the starting point. What they are really after is explaining how cognition emerges within an individual (herself a composite of autopoietic unities) and how individuals then collectively give rise to a social world. Thus if phenomenology could be accused of trying to explain the world as it already is, then Maturana and Varela by contrast seek to explain world building.

Maturana and Varela's quest comes with a strong social and ethical dimension framed around love, responsibility, and care for the other. For them, "love is a biological dynamic" that is essential to world building with others:

> Biology also shows us that we can expand our cognitive domain. This arises through a novel experience brought forth through reasoning, through the encounter with a stranger, or, more directly, through the expression of a biological interpersonal congruence that lets us *see* the other person and open up for him room for existence beside us. This act is called *love*, or, if we prefer a milder expression, the acceptance of the other person beside us in our daily living.[35]

Maturana and Varela insist they are "not moralizing" but simply suggesting that "biologically, without love, without acceptance of others, there is no social phenomenon." They almost sound like Martin Luther King, Jr., who spoke of love "as the supreme unifying principle of life."[36]

But what does autopoiesis really have to do with love? This might be the most enigmatic aspect of Maturana and Varela's project. They claim that "blind to the transparency of our actions, we confuse the image we want to project with the being we want to bring forth. This is a misunderstanding that only the knowledge of knowledge can correct."[37] Perhaps some people do confound the image they want to project with the kind of beings they aspire to be. Why is it, though, that "only the knowledge of knowledge" can resolve such confounds? Why would an epistemic doctrine, presumably the theory of autopoiesis, have such special bearing on world building with others? It's not clear.

Moreover, the problem we had seen with the phenomenological lens—namely, that this frame can further shoehorn individuals into existing oppressive structures—arises for autopoiesis as well. The "structural determinism" of autopoiesis invites an interpretation where organisms lack any discernable agency or autonomy, and react to their environments in structurally determined ways. Such determinism, core to autopoietic theory, is hard to square with Maturana and Varela's vision of love and care for others.

The attempts to computationally model autopoiesis bring this tension to light. While Maturana has shied away from mathematical models, the precision of autopoiesis invites formalization.[38] Economists and social scientists have created formal models of autopoiesis and started to view businesses, institutions, and societies as autopoietic entities. One early attempt to formalize autopoiesis, in the late 1970s, was proposed by the economist Milan Zeleny, who already then noted the similarity between autopoiesis and Friedrich Hayek's conception of the market.[39] Zeleny's efforts exemplify an entire line of work that sees autopoiesis and the neoliberal, self-organizing market as variations of the same basic idea. Zeleny has argued that "the economy is not a machine but an organism."[40] When markets are left to be "free," he claimed, the economy self-maintains and self-regulates without the need for centralized control (much like an organism), and he therefore linked "social autopoiesis" to Hayek's conception of markets.[41] He even described autopoiesis as a way to make notions like Adam Smith's "Invisible Hand" more explicit in order to illuminate "business self-renewal."[42] This view of autopoiesis rehashes the epistemic forgery of neoliberal economics (which also manifests in AI) that the market is a self-organizing and powerful information-processor that stands outside people and institutions.

Theories of living things as complex, self-maintaining systems have been broadly used as metaphors for markets, and vice versa.

Through this move, organisms become akin to individuals competing in markets, while populations of organisms become networks of entrepreneurs. Life itself becomes an economy, and markets get naturalized for merely reflecting the "spontaneous" biological order. This view has brought biologists and business entrepreneurs together. In the late 1980s and early 1990s, as Fred Turner has described, corporate executives and scientists alike—including biologists such as Francisco Varela and Lynn Margulis, as well as AI practitioners Marvin Minsky and Seymour Papert—assembled around these loose metaphors to build their own networks of power.[43] Melinda E. Cooper has similarly argued that theories of life as a self-maintaining system—notably the view of the Earth-as-Gaia, advanced by James Lovelock and Lynn Margulis—lend themselves to neoliberal visions.[44]

In our context, the connection between autopoiesis and neoliberal economic theory is not contrived. Both Hayek's conception of spontaneous order and Maturana and Varela's autopoietic theory commit to a kind of structural determinism. If individuals are viewed as structurally determined entities who bring forth a world, including social relations, it isn't a great leap to apply the same lens to all of society's institutions—much to Maturana's protest.[45]

This is in part why the capitalist eye can easily see the whole world, including businesses, in autopoietic terms. And while Maturana and Varela want to add layers of responsibility, love, and friendship to their structurally deterministic account, it remains unclear how these arise from autopoiesis. Thus in Maturana and Varela's autopoiesis we have both a recognition of an embodied knowing subject and a socially conscious vision of world building—but there is a gap between the two. And like phenomenology, the autopoietic lens lends itself to reinforcing existing power structures.

The theme of world building has nevertheless continued in later work on embodied cognition. I will next turn to work that, inspired by autopoiesis, sought to reframe cognitive science in a way that promotes collective living.

EMBODYING MINDS AND ENACTING WORLDS

In their seminal book *The Embodied Mind* (1991), Francisco Varela, Evan Thompson, and Eleanor Rosch (VTR) offer a wide-ranging critique and reframing of cognitive science. Their book has multiple philosophical and moral layers that defy simple summary. *The Embodied Mind* deconstructs the dominant thinking about cognition and sketches an alternative, embodied program. But rather than providing an alternative to be practiced in the same frame, *The Embodied Mind* seeks to identify the envelope of Western thought responsible for the problematic premises—and break out of it.

At the most basic level, VTR perceptively outline the common epistemic thread running through cognitive science, AI, linguistics, economics and evolutionary biology. They show how all these superficially disparate areas see individuals as atoms motivated by self-interest. This manifests in a view of beings as goal-seekers, processing information and behaving "rationally" in a world from which they are detached; an affair in which bodily aspects are at best marginal. This problematic view, which VTR label "cognitivist," is basically what Winograd and Flores have identified as "rationalistic."

Like Winograd and Flores, or Dreyfus, VTR see the value in phenomenology for shaking off the rationalistic tradition. Yet VTR note that phenomenology does not carry us very far. They critique phenomenologists, such as Maurice Merleau-Ponty, for contradictorily stating the world can be understood only through embodiment, while they themselves only contemplate the world without engaging in actual scientific practice. *The Embodied Mind* has to pick up where phenomenologists failed.

The Embodied Mind charts a path that begins by situating the subject, as a step toward shedding the epistemic forgery of a view from nowhere. The embodied subject knows that her ways of seeing the world are produced by a circular relationship between her own biological structure, on the one side, and her lived experiences in the world, on the other (as shown in figure 6.1). Each side gives rise to the other. But the embodied thinker recognizes that this way of framing things is also a product of that very circularity. She acknowledges, therefore, that our experiences of

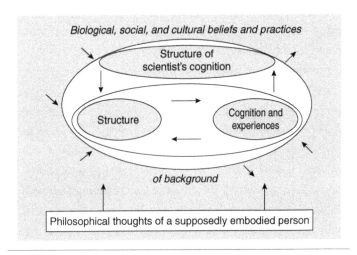

FIGURE 6.1 Model of the embodied subject from *The Embodied Mind*. The embodied thinker is conscious of how ways of seeing the world are produced by a circular relationship between our own biophysical structure, on the one hand, and our experiences and cognitive apparatus, on the other.

the world are built on an infinite regress of such circularities. For VTR, the embrace of circularity is the only way to close the "rift between science and experience in our society." Circularities let us see how an individual "enacts" a world, to use the language of *The Embodied Mind*.[46] Individuals do not bring forth this world alone, however, but collectively—and VTR call this "planetary building." Echoing Maturana and Varela's autopoietic love, planetary building requires "concern for the other with whom we enact a world."[47]

While *The Embodied Mind* aims to situate subjects who enact worlds, the path does not end there. The aim is to dispense altogether with the notion of the subject, or "self," that has dominated Western discourses.[48] Rather than attempt to invent yet another novel framework, they look to mindfulness and Buddhist practices as a way of "letting go of habits of mindlessness, as an unlearning rather than a learning." As they write, such unlearning "is a different sense of effort from the acquiring of something new."

The Embodied Mind thus tries to undo some of the violence that hegemonic scientific accounts do to minds, bodies, and worlds. The result is a rich project that self-consciously grasps at the social envelope in which it operates.

Yet *The Embodied Mind* falls short in situating the context in which cognitive science and AI research takes place. Consider the following example, which shows how the social structures of scientific practice remain unexamined in VTR's account. To illustrate the intellectual terrain of the fields they are concerned with, VTR present a "polar map" (figure 6.2). The main dimensions of this map are fields (e.g., AI, cognitive science, or neuroscience) and epistemic styles (e.g., emergent or cognitivist), and individual researchers are placed on the map as exemplars of different lines of inquiry. Strikingly, all the exemplars are men.[49]

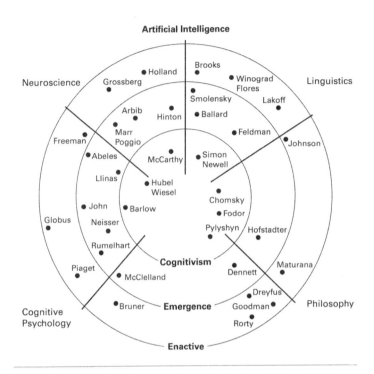

FIGURE 6.2 Conceptual chart from *The Embodied Mind* of fields, epistemic premises, and individual researchers. Original caption: "A conceptual chart of the cognitive sciences today in the form of a polar map, with the contributing disciplines in the angular dimensions and different approaches in the radial axis."

So while *The Embodied Mind* is deeply critical of explicit representations when used as theoretical constructs for explaining the mind, the authors appear blind to the way in which their own representation reinstates the idea that only men define intellectual landscapes.

In other ways, too, VTR reproduce salient aspects of the dominant scientific culture that they aim to go beyond. Although they view their project as "unlearning," they, like Dreyfus, cling to a stubborn pragmatism when it comes to evaluating scientific work. They claim that "cognitive science cannot be separated from cognitive technology"—and therefore, embodied ideas must show their value pragmatically by helping to build "truly intelligent, cognitive artifacts."[50] This pragmatism leads them to search for examples of successful "applied" embodied AI. For VTR, the field of situated robotics—and the work of AI practitioner Rodney Brooks, in particular—provides such an example. Other critics of AI's orthodoxy have also looked to situated robotics as a viable alternative. In the next section I examine the context in which situated robotics developed, in order to see how notions of embodiment work in practice. What kind of "cognitive artifacts" did these ideas help create?

THE MILITARIZED FRAME OF SITUATED APPROACHES TO BODY AND MIND

Critics of AI's dominant streams have looked to situated robotics as a potential alternative, at least partly because in situated robotics the physical body is paramount.[51] By focusing on acting in the world with an actual body, situated robotics looks like the antipode of the rationalistic stance. Alison Adam, for instance, expressed cautious optimism about situated robotics capturing those elements that AI has traditionally neglected.

Yet much like the rest of AI, the situated line of work developed within a military-industrial setting. So while Adam's evocative question regarding alternatives—is seeking a "feminist AI" akin to building a "feminist fighter plane"?—uses military imagery so effectively, critics of AI's dominant, disembodied epistemology often overlook the militarized character of situated approaches.

To contextualize situated robotics, I turn to the work of Rodney Brooks, an AI practitioner and entrepreneur who has spent much of his career at MIT's Artificial Intelligence Laboratory. Brooks's work has captivated many AI critics, partly because of its biological and embodied framing. His robots are built using reusable, autonomous modules—"layers" in his terminology—that interact to produce useful behavior and, by analogy to biological evolution, do so without a guiding hand. These robots lack a centralized, stable representation of the world. Instead, objects in the environment are represented transiently and only as required by action. Brooks was the subject of Errol Morris's documentary *Fast, Cheap, & Out of Control* (1997), which highlighted the bio-feel of this approach. As Brooks put it in the film, "When I think about it, I can almost see myself as being made up of thousands and thousands of little agents, doing stuff almost independently." Brooks has also been a kind of "insider" critic of AI, sometimes lambasting the field for its "hype," which has attracted those seeking alternatives to mainstream AI.[52]

Overall, Brooks's program appealed to AI critics and practitioners not just for its biological flair and epistemic heresy but also for its commercial successes. One of his companies, iRobot (founded in the early 1990s) is known for the Roomba, a floor-cleaning robot and a success story of situated robotics. The Roomba's emergent cleaning behavior arises from interactions between independent agents.[53]

While the Roomba is well-known, the militarized aspects of situated robotics have received less critical attention. Brooks and his colleagues are also in the business of making robots for the battlefield, notably a series of machines known as PackBots. Lucy Suchman has cleared some of the fog over the link between these two wings of situated robotics. Suchman noted how iRobot's marketing materials place the PackBot and the Roomba "side by side and as if at the same scale, the former lending power to the latter, while being rendered more benign in the process."[54] In other words, the friendliness of the Roomba tames PackBots, while the hardcore image of battle-tested robotics may elevate the Roomba, which is otherwise a sluggardly vacuum cleaner.[55]

PackBots were used by the U.S. military in 2003, following the American invasion of Iraq and Afghanistan, and were initially presented as a way to detect chemical and nuclear weapons.[56] This marketing appealed to the pretext given by the George W. Bush administration for invading Iraq (that Saddam Hussein had obtained weapons of mass destruction and hence posed an imminent threat to the United States).[57] The media coverage of these robots emphasized their seamless integration into the battlefield (redolent of Licklider's "Man-Computer symbiosis"). Equipped with many sensors, PackBots could surveil hard-to-reach territories while withstanding explosives, serving as shields for troops on the ground. The marketing was successful, and PackBots have since been bought and emulated by various armies. While the actual capacities of PackBots are difficult for outsiders to assess, they are sold as "platforms" that can be extended by others, and notably, PackBots have been stocked with machine guns that can evidently fire one million rounds per minute.[58]

PackBots are not an isolated example of embodied and situated AI's entanglement with warfare. Though the aura of embodiment may give a different impression, these research programs developed within the same imperial contexts as their rationalistic counterparts. Practitioners in the situated and embodied streams, like those in the rationalistic tradition, articulated early on how their work can advance military aims. And for their part, military powers were able to embrace a transition in metaphor and language: away from centralized command-and-control and toward decentralized embodiment. Warfare would become a situated affair, and the frameworks of situated and embodied cognition would play a more prominent role in imperial visions.

EMBODIED WAR

The concepts associated with embodied cognition tend to flow between the worlds of biology and computing. In the 1990s, as the field of "artificial life" gained attention, concepts such as embodiment, complexity, emergence, and decentralization became focal points of biologically inspired computing. These notions were developed in large part through computational simulation at places like the Santa Fe Institute in New Mexico (a center devoted to computational science founded by scientists who worked on the atomic bomb at Los Alamos National Lab). This line of inquiry became identified with certain formal frameworks, such as cellular automata and genetic programming, which aimed to capture *in silico* the essential aspects of biological evolution.

Various commentators saw these bio-inspired computing frameworks as alternatives to the conventional digital and sequential modes of computing that have long served military aims and capitalist production. Media theorist Tiziana Terranova, for one, saw political promise in biological computing frameworks such as cellular automata. Biological computing of this sort, Terranova argued, is a promising attempt to "hack the social at its most fluid and least stratified, wherever it escapes the constrictions of rigid forms of organization but also of identity and class."[59] In narrating the history of British cybernetics, historian Andrew Pickering was even more optimistic about decentralized and bio-inspired frameworks such as cellular automata, arguing they provide "nonmodern ontology" and sharp counter to ordinary science. For Pickering, the epistemic premises that animate these frameworks, and the practices around them, hold revolutionary potential. He went as far as to suggest these frameworks should be introduced into school curricula "beginning at an early age."[60] Other critics have painted similarly rosy pictures of related computing frameworks, suggesting they lead to "truly liberating paths."[61]

Yet these alternative formulations, I would argue, have been realized and developed—without needing contortion—in the service of imperial and capitalist projects. The institutional setting in which these streams have emerged has been largely neglected in these optimistic assessments. It is crucial to explore this context in order to see how these frameworks' epistemic potential, as articulated by enthusiastic commentators, compare with their actual practice. This comparison cannot be made without appreciating that the military-industrial sphere can change its epistemic mood, too. For instance, in chapter 1 we encountered an air force colonel who saw the need for centralized, "Cartesian" control of the battlefield, as opposed to the distributed, decentralized modes of computing associated with cybernetics. But that was in the 1950s, and military epistemology has since shifted. The language of embodiment and emergence, developed in similar social contexts as its "Cartesian" computing rival, has since taken a more prominent role.

The work of Paul Van Riper, a retired marine lieutenant general and Vietnam War veteran, exemplifies this turn. Van Riper has been a vocal promoter of an embodied, emergent conception of war. In his telling, the command-and-control frame used by Vietnam War era analysts has proven to be a failure. According to Van Riper, war—unlike factory production—could not be centrally planned. His argument against central planning drew on the work of neoliberal economist Friedrich Hayek, who famously argued against centrally planned economies. In a reflection on war in the twenty-first century, Van Riper cites Hayek's observation, from the book *The Fatal Conceit: The Errors of Socialism*, that "nobody can communicate to another all he knows, because much of the information he can make use of, he himself will elicit only in the process of making plans of action."[62] For Hayek, knowledge can be elicited only through behavior (response to price signals in the market). For Van Riper, war is similarly decentralized, emergent, and defying of central management. In the mid-1990s Van Riper even participated in live fire military exercises with marines working alongside Wall Street stock traders, with the hope that the intuitive, situated behavior of traders will inspire soldiers' decision making in battle.[63]

This turn to an embodied epistemology of war brought a new wave of military analysts. Their new understanding of war is exemplified by military analyst Andrew Ilachinski's book *Artificial War* (2004), a culmination of over a decade of research into the decentralized battlefield. Van Riper wrote a glowing forward to *Artificial War* where he argued that Ilachinski, unlike older generations of analysts, understood war as it really is. According to Van Riper, analysts of the Vietnam War period have merely produced "*descriptions of what they wish war to be*, not the terrible, brutal, bloody phenomenon that exists in the real world." But in the twenty-first century, van Riper writes, the United States faces perpetual war "with a tenacious and dangerous enemy," which demands new theoretical foundations. Van Riper predicted that when historians look back on our times, they will identify Ilachinski as the "Father of Military Complexity Research" who delivered the new foundations for the military. Subsequently, "an entire new way of thinking soon took hold. Phrases such as 'battle management' and 'fight like a well-oiled machine' disappeared. Marines recognized that nonlinear phenomena are not subject to the sort of control the term 'management' imparts and military units are *complex adaptive systems* not 'machines.'"[64]

In *Artificial War*, Ilachinski articulates that alternative framing of war. In his words, the alternative demands moving away from thinking of battle as "collision between Newtonian billiard-balls" and toward battle as "self-organized ecology of living, viscous fluids." For Ilachinski, this is a shift from a "Newtonian" to a "Heraclitan" worldview, which requires changing all metaphors and expectations. Whereas prior "Newtonian" conceptions of the battlefield were "closed system," "stable," "predictable," "reductionist," and premised on "linear causation," the Heraclitan formulation was "open," "dynamic," "unpredictable," "holistic," and premised on "circular causality," concerned not with "being" but "becoming."[65] The dynamics of the battle would no longer be seen as controllable in top-down manner by individual entities, but rather as emergent and even "collectivist" (see table 6.1). Ilachinski explained that he was led to this "epiphany" through a study of cellular automata, a framework that he thought captured the decentralized and emergent nature of war.[66]

Ilachinski's study is based on computational simulation. Typically, two warring troops are simulated, the "Reds" and the "Blues." Troops are assigned "personalities" (Ilachinski's term) that determine how they react, statistically speaking, to different battle scenarios. War then unfolds as a stochastic simulation. The result is "emergent": neither the behavior of individual soldiers nor the troop configuration as a whole are directly programmed. And unlike in some traditional cartoons of battle, the troop does not move as a single unit but can disperse into multiple small groups. According to Ilachinski, the troop could even be viewed as an autopoietic unity, with war producing what he calls "autopoietic skirmishes": scenarios where the overall configuration of troops remains stable even as individual soldiers continually change positions.

TABLE 6.1

General Property of Complex Systems	Description of Relevance to Land Warfare
Nonlinear interaction	Combat forces composed of a large number of nonlinearly interacting parts; sources include feedback loops in C2 hierarchy, interpretation of (and adaptation to) enemy actions, decision-making process, and elements of chance.
Nonreductionist	The fighting ability of a combat force cannot be understood as a simple aggregate function of the fighting ability of individual combatants.
Emergent behavior	The global patterns of behavior on the combat battlefield unfold, or emerge, out of nested sequences of local interaction rules and doctrine.
Hierarchical structure	Combat forces are typically organized in a command and control (fractal-like) hierarchy.
Decentralized control	There is no master "oracle" dictating the actions of each and every combatant; the course of a battle is ultimately dictated by local decisions made by each combatant.
Self-organization	Local action, which often appears "chaotic," induces long-range order.
Nonequlibrium order	Military conflicts, by their nature, proceed far from equilibrium; understanding how combat unfolds is more important than knowing the "end state."
Adaptation	In order to survive, combat forces must continually adapt to a changing environment, and continually look for better ways of adapting to the adaptation pattern of their enemy.

General Property of Complex Systems	Description of Relevance to Land Warfare
Collectivist dynamics	There is a continual feedback between the behavior of (low-level) combatants and the (high-level) command structure.

Source: Table reproduced with permission from CNA report, copyright, 1996 the CNA Corporation. All rights reserved.

Note: Embodied and situated language for war, described by Andrew Ilachinski in *Artificial War: Multiagent-Based Simulation of Combat* (Singapore: World Scientific, 2004).

These alterative conceptions of war, promoted for years by Van Riper, were basically internalized by the Washington establishment in its global "War on Terror." Only days following the attacks of September 11, 2001, the *Washington Post* echoed Van Riper in describing the new conditions the United States faced: "This conflict is not only unlike any faced before by the United States, but also quite different from its closest correlates elsewhere. In Vietnam—as well as Northern Ireland and Israel—the enemy was less diffuse in its identity and more specific in its aims of political control."[67] This new "enemy" is seen as decentralized and fluid, as in Ilachinski's simulations. Computational simulation had in fact played a role in preparing the U.S. invasion of Iraq. In 2002 the U.S. government staged the "Millennium Challenge," an exercise meant to train the American military for war in Iraq. Paul Van Riper, commanding the Reds, took on the role of Saddam Hussein, fighting against the Blues (who stood for the U.S. military). This 250 million dollar "war game" was not merely theoretical: troops were deployed, while computational simulation was used to guide and interpret each side's moves.[68] The Millennium Challenge was an opportunity for Van Riper to enact his model of the "enemy" and practice what he viewed as unconventional warfare (in the end the Blues prevailed, though Van Riper protested that the game was rigged in favor of the U.S. military).

When the Iraq invasion became reality, it fueled more simulations of war. The geocoordinates of U.S.-led coalition troops became "real-world data" that Ilachinski used to argue that his framework recapitulates empirical troop dynamics. And when the situation for the American military in Iraq turned out not to unfold as advertised by the government, Van Riper—who had urged for more troops on the ground—criticized the Bush administration for misunderstanding war.[69]

Nevertheless, the attention given by the media and political establishment to formulations of war advanced by the likes of Van Riper should not be overstated. There has not been a clear and consistent transition from the command-and-control mindset to one in which war is embodied. Imperial projects need not be cohesive in that way; the "old" metaphors live on. Contemporary books in the genre of military information management refer to the soldier as "knowledge worker."[70] This phrase can be casually tossed thanks in part to the work of "symbolic" AI practitioners, whose epistemic narratives play alongside embodied conceptions. The war industry has already served as a site for blending these epistemologies and practices, as we will see in the next section.

SYNTHESIZING THE ABSTRACT AND BODILY THROUGH WAR

A long-running criticism leveled against AI practitioners is that they have neglected the embodied, situated, cultural, and emotional aspects of human life in favor of disembodied abstraction. This critique gives the impression that discontents with AI could be remedied by sowing together these artificially separated threads. But what I would like to suggest is that the war industry has already synthesized these worlds. Driven by U.S. imperial aims, the abstract, universalist AI that did not concern itself with bodies and cultures, on the one hand, and the embodied and situated approaches on the other, have come together.

Historically, the war industry has catalyzed such interdisciplinary crossings. As Peter Galison has observed, during World War II, scientists, mathematicians, and engineers working on calculations for the atomic bomb crossed disciplinary boundaries through shared interests in Monte Carlo simulations performed on computers.[71] That these different participants were committed to different epistemic doctrines and methods (what philosophers of science might have labeled as distinct "paradigms"), or came from different intellectual traditions, mattered less in practice. The shared medium (in this case, the computer), the overarching war aims, and the social structures provided by the war industry were enough to suspend these epistemic and cultural differences.

Within the war industry, a similar phenomenon has taken place around AI and cognition. The creation of immersive soldier training environments has been an obvious meeting point for seemingly opposed streams. To train soldiers for combat, immersive virtual and semivirtual environments have been developed, which require detailed rendering of characters and landscapes, as well as narratives that capture the audience's attention. This demands expertise from designers, social scientists, and other experts outside of AI's traditional practice, who are tuned to the embodied nature of human experience. But simulation of abstract reasoning and planning is also needed to create military scenarios that do not feel too preprogrammed, and this part draws on work from AI's rationalistic tradition. Military systems, then, combine these elements.

This synthesis was mediated through a set of alliances between the entertainment industry, the military, and the media. Soldier training environments, for instance, require the know-how of the video gaming industry, which is also in the business of creating immersive experiences. For both the military and entertainment industry, attention to detail, narrative, and bodies is crucial. Indeed, these industries routinely collaborate and borrow from one another. The resulting creations in turn inspire media depictions of war. This nexus of war, gaming, and media has been called "militainment" by the media scholar Roger Stahl. "Militainment," according to Stahl, enables multiple flows: "Wartime news looks like a video game; video games restage wartime news. Official military training simulators cross over into commercial entertainment markets; commercial video games are made useful for military training exercises. Advertisements sell video games with patriotic rhetorics; video games are mobilized to advertise patriotism."[72] These flows, as he argued, serve multiple ends: training and recruitment for the military, profits for the gaming industry, and inducement for citizens to see themselves as actors in a militarized world through virtual immersion.

Through "militainment," the disembodied and abstract wing of AI and cognitive science and the embodied and social world of immersion have been joined. The merger is exemplified by the work of the University of Southern California's Institute for Creative Technologies (ICT), which Stahl has described as "a motley collection of Hollywood talent, academics, toymakers, and game industry insiders [working] to assist the military."[73] Among the academics, there are AI practitioners and cognitive scientists, as well as linguists and anthropologists. Although it is part of the university and draws on its students and faculty members, the ICT was created by the U.S. Army. The institute's goals include both serving the military and making useful products for the entertainment industry.[74]

Many ICT projects focus on creating immersive training environments such as the one shown in figure 6.3. In this semivirtual environment, an armed soldier is navigating a studio meant to look like a home in Iraq or Afghanistan.[75] A projected screen shows interactive virtual characters, in this case a woman wearing a head covering standing next to a child. As soldiers navigate these semivirtual environments, sensors collect biometric and haptic data about their behavior (for use in later "performance" analysis). To make such environments more realistic, the ICT has developed a portfolio of characters, which it calls "Virtual Humans," corresponding to distinct stereotyped bodies, gestures, and cultures.[76] These virtual characters are used to prepare soldiers for what the military sees as the more "social" and "cultural" elements of war. In virtual training environments, this entails staging scenarios where soldiers have to police or gather information from local populations so as to mimic the activities of occupying American troops.[77] In one training scenario, for example, soldiers meet a local police officer in order to achieve a military aim and demonstrate fluency with the local scene. In this instance, ICT researchers coded variation into the police officer character along three dimensions: cultural ("Iraqi vs. German"), religious ("Sunni vs. Shia"), and personality ("introvert vs. extrovert").[78]

AI practitioners and cognitive scientists working on these projects see them as an opportunity to incorporate cultural, emotional, and bodily aspects of human life into their work (which they acknowledge their fields have mostly ignored).[79] Such

FIGURE 6.3 Screenshot from a promotional video by the
University of Southern California's Institute for Creative Technologies
showing a soldier-training environment modeled after
a home. Virtual characters are projected on a screen (a woman
wearing a niqab standing next to a child).

projects are also seen as highly "interdisciplinary" because they
involve linguists, anthropologists, and even screenwriters, who
can fill in the contextual detail—and Hollywood flair—needed
for staging war in foreign lands (as envisaged by the U.S. military, at least). Embodiment, affect, and narrative matter greatly in
these projects, since the environments are judged by how people
(notably, soldiers in training) experience them rather than by
abstract benchmarks normally used to evaluate AI systems.

Under the hood, though, these simulated environments frequently use more traditional AI systems to handle abstract reasoning and planning. For instance, cognitive architectures such
as Soar, which typify the "symbolic" lineage of AI, have been
integrated with military simulations such as those used by ICT.[80]
Cognitive architectures are used as the "reasoning engine" that

drives virtual characters in highly detailed, semivirtual environments. AI practitioners engaged in such work do not view it as a clash between rationalistic and embodied approaches but rather as a synthesis.[81] Soldier training, then, is one arena where AI practitioners, working with other academics and experts, have paid close attention to elements of embodiment, emotion, and culture.

One the one hand, it is easy to critique how these systems incorporate cultural and emotional elements. "Culture," here, is simply another variable that the master eye, forging a view from nowhere, codifies. And the computational representation of any such variable naturally reflects stereotypes constructed to serve military aims. It is, after all, engineers and social scientists working in military-industrial-academic spaces who determine the "differences" between, say, German and Iraqi police officers, or Shia and Sunni Muslims.

But on the other hand, it is worth asking: Is a fundamentally different encoding of "culture" in a computer program really possible here? In the contexts in which these computing systems are built, it seems inescapable that attempts to capture what's considered cultural, emotional, or bodily would end up objectifying people and communities in ways that suit imperial and capitalist aims—especially when even the practitioners of situated cognition and AI, who build these systems, have not situated their own inquiries.

UNSITUATED INQUIRIES AND NEGLECTED WORLD BUILDING

This chapter has explored the situated and embodied streams as alternative paths within AI's orbit. These "dissident" streams were promising. They offered radically different epistemologies from those that have dominated AI and cognitive science. And crucially, they seem to have aspired to more than just a different research program: they spoke of a social vision concerned with world building, collective living, and caring for others.

But while the language of situated and embodied cognition evokes a socially conscious way of being, I would argue that this has so far been mostly a mirage. These streams have not historically served collective living. Embodied and situated cognition were also part of the imperial and capitalist machine, and these streams' language of collectivist dynamics, embodiment, decentralization, and emergence could be readily absorbed by military generals. Likewise, the conceptual frameworks offered by embodied and situated perspectives happily reinforced a neoliberal vision of the individual as entrepreneur. One might have hoped that a more integrative scientific practice—one that seeks to link mind and body, reason and emotion, individual and collective—would yield different results, but this does not appear to be the case. The war industry, as we have seen, has already gone to great lengths to sow all these elements together.

The trouble is that the situated approaches in AI's orbit have been practiced in a desperately unsituated way. These approaches fixated on only a narrow sliver of epistemic space. The capitalist and imperial institutions in which researchers operate were cast aside, even though this context shapes the paths of inquiry. All this suggests that simply choosing a different epistemic orientation cannot generate substantively different systems and practices than the ones AI and the cognitive sciences have produced so far. Different social structures are also needed. Thus we are left with a glaring gap between the ethical and socially conscious visions found within embodied cognition, and their actual realizations in the service of empire and capital. As a result, the powerful work of caring for others and collective living has been neglected.

And while the streams of situated and embodied cognition offer ways to partially "unlearn" the rationalist tradition, a perhaps more far-reaching understanding of minds and bodies was already available elsewhere. In his book on imperial conquest, *Columbus and Other Cannibals* (1978), Jack Forbes manages, in the span of several paragraphs, to distill and even go beyond what dissenting AI practitioners and cognitive scientists have been grasping at. Forbes writes, "I can lose my hands, and still live. I can lose my legs and still live. I can lose my eyes and still live. I can lose my hair, eyebrows, nose, arms, and many other things and still live. But if I lose the air I die. If I lose the sun I die. If I lose the earth I die. If I lose the water I die. If I lose the plants and animals I die." As he notes, this raises a deep question about embodiment: "All of these things are more a part of me, more essential to my every breath, than is my so-called body. *What is my real body?*"[82] Some streams of cognitive science have viewed parts of the material world as essential to cognitive function (recognizing, for instance, that people use writing as a form of memory). But this is not the same as Forbes's view, which sees the earth as essential to human life and refuses to see the earth apart from its history—a history that includes the plunder of nature and dispossession of people brought about by imperialism and the pursuit of capital.

Since the situated and embodied streams have not fully situated their own positions, they remain underdeveloped with respect to the issues Forbes raises. Some thinkers in these traditions have made nods to a more reflective stance. Humberto Maturana and Ximena Paz Dávila, for example, have argued that knowing "is not looking at things as such, but rather knowing the bases from which one affirms that something is and being willing to show it." For this, they say one must "abandon certainties in order to look and assume what one sees from the standpoint of its doing, without supposing that this vision is independent from what one does."[83] But when these ideas are not part of the practice, situated and embodied inquiries remain unaware of their own imperial and capitalist envelope. They then continue to perpetuate, albeit in different form, long-running destructive projects and epistemic forgeries.

7

A GENERATIVE REFUSAL

But not yet have we solved the incantation of this whiteness, and learned why it appeals with such power to the soul. . . . Is it that by its indefiniteness it shadows forth the heartless voids and immensities of the universe, and thus stabs us from behind with the thought of annihilation, when beholding the white depths of the milky way? Or is it, that as in essence whiteness is not so much a color as the visible absence of color, and at the same time the concrete of all colors; is it for these reasons that there is such a dumb blankness, full of meaning, in a wide landscape of snows—a colorless, all-color of atheism from which we shrink?

. . . like wilful travellers in Lapland, who refuse to wear colored and coloring glasses upon their eyes, so the wretched infidel gazes himself blind at the monumental white shroud that wraps all the prospect around him. And of all these things the Albino Whale was the symbol. Wonder ye then at the fiery hunt?
—Herman Melville, *Moby-Dick*

We prepare to part company with American critical academics, to become unreliable, to be disloyal to the public sphere, to be

obstructive and shiftless, dumb with insolence in the face of the
call to critical thinking.

—Stefano Harney and Fred Moten

I have argued in this book that artificial intelligence is a technology of whiteness: malleable, contested, and continually remade to serve imperial and capitalist aims. Whiteness is artificial, and so perhaps it is natural that AI has mirrored it so well.

While the endeavor's offerings were always a moving target, AI's recurring "revolutions" were staged with remarkable consistency. And when this nebulous technology broke down, raising questions about its utility to invested powers, practitioners would help connect the dots for their patrons by formulating their work around imperial and capitalist visions and offering new computational engines. But new computational engines came with old epistemic forgeries, and AI has continually produced racial, gendered, and classed models of the self. I have argued that the nebulous and malleable character of the endeavor, and its models of the self, indicate that AI reproduces the form of whiteness as an ideology.

AI's malleability and incoherence, like that of whiteness, has served destructive ends. Since the 2010s, as we saw, its rebranding brought a slew of initiatives that crisscross state-military, corporate, and academic worlds. These initiatives sounded as nebulous as their subject matter. Yet throughout this book I have tried to more explicitly link the nebulous façade and abstract ideals ("ethical AI for everyone's benefit") to ongoing, tangible political projects. These projects include advancing neoliberal policies in a variety of arenas, from education to science; the accumulation of land and its conversion to real estate at the expense of communities; and the attempts to naturalize and broaden the prison-industrial complex—sometimes through a carceral-positive logic that insidiously hijacks the language of radical social movements.

Our tour has also taken us to streams in AI's orbit that offer different orientations, at least superficially. These streams emphasize the situated and embodied elements of thought and action. They were promising not only because they could help deflate AI's prevailing epistemic forgeries but also because they invoked notions such as world building, collective living, and caring for others. Unfortunately, those aspects were largely neglected. These streams have not situated themselves within imperial and capitalist institutions or reckoned with their own history.[1] And so the embodied and situated lines of inquiry developed as another weapon for the militarized world, and another collection of metaphors to naturalize the accumulation of capital.

THE LIMITS OF EXPOSITION

As I mentioned at the outset, AI isn't a deck of lies that would topple if the truth were exposed (as Edward Said wrote of Orientalism). And contrary to the professional academic impulse, probably the last thing that is needed is a new subfield of "critical" AI studies.[2]

Indeed, in recent decades there have been pleas for AI practitioners to adopt more "critical" or "ethical" stances alongside attempts to sketch various "critical technical practices." These were accompanied by calls for more collaboration between AI practitioners and the social scientists who study them. Such pleas reproduce the problematic fixation on "AI" that benefits corporations and the national security state, even if they desperately try to invert its valence ("AI for social justice" rather than "AI for war"). Since AI isn't the general-purpose technology experts present it as but a technology of whiteness, the attempted inversion becomes another justification for AI's expert industry and its initiatives.

Such proposals flow from the sociological frame with which academics often approach AI, computing, and the sciences generally. This frame's attempt to show there are no boundaries remaining—between the social and technical or the natural and cultural—has produced a picture of a world made up of actors, networks, and devices. This picture is eerily similar to the neoliberal vision in which people are entrepreneurs, building portfolios and forming alliances in order to cater to an ever-changing market. Institutional power and history recede; we are left with networks of enterprising individuals and their sociotechnical imaginaries, and the politics baked into gadgets. By better navigating these networks, the ship could apparently be steered in a more "critical" or "ethical" direction.

Yet troubles lie in the very institutions that this logic seeks to further interweave and extend. Much violence emerges from what is held up as the site of "knowledge production"—the academy, allied with corporations and the state—that stages AI's perpetual revolutions. Therefore I want to conclude by considering other modes of action, grounded in this work's premise that AI is tethered to whiteness, its political projects, and attendant institutions.

UNIVERSITIES AND A
GENERATIVE REFUSAL

The old question that this work returns to is: How can whiteness be resisted? It is a question many have grappled with. Since the ideology of whiteness is backed by institutional power and a long history, resisting it is not simply a matter of individual choice, as so many have pointed out. Individuals, however, certainly do become, to use George Lipsitz's phrase, "possessively invested" in whiteness. As Lipsitz notes, "The artificial construction of whiteness almost always comes to possess white people themselves unless they develop antiracist identities, unless they disinvest and divest themselves of their investments in white supremacy."[3]

The experts and institutes we have encountered in this book are possessively invested in AI like they are in whiteness. And a disinvestment in whiteness would entail disinvesting in AI and its epistemic forgeries, as well as the expert industry and institutions that sustain it.

This brings us back to the academy. Throughout this book we have seen the central roles that American universities play in the making of AI. They have provided a flexible meeting point for the corporate world, the national security state, and the realm of scholarship and academic expertise, catering to every wing of institutional power. They have pushed forward the propagandistic discourse on AI and used it to cement partnerships that cede even more control to military-industrial powers. The nebulous air about these initiatives stands in contrast to the tangible projects that happen within and alongside them—notably, global projects of land accumulation and dispossession of people from their homes, and the naturalization of incarceration. Universities have long participated in these projects; the rubric of "AI" only sanctions their latest manifestations.

One also cannot help but notice the similarity between the nebulous subject matter of these initiatives (AI) and the means by which they are formed (as discussed in chapter 2). These initiatives depend on nebulous and opaque partnerships and financial instruments; those same instruments that universities and their partners use to convert land into real estate. This illustrates how the university, as Sandy Grande wrote, is "a site where the logics of elimination, capital accumulation, and dispossession are reconstituted."[4] AI, as we have seen, has been one vehicle for advancing these logics in a range of arenas.

When the neoliberal logic surrounding the university pushes for more partnerships, more interdisciplinary collaborations, and the creation of more institutes that naturalize the military-industrial-academic machine, it seems to me that a different disposition—one of *refusal*—becomes even more essential.

Refusal is not just a rejection of the neoliberal glue. A refusal can be generative. It is a switch that can lead into what Audra Simpson has called, in a different context, "the productive ambit of refusal."[5] Building on Simpson's thread, Grande has called for a refusal of the university, which opens opportunities "for coalition and collusion within and outside the university."[6]

Refusal is grounded in the recognition of institutional violence and its history, which cannot be denied in the case of the university and its allies. This recognition also helps one think more clearly about what takes place inside these compromised spaces. As Stefano Harney and Fred Moten put it: "It cannot be denied that the university is a place of refuge, and it cannot be accepted that the university is a place of enlightenment."[7] Harney and Moten shift the focus to what happens underneath and in spite of the university, what they call "*the undercommons of enlightenment.*" The undercommons is both a way of being and a space of possibility that does not seek recognition from the university but also does not frame itself in opposition to it.[8] In the undercommons, maroon communities engage not in "policy" but in fugitive planning and study. And while the university feeds on the labor of the undercommons, it could never embrace it or even acknowledge its existence.[9] In other words, what the undercommons offers cannot be (and does not seek to be) institutionalized in the form of new academic initiatives, inter-disciplinary centers or policy proposals.

When Henry Kissinger comes to campus to warn about "AI" bringing an end to the Enlightenment—and the university offers the ethical capitalism of billionaires to the rescue—I think of the undercommons. In the undercommons, alternatives are being sketched to the concrete and destructive projects described in this book, such as the investments in the prison-industrial complex, in companies that plunder the earth, in the debt of Puerto Rico, in the surveillance of populations across the world (from the United States to Palestine and China), or in systems that render workers precarious and disposable.

This book is anchored partly in the refusal to see these projects as tangential to AI, whose surrounding discourses prioritize abstraction and aloof imperial fantasies of the sort articulated by Kissinger. Such refusal entails joining the coalitions that struggle against, and exist in spite of, the concrete realities that the orbit of AI works hard to sanction.[10] Embedded here is also an act of "disloyalty," to borrow Harney and Moten's term, to fields and disciplines.[11] Loyalty to fields and disciplines would require that AI remain in the realms of cognition, information-processing, sociotechnical systems, posthumanism, Man-Computer symbiosis, and cyborgs—unsullied by the practical, messy, opaque, and bureaucratic projects described above. Disloyalty muddies AI's cerebral reputation by refusing to see these projects as background noise.

THE SAILING SHIP OF EMPIRE AND CAPITAL

In a world far from that of social scientists and sociotechnical imaginaries, professional codes of ethics, and bureaucratic

frameworks of accountability, we have Captain Ahab leading the
Pequod in Herman Melville's monumental book *Moby-Dick*
(1851).

By standard readings, Ahab is a madman. He represents
hubris, obsession, the human fear of and need to conquer nature.

But I bring up Ahab because, as Toni Morrison has argued
and contrary to canonical interpretations, the journey of the
Pequod is about dismantling whiteness. Ahab and his "multira-
cial" crew were out to slay whiteness, imbibed by the white whale.
Like whiteness, the whale is elusive, enormous, inaccessible, and
desirable (to some). Melville's narrator, Ishmael, describes the
emptiness of whiteness, which nonetheless has real consequences.
Whiteness is thus "not so much color as the visible absence of
color, and at the same time the concrete of all colors"; whiteness
is "dumb blankness" and yet "full of meaning."[12]

In Morrison's reading, "Melville's 'truth' was his recognition
of the moment in America when whiteness became ideology."
Melville, Morrison writes, found himself "overwhelmed by the
philosophical and metaphysical inconsistencies of an extraordinary and unprecedented idea that had its fullest manifestation
in his own time in his own country"—this idea being "the successful assertion of whiteness as ideology."[13]

Ishmael takes us through a wide range of disciplines—science,
philosophy, theology, and history—because all these play into
the making of whiteness. It is the enormity of the system to be
pulled apart that drives Ahab mad ("of all these things the
Albino Whale was the symbol. Wonder ye then at the fiery
hunt?").[14] Morrison's interpretation of Ahab's quest captures the
totalizing and nebulous quality of whiteness as well as the practical role it plays in guiding and even imbuing with meaning
the lives of those racialized as white. As she writes, "If the
white whale is the ideology of race, what Ahab has lost to it is

personal dismemberment and family and society and his own place as a human in the world." Ahab's audacity (and folly) was to think he could take on this beast alone, a quest that left him "navigating between an idea of civilization that he renounces and an idea of savagery he must annihilate, because the two cannot coexist. The former is based on the latter." In Melville's twist, however, "savagery" does not have its usual racist meaning, but instead it is "white racial ideology that is savage."[15]

With Morrison's reframing, Melville's chapters on the contradictory physiology of the whale ("classification of the constituents of a chaos"),[16] the animal's religious significance, and the folklore surrounding it receive new cogency and force. Indeed, Ishmael can be said to give us a tour of the "makeshift patchwork" of whiteness, to use Cedric Robinson's term, delivered through the ineffable white whale.

In the background of each chapter in this book, I imagined the *Pequod* on its anguished journey, one that seems endless but comes to an unsatisfying end. Melville gives a sense of what the journey entails, and importantly, what must be refused along the way.

In the final stretch, days before Ahab will disappear into the sea, the *Pequod* encounters several ships. One is the *Bachelor*. Overflowing with lucrative spermaceti oil, the *Bachelor* is the ship of capital, with all its imperial and gendered connotations. On board the *Bachelor* "the mates and harpooneers were dancing with the olive-hued girls who had eloped with them from the Polynesian Isles." It is a ship that sails "joyously, though somewhat vain-gloriously," its surplus oil burning, and the jaws of its latest kill on display. The *Bachelor* calls out to the *Pequod*— "Come aboard, come aboard!"—inviting the crew to share in the profits and reap the rewards of imperial expeditions. Ahab, "madman" as he is, refuses. And so they parted; the *Bachelor* sailing "cheerily before the breeze" while the *Pequod* "stubbornly fought against it."[17]

What did the *Pequod* give up? Or rather, in dismantling whiteness, what must go? Clearly, the offerings of capital and empire must be refused.

In our context, this would mean thinking and acting in reparative rather than entrepreneurial terms.[18] It would mean refusing AI—the concept, the associated epistemic forgeries and models of the self, as well as the institutions that sustain these. Take, for instance, the slew of "AI" partnerships, which revolve around institutions that destroy, plunder, and dispossess. Consider refusing, or better yet dissolving, all these and using their resources (but not their energies) to repair communities and rematriate lands. Envision the alternative coalitions that may arise. One could ask: But if we go down this path, where would it all end? One possibility is that it doesn't.

Refusing AI is only part of refusing whiteness, as an ideology and institutional logic, while recognizing that such acts can be realized only collectively. Refusal is not the end, just the continuation of something different.

ACKNOWLEDGMENTS

This book would not have been possible without the help and support of many people.

I would like to thank those who generously agreed to be interviewed as part of my research: Noam Chomsky, Jacinta Gonzaléz, Jonathan Gratch, W. Lewis Johnson, Hamid Khan, John Laird, Humberto Maturana, Lenny Siegel, Michael van Lent, and Terry Winograd. I have taken their words seriously, even if not all their voices made it into the text. For access to archival materials, I thank Miles Crowley and the staff of MIT Archives, and the librarians at Harvard University. For permission to reprint materials, I thank the Newell and Simon families, University of Chicago, the Computer History Museum, CNA, Fight for the Future, NWDC Resistance, Mijente, and Stop LAPD Spying Coalition. While writing this book I was a departmental fellow in systems biology at Harvard Medical School and in 2016–2017 also held an unpaid fellowship at the Berkman Klein Center for Internet & Society.

It has been a pleasure working with Columbia University Press. I am grateful to Eric Schwartz and Lowell Frye for believing in this project from the beginning, and for their insightful guidance throughout the process. I thank the two anonymous reviewers of the manuscript for their critiques and suggestions.

I also thank Anita O'Brien for outstanding and careful copyediting, Zachary Friedman for marketing copy, and Susan Pensak for coordinating the production of this book.

I am also deeply indebted to Jessie Kindig for her brilliant editorial suggestions, which greatly improved this book.

I thank Lukas Rieppel, Joan Richards, and the Brown University STS group for helpful discussions on parts of this work, and Chris Lydon, Mary McGrath, and the rest of the ROS crew for a chance to talk through some of these ideas. I also thank Walter Fontana for many illuminating conversations on biology and computation, and for his adventurous intellectual spirit.

I thank the family and friends who have helped me cope with and sometimes laugh about the tech-(dys)topian world: Ariella Azoulay, Andrew Bolton, Nazim Bouatta, Vincent Butty, Eric Jonas, Ulrich Matter, Katherine McConachie, Adi Ophir, Ruth Perry, Grif Peterson, Matthew Ricci, and Lauren Surface. Thanks to Ariella, Grif, Matt, and Lauren for their insightful comments on drafts of this work. I also thank Grif, Ulrich, and Ruth for being partners in crime on several projects loosely related to this book. Special thanks to Ruth for putting up with my ramblings about Melville and whiteness, and for directing me to Toni Morrison's treatment of the topic—a reference that literally changed my life. I also thank Ariella and Adi for being intellectual role models in the truest sense.

I thank my parents, Orly Azoulay and Jacob Katz, and my sister, Shira Wasserman, for their endless love, support, and encouragement, as well as the more recent members of the family, Shelley Fitzer Surface and Tim Surface. Finally, my infinite gratitude to Lauren and Azoul for the daily joys and sweetness of life. And to Lauren, for her love, friendship, support, and inspiration, which I could never capture with words.

NOTES

INTRODUCTION

1. Arjun Kharpal, "Stephen Hawking Says A.I. Could Be 'Worst Event in the History of Our Civilization,' " CNBC, November 6, 2017.
2. David Meyer, "Vladimir Putin Says Whoever Leads in Artificial Intelligence Will Rule the World," *Fortune*, September 4, 2017.
3. Museum of Modern Art (MoMA), "MoMA R&D: AI—Artificial Imperfection" (New York: MoMA, 2018).
4. Jess Cartner-Morley, "Do Robots Dream of Prada? How Artificial Intelligence Is Reprogramming Fashion," *Guardian*, September 15, 2018.
5. Max Tegmark, *Life 3.0: Being Human in the Age of Artificial Intelligence* (New York: Knopf, 2017); New York University, "New Artificial Intelligence Research Institute Launches," November 20, 2017, https://engineering.nyu.edu/news/new-artificial-intelligence-research-institute-launches; Ahmed Alkhateeb, "Can Scientific Discovery Be Automated?," *Atlantic*, April 25, 2017; Arun Vishwanath, "When a Robot Writes Your News, What Happens to Democracy?," CNN, February 27, 2018.
6. Ian Sample, "AI Will Create 'Useless Class' of Human, Predicts Bestselling Historian," *Guardian*, May 20, 2016; Vikram Barhat, "China Is Determined to Steal A.I. Crown from US and Nothing, Not Even a Trade War, Will Stop It," CNBC, May 4, 2018; Michael Auslin, "Can the Pentagon Win the AI Arms Race?," *Foreign Affairs*, October 19, 2018; Kelsey D. Atherton, "Are Killer Robots the Future of War? Parsing the Facts on Autonomous Weapons," *New York Times*, November 15, 2018.
7. Jeff Nesbit, "We All May Be Dead in 2050," *U.S. News & World Report*, October 29, 2015.

8. Even scholars in science and technology studies and historians of computing who see themselves as providing critical counters to the rhetoric of entrepreneurs and computing practitioners often treat "AI" as a coherent, transformative force (without really scrutinizing the label nor the timing of its reappearances). See, e.g., Lucy Suchman, Lilly Irani, and Peter Asaro, "Google's March to the Business of War Must Be Stopped," *Guardian*, May 16, 2018; Marie Hicks, "Why Tech's Gender Problem Is Nothing New," *Guardian*, May 13, 2018.

9. Gian-Carlo Rota, "The End of Objectivity," *The Legacy of Phenomenology: Lectures at MIT* (Cambridge, Mass.: MIT Mathematics Department, 1991), 174.

10. *Singju Post*, "Artificial Intelligence Is the New Electricity," January 23, 2018.

11. Pamela McCorduck's history of AI is a paradigmatic example; see McCorduck, *Machines Who Think: A Personal Inquiry Into the History and Prospects of Artificial Intelligence* (New York: Freeman, 1979). McCorduck's narrative is based on interviews with a close-knit circle of men—Herbert Simon, Allen Newell, John McCarthy, and Marvin Minsky, among others—all affiliated with McCorduck's collaborator Edward Feigenbaum. These are AI's celebrated protagonists, with whom McCorduck sides, while being harshly critical of the two dissenting voices featured in the book (Joseph Weizenbaum and Hubert Dreyfus). Although McCorduck in no way conceals her admiration for AI and its most famous practitioners, her account continues to be cited as an authoritative history of AI. We will encounter other triumphalist histories of AI, written and praised by prominent practitioners, throughout this book.

12. Allen Newell, "AAAI President's Message," *AI Magazine* 1, no. 1 (1980): 4.

13. Alison Adam, *Artificial Knowing: Gender and the Thinking Machine* (New York: Routledge, 2006).

14. Toni Morrison, "Unspeakable Things Unspoken: The Afro-American Presence in American Literature," Tanner Lectures on Human Values, 1988.

15. Cheryl I. Harris, "Whiteness as Property," *Harvard Law Review* 106, no. 8 (1993): 1714–91.

16. Edward W. Said, *Orientalism* (1978; New York: Knopf, 2014), 6.

17. Dismissals of AI as hype or a marketing trick get in the way of this analysis. To say AI is an "overhyped technology" does not tell us what kind of technology it is, how it functions, what sustains it, and the purposes it serves. "Hype" also masks AI's imperial origins and its racial, gendered,

and classed epistemologies, making it seem as if it were a neutral body of technical knowledge whose importance is simply exaggerated.

18. Silvia Federici, *Caliban and the Witch* (New York: Autonomedia, 2004); Anne McClintock, "Imperial Leather," in *Imperial Leather: Race, Gender, and Sexuality in the Colonial Contest* (New York: Routledge, 2013).

19. Harris, "Whiteness as Property"; George Lipsitz, *The Possessive Investment in Whiteness: How White People Profit from Identity Politics* (Philadelphia: Temple University Press, 2009).

20. As Paul N. Edwards argued in his book *The Closed World: Computers and the Politics of Discourse in Cold War America* (Cambridge, Mass.: MIT Press, 1997), a Cold War–era imperial logic shaped the field of computing, including AI's formation, in the 1950s. In the "closed world" frame he described, all projects are viewed as part of a grand struggle between warring empires—a frame that the computer imbibed. AI is undoubtedly animated by such imperial logics and their accompanying capitalist visions in ways I will describe in this book. But not all the vast commentary on AI fits within a Cold War–like frame, either. One should consider how AI's shifting nebulosity allows it to adapt to new conditions.

21. Cedric J. Robinson, *Forgeries of Memory and Meaning: Blacks and the Regimes of Race in American Theater and Film Before World War II* (Chapel Hill: University of North Carolina Press, 2007), xii.

22. Lipsitz, *The Possessive Investment in Whiteness*, 1.

23. Robin DiAngelo, "White Fragility," *International Journal of Critical Pedagogy* 3, no. 3 (2011): 54–70.

24. As several media scholars have argued, race (or racial categories) can be usefully analyzed as technologies. This framing emphasizes the fact that race is a flexible tool for doing (in my view, violent) things in the world. My thinking in this book draws on different accounts of whiteness and race that do not necessarily invoke "technology" but certainly do highlight how these concepts and the systems of power behind them are dynamic and malleable. The idea of race as a technology is nonetheless worthwhile and relevant. As Wendy H. K. Chun has argued, the notions of "race as biology and race as culture are similarly mobile and flexible technologies." This framing, as Chun writes, helps dispense with essentialist notions: "Focusing on race as a technology, as mediation, thus allows us to see the continuing function of race, regardless of its essence." Chun, "Introduction: Race and/as Technology; Or, How to Do Things to Race," *Camera Obscura: Feminism, Culture, and Media Studies* 70, no. 1 (24) (2009). However, the idea of race as technology can go in directions I shy away from. In particular, I reject the line of reasoning that suggests that since

race is a technology and technologies have multiple uses, then perhaps racial categories are not inherently oppressive and can instead be put to subversive and liberatory uses by creative individuals. This sounds to me like the point, identified by David Graeber, where neoliberalism and postmodern critique become mirror images of each other: both see the world as bound by totalizing systems of power, and fixate on action at the individual level. In the case of former, taking action means becoming an entrepreneur, and in the latter it means "fashioning of subversive identities." Graeber, *Toward An Anthropological Theory of Value: The False Coin of Our Own Dreams* (New York: Palgrave, 2001), x. Whiteness derives its force from violent institutions with a long history, and so subverting or challenging it cannot simply be a matter of individual practice. My argument in this book is rather that AI—a much narrower thing than whiteness or "race"—should be seen as a technology that not only serves the racial ideology of whiteness but also mimics it in form by itself being hollow, flexible, and subservient to imperial and capitalist interests. I invoke "technology" in part to emphasize la paperson's important observation that technologies of oppression are trafficked across distinct spheres (from the military to universities, for instance), an observation that applies well to AI as understood here. See la paperson, *A Third University Is Possible* (Minneapolis: University of Minnesota Press, 2017), 1–14.

25. Judith Squires, "Fabulous Feminist Futures and the Lure of Cyberculture," in *The Cybercultures Reader*, ed. David Bell and Barbara M. Kennedy (New York: Routledge, 2000).

26. See Lawrence Weschler, *And How Are You, Dr. Sacks? A Biographical Memoir of Oliver Sacks* (New York: Farrar, Straus and Giroux, 2019), 198, 275. Sacks did not mince words about AI: "Everything to do with AI is Golemmaking. . . . It's worse than perverted: It's sinister."

27. I do have strong reservations about the intense focus on the individual in these arguments.

28. To state the obvious, forgoing whiteness is not only an individual decision but part of a struggle to dismantle the structures of white supremacy that make being "white" possible.

29. Susan Slyomovics, "French Restitution, German Compensation: Algerian Jews and Vichy's Financial Legacy," *Journal of North African Studies* 17, no. 5 (2012): 881–901.

30. For a wide-ranging discussion of what Roger Azoulay and others like him had erased by complying with the imperial project, see Ariella Aïsha Azoulay, *Potential History: Unlearning Imperialism* (New York: Verso Books, 2019), chap. 1.

1. IN THE SERVICE OF EMPIRE

1. Herman Melville, *Moby-Dick, Or, The Whale*, Modern Library Classics (1851; New York: Penguin, 2000), 190.

2. Stuart W. Leslie, *The Cold War and American Science: The Military-Industrial-Academic Complex at MIT and Stanford* (New York: Columbia University Press, 1993); Paul N. Edwards, *The Closed World: Computers and the Politics of Discourse in Cold War America* (Cambridge, Mass.: MIT Press, 1997).

3. W. H. Tetley, "The Role of Computers in Air Defense," in *Papers and Discussions Presented at the December 3–5, 1958, Eastern Joint Computer Conference: Modern Computers: Objectives, Designs, Applications*, 1958, 15–18.

4. Edwards, *The Closed World*, 43.

5. See Robert M. Yerkes's report from 1921 on psychologists' services to the military, "Psychological Examining in the United States Army," in *Readings in the History of Psychology*, ed. Wayne Dennis (New York: Appleton-Century-Crofts, 1948), 528–40.

6. Nils J. Nilsson, *The Quest for Artificial Intelligence* (Cambridge: Cambridge University Press, 2009), 53.

7. Peter Galison, "The Ontology of the Enemy: Norbert Wiener and the Cybernetic Vision," *Critical Inquiry* 21, no. 1 (1994): 228–66.

8. See V. Rajaraman, "John McCarthy—Father of Artificial Intelligence," *Resonance* 19, no. 3 (2014): 198–207. To McCarthy's disappointment, the collection coedited with Shannon, published under the heading "Automata Studies," ended up attracting conventional cyberneticians. James Fleck, "Development and Establishment in Artificial Intelligence," in *Scientific Establishments and Hierarchies*, ed. N. Elias, H. Martins, and R. Whitley (New York: Springer, 1982), 169–217.

9. See Association for Computing Machinery, "1971 A. M. Turing Award Citation for John McCarthy." The citation also notes McCarthy's previous disappointment with "Automata Studies": "Having noticed that the title of the Automata Studies book didn't stir up much excitement, when he [McCarthy] subsequently moved to Dartmouth College he introduced the name artificial intelligence at a 1956 conference there and saw that it was embraced both by people working in the field and the general public."

10. James Moor, "The Dartmouth College Artificial Intelligence Conference: The Next Fifty Years," *AI Magazine* 27, no. 4 (2006): 87.

11. Moor, 87.

12. Martin Shubik, "Bibliography on Simulation, Gaming, Artificial Intelligence and Allied Topics," *Journal of the American Statistical Association* 55, no. 292 (1960): 736–51.

13. Seymour Papert, "The Summer Vision Project," Vision Memo No. 100, MIT Artificial Intelligence Group, July 1966.

14. Flo Conway and Jim Siegelman, *Dark Hero of the Information Age: In Search of Norbert Wiener—Father of Cybernetics* (New York: Basic Books, 2005), 321.

15. Patrick H. Winston, oral history interview, Charles Babbage Institute, University of Minnesota, 1990, 19.

16. Conway and Siegelman, *Dark Hero of the Information Age*, 321.

17. A. Müller and K. H. Müller, eds., *An Unfinished Revolution? Heinz Von Foerster and the Biological Computer Laboratory, BCL, 1958–1976*, Complexity, Design, Society (Vienna: Edition Echoraum, 2007), 60–61.

18. See Defense Advanced Research Projects Agency, "DARPA Artificial Intelligence Grants Records, 1963–2017 (Case No. 19-F-0077)," March 15, 2019.

19. According my analysis of DARPA's funding records, it was not until 1972 that a university other than MIT or Stanford (Carnegie Mellon University) was awarded an AI grant. These three schools continued to receive most of DARPA's AI grants. It was only in the mid-1980s that the agency began giving such grants to other institutions, such as Columbia University, the University of Maryland, the University of Southern California, and California Institute of Technology.

20. Perhaps the most sophisticated of these classifications is the polar map given in *The Embodied Mind*, which attempts to organize the work of individual influential researchers (e.g., McCarthy, Simon, Newell) along fields (e.g., cognitive psychology, neuroscience, artificial intelligence) and epistemic premises/styles (e.g., cognitivism, emergence, enaction). See Francisco J. Varela, Evan Thompson, and Eleanor Rosch, *The Embodied Mind: Cognitive Science and Human Experience* (Cambridge, Mass.: MIT Press, 2017), 7. H. R. Ekbia offers another taxonomy of streams within AI, such "problem solving," "supercomputing," "cybernetic," "knowledge-intensive," "case-based," "connectionist," "dynamical," "embodied," and "analogical." See Ekbia, *Artificial Dreams: The Quest for Non-Biological Intelligence* (Cambridge: Cambridge University Press, 2008), 18.

21. Sometimes referred to as "Good Old-Fashioned AI."

22. Indeed, already in the 1960s, AI practitioners interested in building robots were thinking of ways to combine symbolic structures with probabilistic inference and statistics. A report in 1969, for instance, points out that "since 'facts' obtained from either the [robot's] model or the subroutines are subject to error, it is natural to accompany them by some confidence or probability measure." Nils J. Nilsson, *A Mobile Automaton: An Application of*

Artificial Intelligence Techniques (Menlo Park, Calif.: Stanford Research Institute, 1969).

23. Robert L. Chapman et al., "The Systems Research Laboratory's Air Defense Experiments," *Management Science* 5, no. 3 (1959): 250–69.

24. Allen Newell and Herbert A. Simon, *Human Problem Solving* (Englewood Cliffs, N.J.: Prentice-Hall 1972), 9.

25. Herbert A. Simon and Allen Newell, "Heuristic Problem Solving: The Next Advance in Operations Research," *Operations Research* 6, no. 1 (1958): 1–10.

26. In an early report about GPS, Newell and Simon also wrote: "Realizing programs like GPS on a computer is a major programming task. Much of our research effort has gone into the design of programming languages (information-processing languages) that make the writing of such programs practicable." Allen Newell, John C. Shaw, and Herbert A. Simon, *Report on a General Problem-Solving Program*, Memo P-1584 (Santa Monica, Calif: RAND Corporation, 1958).

27. The pair wrote that their work should be seen as "nonstatistical" and "makes very little use of the standard statistical apparatus." For Newell and Simon, mental "content," made of "diverse meaningful symbolic structures," nearly defied reduction to numbers. Newell and Simon, *Human Problem Solving*, 13. They equated symbolic computation with AI, as they made clear in their A. M. Turing Award lecture in 1976: "Artificial intelligence research is concerned with how symbol systems must be organized in order to behave intelligently." Allen Newell and Herbert A. Simon, "Computer Science as Empirical Inquiry: Symbols and Search," *Communications of the ACM*, no. 3 (1976): 113–26.

28. Alison Adam, *Artificial Knowing: Gender and the Thinking Machine* (New York: Routledge, 2006).

29. Simon and Newell, "Heuristic Problem Solving."

30. Feigenbaum's colleague Joshua Lederberg was involved with NASA's Mariner mission to Mars, which involved spacecrafts equipped with mass spectrometers. Lederberg proposed to Feigenbaum the problem of computationally identifying chemical structures from mass spectrometry data, and this initiated their collaboration on DENDRAL. Robert K. Lindsay et al., "DENDRAL: A Case Study of the First Expert System for Scientific Hypothesis Formation," *Artificial Intelligence* 61, no. 2 (1993): 209–61.

31. Meta-DENDRAL was a system Edward Feigenbaum and colleagues developed explicitly for this purpose. See Lindsay et al., "DENDRAL."

32. Edward A. Feigenbaum, *Knowledge Engineering: The Applied Side of Artificial Intelligence* (Stanford, Calif.: Stanford University, 1980).

244 ࠍ I. IN THE SERVICE OF EMPIRE

33. Pamela McCorduck, *Machines Who Think: A Personal Inquiry Into the History and Prospects of Artificial Intelligence* (New York: Freeman, 1979), 272.

34. McCorduck, 284.

35. Systems such as DENDRAL were not instantly popular, according to Feigenbaum. One reason he gave was the lack of computers suited for running Lisp programs like DENDRAL: "[Lisp programs in] which most AI work has been done, have been pasted on top of the instruction code of conventional computers. That is a mistake. We need specialized symbol processing devices." Feigenbaum, *Knowledge Engineering*.

36. McCorduck, *Machines Who Think*, 284.

37. Paul Armer, who worked at RAND at the time, described the internal reaction to Dreyfus's report in an interview with Pamela McCorduck: "I thought it [Dreyfus's report] was lousy philosophy. And, further, he had decided he was really going to attack. . . . I had a big squabble with some other people in the department who liked the paper and who kept pinning me to the wall with my own pronouncements about censorship and how bad it is to have yes-men around. . . . So eventually it came out. I suppose I delayed publication on it for nine months or so." McCorduck, 195.

38. For the acrimonious exchanges between Hubert Dreyfus and Herbert Simon, as well as Seymour Papert and Dreyfus, see McCorduck, 198–200. According to Feigenbaum and McCorduck, the "anti-AI philosophers" (presumably Dreyfus is in this class) "were by turns amusing, impenetrable, and disputatious." Edward A. Feigenbaum and Pamela McCorduck, *The Fifth Generation: Artificial Intelligence and Japan's Computer Challenge to the World* (Boston: Addison-Wesley, 1983), 33.

39. James Lighthill, *A Report on Artificial Intelligence* (London: UK Science and Engineering Research Council, 1973).

40. A well-known textbook on AI notes in passing that "to save embarrassment," after the Lighthill report, "a new field called IKBS (Intelligent Knowledge-Based Systems) was invented because Artificial Intelligence had been officially canceled." This enabled researchers to get back the funding apparently slashed as a result of Lighthill's critique. See Stuart Russell and Peter Norvig, *Artificial Intelligence: A Modern Approach*, 2d ed. (Englewood Cliffs, N.J.: Prentice Hall, 2002), 23.

41. Heilmeier was probably not as hostile to the AI field as some practitioners made him out to be. For one, he has stated that advances made in "nonnumerical mathematics," including the feat of outdoing experts in interpreting mass spectroscopy data (an allusion to DENDRAL), have made AI intensely appealing to the Pentagon. See Paul Dickson, *The Electronic Battlefield* (Bloomington: Indiana University Press, 1976). And as Patrick

Winston noted, "Here is a guy [Heilmeier] who was feared by the artificial intelligence laboratories while he was in charge, who when he left DARPA, carried the AI crusade on himself at TI [Texas Instruments]." Winston, oral history interview.

42. Allen Newell, "Newell Comments Concerning Roadmap of DARPA Funding of AI," letter, November 3, 1975, in Edward A. Feigenbaum Papers, Stanford University, SC0340, B6, F11.

43. Nilsson, *The Quest for Artificial Intelligence*, 246.

44. See Nils J. Nilsson, *Artificial Intelligence—Research and Applications*, vol. 2, May 1975. AI has been depicted elsewhere as a kind of "stack" organized around the Pentagon's aims. See, for example, Edward A. Torrero, *Next-Generation Computers*, Spectrum Series (New York: Institute of Electrical and Electronics Engineers, 1985), 146.

45. Peter E. Hart and Richard O. Duda, *PROSPECTOR—A Computer Based Consultation System for Mineral Exploration* (Menlo Park, Calif.: SRI International, 1977).

46. Peter E. Hart, *Artificial Intelligence* (Menlo Park, Calif.: Stanford Research Institute, 1976).

47. Leslie, *The Cold War and American Science*, 252.

48. Edwards, *The Closed World*, 18.

49. Robert Trappl, *Impacts of Artificial Intelligence* (Amsterdam: North Holland, 1986), 6.

50. Allen Newell, "AAAI President's Message," *AI Magazine* 1, no. 1 (1980): 1–4.

51. William Stockton, "Creating Computers That Think," *New York Times Magazine*, December 7, 1980.

52. Feigenbaum and McCorduck, *The Fifth Generation*, xvi.

53. Feigenbaum and McCorduck, xvi, xviii.

54. Pamela McCorduck, "Selling Concept of 'Fifth Generation' Book to Publishers," letter, January 19, 1982, in Edward A. Feigenbaum Papers, 1950–2007, Stanford University, SC0340, Accession 2005-101, Box 37, Folder 5.

55. See George Lipsitz, *The Possessive Investment in Whiteness: How White People Profit from Identity Politics* (Philadelphia: Temple University Press, 2009), chap. 4.

56. Feigenbaum and McCorduck, *The Fifth Generation*, 14.

57. A *New York Times* article about the state of Japan's Fifth Generation Project hinted at this: "Some American computer scientists say privately that some of their colleagues did perhaps overstate the scope and threat of the Fifth Generation Project. Why? In order to coax more support from the United States Government for computer science research." Andrew

Pollack, "'Fifth Generation' Became Japan's Lost Generation," *New York Times*, June 5, 1992.

58. Feigenbaum and McCorduck were not alone in their views, of course. Various practitioners, as well as organizations such as the Institute of Electrical and Electronics Engineers (IEEE), contributed to the propaganda campaign. An IEEE publication titled *Next-Generation Computers* is filled with various thoughts on how to maintain U.S. hegemony and keep competitors at bay. An article by Trudy E. Bell, an IEEE editor, suggests that Japan is "developing fifth-generation technology to meet the social needs they anticipate in the next decade. The Japanese also anticipate that exporting fifth-generation technology will improve their world economic position," whereas "the United States is primary concerned with maintaining its own world leadership in information technology. The United States is also concerned with the applications of fifth-generation computing technology to national security, to build up its strategic strength with respect to the USSR and the communist-bloc nations." Bell goes on to say that "the U.S. goal is to build up a greater common pool of knowledge about individual systems, both for the military and also for the use of private companies in further developing products in the usual competitive free market." Trudy E. Bell, "The Teams and The Players," in *Next-Generation Computers*, ed. Edward A. Torrero, Spectrum Series (Institute of Electrical and Electronics Engineers, 1985), 13. Like AAAI, IEEE gives DARPA ample space to disseminate its "strategic plan for the development and application of next-generation technology for the military" (Torrero, 146–90).

59. Alex Roland and Philip Shiman, *Strategic Computing: DARPA and the Quest for Machine Intelligence, 1983–1993* (Cambridge, Mass.: MIT Press, 2002), 91–92.

60. Roland and Shiman, 92.

61. In 1986 a reporter reviewing the state of MCC wrote: "Where is MCC today? . . . No longer is the company chasing the elusive computer that was to revolutionize the industry by incorporating artificial intelligence and making decisions based on reasoning." Yet the same article states MCC is building a program to emulate commonsense "this year." See Mark A. Fischetti, "A Review of Progress at MCC: Although Its Current Objectives Do Not Include 'Beating Japan,' This US Organization Is Positioned to Help Industry Do So," *IEEE Spectrum* 23, no. 3 (1986): 76–82.

62. Mark A. Fischetti, "The United States," *IEEE Spectrum* 20, no. 11 (1983): 52.

63. Philip M. Boffey, "Software Seen as Obstacle in Developing 'Star Wars,'" *New York Times*, September 16, 1986.

64. Rodney A. Brooks et al., *Panel Review of the Semi-Automated Forces* (Alexandria, Va.: Institute for Defense Analyses, September 1989), D4.

65. Brooks et al., C4.

66. Brooks et al., C16.

67. Terry Winograd, *Strategic Computing Research and the Universities* (Stanford, Calif.: Stanford University, March 1987).

68. This was part of broader resistance among scientists, notably physicists, to Reagan's Star Wars program and related initiatives. See Sigrid Schmalzer, Daniel S. Chard, and Alyssa Botelho, *Science for the People: Documents from America's Movement of Radical Scientists*, Science/Technology/Culture Series (Amherst: University of Massachusetts Press, 2018), 79–83.

69. Joseph Weizenbaum, "Computers in Uniform: A Good Fit?," *Science for the People* 17, no. 1 (1985): 26–29.

70. As Weizenbaum put it, "If a student were to come to an AI laboratory and were to want to work on something that couldn't be justified in these terms, that had nothing to do with these things I have been speaking of, it is not that the money couldn't conceivably be found, but that the supervisors couldn't be found because the whole laboratory is already soaked up by this enormous effort."

71. John McCarthy, *Defending AI Research: A Collection of Essays and Reviews* (Stanford, Calif.: CSLI Publications, 1996).

72. In reviewing concerns regarding "military applications" of AI, Robert Trappl wrote that one danger of automated weapons (e.g., implemented using expert systems) is that "the use of such systems would make it easier for an opponent to predict the behavior of his antagonist (and to take counter-measures) than is presently the case with human decision makers," if the "opponent" knew the rules by which the automated weapon system behaves and had access to faster computers. Trappl also raised another concern: "A second danger lies in the fact that it is almost impossible to fully debug such complicated programs, and under battle conditions there would be too little time to rectify obviously incorrect actions." Both concerns are tactical; they question the effectiveness of "AI-driven" weaponry but not the broader aims these systems serve. Trappl, "Impacts of Artificial Intelligence: An Overview," in *Impacts of Artificial Intelligence*, ed. Robert Trappl (Amsterdam: North Holland, 1986), 37.

73. Ronald Rosenberg, "AI Alley's Longest Winter," *Boston Globe*, December 18, 1988.

74. William Bulkeley, "Bright Outlook for Artificial Intelligence Yields to Slow Growth and Big Cutbacks," *Wall Street Journal*, July 5, 1990.

75. Rosenberg, "AI Alley's Longest Winter."

76. Pamela K. Coats, "Why Expert Systems Fail," *Financial Management* 17, no. 3 (1988): 77–86.

77. Alan Bundy, "What Kind of Field Is AI?," in *The Foundations of Artificial Intelligence: A Sourcebook*, ed. Derek Partridge and Yorick Wilks (Cambridge: Cambridge University Press, 1990); Eric Dietrich, "Programs in the Search for Intelligent Machines: The Mistaken Foundations of AI," in *The Foundations of Artificial Intelligence: A Sourcebook*, ed. Derek Partridge and Yorick Wilks (Cambridge: Cambridge University Press, 1990).

78. Roger M. Needham, "Is There Anything Special About AI?," in *The Foundations of Artificial Intelligence: A Sourcebook*, ed. Derek Partridge and Yorick Wilks (Cambridge: Cambridge University Press, 1990).

79. Pollack, "'Fifth Generation' Became Japan's Lost Generation."

80. George Johnson, "Artificial Brain Again Seen as a Guide to the Mind," *New York Times*, August 16, 1988.

81. Seymour Papert, "One AI or Many?," in *The Artificial Intelligence Debate: False Starts, Real Foundations*, ed. Stephen Graubard (Cambridge, Mass.: MIT Press, 1988), 241–67.

82. A DARPA paper in 1991 describes the agency's recent effort to explore the viability of neural networks for military use. The report does not mention "artificial intelligence" nor simulation of human minds but presents neural networks as a data analysis technique to be compared with other statistical methods (such as Bayesian classifiers). See B. L. Yoon, "DARPA Artificial Neural Network Technology Program," in *1991 International Symposium on VLSI Technology, Systems, and Applications*, 1991, 61–63.

83. George Johnson, "Japan Plans Computer to Mimic Human Brain," *New York Times*, August 25, 1992.

84. See Philip E. Agre, "Toward a Critical Technical Practice: Lessons Learned in Trying to Reform AI," in *Social Science, Technical Systems, and Cooperative Work: Beyond the Great Divide*, ed. G. Bowker, S. L. Star, L. Gasser, and W. Turner (Abingdon, UK: Taylor & Francis, 1997). While Agre is critical of the field of "AI" as well as the concept, his account nonetheless privileges the technical elements of computing systems. For Agre, there must be a certain fit between the structure of the computer program and the AI narrative (which invokes concepts like beliefs, reasoning, desires, and so forth) that is attached to it. He is certainly right that the relationship between these two is not entirely arbitrary, and this fit shapes how certain audiences will respond to narratives that invoke AI. As examples reviewed in this book show, however, what counts as AI is not so determined by what is really "in" the software; the trajectory of AI is animated by ideologies and politics that go far beyond any technical practice.

Perhaps by focusing so much on the structure of software, Agre also misses the racial, gendered, and imperialist elements of AI as a "discursive practice."

85. Reflecting on the popularity of one of his publications, Agre noted that it "has been extensively cited, but one reason for this paper's popularity is that our innovations in models of situated activity happened to coincide with a shift in military strategy toward autonomous battlefield robots under the Strategic Computing Initiative." Through the usual cooperation between AI practitioners and the Pentagon, Agre felt that his own alternative vocabulary got co-opted: "There immediately ensued, with scant and mostly disruptive participation from us, another round of consensus-building between ARPA and the AI community about the necessity of 'autonomous agents' and 'reactive planning.'" Agre, "Toward a Critical Technical Practice," 153.

86. United States Department of Commerce, Office of Industrial Resource Administration, *Critical Technology Assessment of the U.S. Artificial Intelligence Sector*, August 1994, xi.

87. This view is repeated in many accounts, not just by military analysts and pundits but also media scholars. For an analysis of the deaths and devastation in the Gulf—enabled by many "dumb" rather than "smart" bombs— and a critical reading of human rights groups' narratives of the war, see Norman G. Finkelstein, "Middle East Watch and The Gulf War," *Z Magazine* (1992): 15–19.

88. A report in *AI Magazine* on AI's contributions to the Gulf War, for example, states that the Pentagon no longer just focuses on "the battlefield but rather on the all encompassing battlespace of highly complex physical, psychological, and electronic 'theatre.' Military power is more than brute force or orchestrated mechanical might now. It involves international coalitions of forces with military, electronic, mechanical and humanitarian capabilities that can effectively quell crises under the intense scrutiny of international monitors and the media's watchful eye." Sara Reese Hedberg, "DART: Revolutionizing Logistics Planning," *IEEE Intelligent Systems* 17, no. 3 (2002): 81–83.

89. Authored by an AI practitioner and business entrepreneur, Crevier's book is premised in prominent practitioners' telling of their own history, some of whom gave enthusiastic blurbs for the book—such as Minsky, Moravec, and Feigenbaum (alongside the *Wall Street Journal*). The book presents AI and the military-industrial powers who support it in utopian tones. According to Crevier, AI will transform all of society, usually for the better, and eventually make "us" immortal by "downloading" human bodies into

electronic hardware: "AI may lift us into a new kind of existence, where our humanity will be not only preserved but also enhanced in ways we can hardly imagine." Daniel Crevier, *AI: The Tumultuous History of the Search for Artificial Intelligence* (New York: Basic Books, 1993), 340.

90. Crevier writes: "The allied forces in the gulf owed their overwhelming superiority largely to sophisticated computer technology. AI played no small part in this success." He then turns to his interviewee, Winston: "'Some of the things we did did have a significant impact in Saudi Arabia,' Patrick Winston of MIT told me, 'but these were not necessarily the things we thought they would be.'" Crevier does not explore this point further; the unintended consequences are left to the reader's imagination. See Crevier, 314.

91. Crevier, 314 (italics added).

92. Crevier, 315.

93. The system was originally called SOR ("State, Operator and Result") and later renamed Soar. See a biography of Allen Newell coauthored by John Laird for a timeline of Laird and Newell's collaboration on Soar: John E. Laird and Paul S. Rosenbloom, "In Pursuit of Mind: The Research of Allen Newell," *AI Magazine* 13, no. 4 (1992): 17–45.

94. See John Laird and Michael Van Lent, "Human-Level AI's Killer Application: Interactive Computer Games," *AI Magazine* 22, no. 2 (2001): 15. This argument about the inadequacy of looking at individual tasks echoes an influential paper by Allen Newell in which he argues that studying individual psychological tasks and their solutions may not necessarily lead to a satisfying "holistic" understanding of cognition. See Newell, "You Can't Play 20 Questions with Nature and Win: Projective Comments on the Papers of This Symposium," *Visual Information Processing* (1973): 283–308.

95. Laird and Van Lent, "Human-Level AI's Killer Application."

96. A report by the Soar group described the high level of detail of Soar-based military simulations and contrasted them with typical approaches in AI: "Early AI systems solved problems that were only in their own 'mind.' That approach ignores many difficult issues in integrating an intelligent system into a dynamic environment where there are a variety of sensors and motor systems. In this project, our AI system was embedded in a realistic real-time simulation of a battlefield, which included a large detailed terrain database. The terrain database was 575 megabytes (3.7 G for visualization) that covered 500 x 775 square kilometers. The database included 13.5K buildings, 20K destructible objects, runways, roads, bridges, bushes, rivers, bodies of water, etc. During the exercise there were up to 3,700 computer-generated vehicles that covered all U.S. military services as well

as opposition forces. The simulation was completely distributed, running on over 300 computers at six sites. Time in the simulation corresponded to time in the real world, and active-duty military personnel participated in the simulation by observing the battles via simulated messages and sensors and giving real-world commands to the computer-generated forces. Our participation involved fielding all of the U.S. fixed-wing aircraft, which included up to 100 airplanes flying at one time, distributed across 20–30 machines." John E. Laird and Randolph M. Jones, "Building Advanced Autonomous AI Systems for Large Scale Real Time Simulations," in *Proceedings of the 1998 Computer Games Development Conference* (Long Beach, Calif.: Miller Freeman, 1998), 365–78.

97. For technical overviews of these probabilistic models written at a time when they were becoming hugely popular, see David Heckerman, "Bayesian Networks for Data Mining," *Data Mining and Knowledge Discovery* 1, no. 1 (1997): 79–119; Kevin Patrick Murphy, "Dynamic Bayesian Networks: Representation, Inference, and Learning," Ph.D. dissertation, University of California, Berkeley, 2002.

98. Sara Reese Hedberg, "Is AI Going Mainstream as Last? A Look Inside Microsoft Research," *IEEE Intelligent Systems and Their Applications* 13, no. 2 (1998): 21, 23.

99. In *The Master Algorithm*, Pedro Domingos describes a literal marriage ceremony: "Praedicatus, First Lord of Logic, ruler of the symbolic realm and Protector of the Programs, says to Markovia, Princess of Probability, Empress of Networks: 'Let us unite our realms. To my rules thou shalt add weights, begetting a new representation that will spread far across the land.' The princess says, 'And we shall call our progeny Markov logic networks [a formalism developed by Domingos and colleagues].'" Domingos, *The Master Algorithm: How the Quest for the Ultimate Learning Machine Will Remake Our World* (New York: Basic Books, 2015), 246, 21.

100. Domingos, 21.

101. Paul J. Springer, *Military Robots and Drones: A Reference Handbook*, Contemporary World Issues (Santa Barbara, Calif.: ABC-CLIO, 2013).

102. For instance, Edward Feigenbaum served as chief scientist for the U.S. Air Force (1994–1997) and later received the air force's "Exceptional Civilian Service Award." See IEEE Computer Society biography of Feigenbaum, https://www.computer.org/web/awards/pioneer-edward-feigenbaum.

103. Springer, *Military Robots and Drones*.

104. For discussion of the use of drones by Israel, see Anshel Pfeffer, "WikiLeaks: IDF Uses Drones to Assassinate Gaza Militants," *Haaretz*, September 2, 2011; Cora Currier and Henrik Moltke, "Spies in the Sky:

Israeli Drone Feeds Hacked by British and American Intelligence," *Intercept*, 2016. The Israeli Army used drones to fire tear gas at protestors and journalists in Gaza, as documented by various news agencies. Tear gas is sometimes dispensed using the "Cyclone Riot Control Drone System" manufactured by the Israeli company ISPRA.

105. Russia deploys "Robojeep" units, armed robots that patrol its nuclear facilities and are reportedly capable of automatically identifying and shooting a target. See David Hambling, "Armed Russian Robocops to Defend Missile Bases," *NewScientist*, April 23, 2014. South Korea employs an automated kill zone in the DMZ, similar to the one used by Israel in Gaza. Thirty-some nations are thought to have such "autonomous" weapons, depending on the definition. Ronald C. Arkin, *A Robotocist's Perspective on Lethal Autonomous Weapon Systems*, United Nations Office of Disarmament Affairs (UNODA) Occasional Papers, 2018, 35–47.

106. Shoshanna Solomon, "Military Sees Surge in AI Use, but Not Yet for Critical Missions," *Times of Israel*, October 29, 2018.

107. According to a Reuters report, the U.S. government is concerned about "China's interest in fields such as artificial intelligence and machine learning. . . . The worry is that cutting-edge technologies developed in the United States could be used by China to bolster its military capabilities and perhaps even push it ahead in strategic industries." An unpublished Pentagon report described by Reuters suggests that the Committee on Foreign Investment in the United States (CFIUS)—which has the power to limit foreign acquisitions of U.S. companies—is not suitable for blocking Chinese advancement. Republican senator John Cornyn and Democratic senator Dianne Feinstein warned that "as we speak, China is using any means available to turn our own technology and know-how against us and erase our national security advantage. This weaponizing of investment is aimed at vacuuming up U.S. industrial capabilities in cutting-edge technologies such as artificial intelligence (AI) and robotics, which have obvious and important military applications." They proposed legislation that would extend CFIUS powers so as to limit Chinese activities. See Phil Stewart, "U.S. Weighs Restricting Chinese Investment in Artificial Intelligence," *Reuters*, June 13, 2017.

108. Drew Harwell, "Defense Department Pledges Billions Toward Artificial Intelligence Research," *Washington Post*, September 7, 2018.

109. Will Knight, "China Has Never Had a Real Chip Industry. Making AI Chips Could Change That," *MIT Technology Review*, December 14, 2018.

110. Emily Parker, "How Two AI Superpowers—the U.S. and China—Battle for Supremacy in the Field," *Washington Post*, November 2, 2018.

111. David Ignatius, "China's Application of AI Should Be a Sputnik Moment for the U.S. But Will It Be?," *Washington Post*, November 7, 2018.

112. David Ignatius, "The Chinese Threat That an Aircraft Carrier Can't Stop," *Washington Post*, August 7, 2018.

113. Edward W. Said, *Culture and Imperialism* (1993; New York: Vintage Books, 2012), 285.

114. See UK Department for Business, Energy & Industrial Strategy and Department for Digital, Culture, Media & Sport, *AI Sector Deal*, policy paper, April 26, 2018, https://www.gov.uk/government/publications /artificial-intelligence-sector-deal/ai-sector-deal. This UK government report likens AI to the printing press: "At the same time, tools for processing and making sense of large quantities of data have developed exponentially—with artificial intelligence (AI) representing the latest leap. In the same way that Gutenberg's press ushered in a new era of growth, data-driven technologies such as AI will underpin our future prosperity." The report was compiled by academics, government officials, and Facebook's vice president of AI research.

115. Nicholas Thompson, "Emmanuel Macron Talks to WIRED About France's AI Strategy," *Wired*, March 31, 2018.

116. Michael C. Horowitz, "Artificial Intelligence, International Competition, and the Balance of Power," *Texas National Security Review* 1, no. 3 (2018); Gregory C. Allen et al., *Strategic Competition in an Era of Artificial Intelligence*, Artificial Intelligence and International Security (Washington D.C.: Center for New American Security, 2018).

117. Henry A. Kissinger, "How the Enlightenment Ends," *Atlantic*, June 15, 2018.

118. Greg Grandin, *Kissinger's Shadow: The Long Reach of America's Most Controversial Statesman* (New York: Holt, 2015), 226.

2. IN THE SERVICE OF CAPITAL

1. Philip Mirowski, *Machine Dreams: Economics Becomes a Cyborg Science* (Cambridge: Cambridge University Press, 2002), 535.

2. I use "entrepreneur" here to refer to the neoliberal notion of the "self-as-entrepreneur." This is the idea that people should conceive of themselves as builders of portfolios whose worth is continually evaluated by some totalizing "market." In this framework, all individuals should aspire to be entrepreneurs, and all social things should be enterprises. See Michel Foucault, *The Birth of Biopolitics* (1979; New York: Palgrave Macmillan, 2008); Wendy Brown, *Undoing the Demos: Neoliberalism's Stealth Revolution* (New York: Zone Books, 2015).

3. These technical explanations for AI's sudden rise mostly appear as short asides in AI commentaries. *Wired* magazine alludes to "post-paucity computing" being a key driver of AI's supposed feats, using "AI" interchangeably with "neural networks." See David Weinberger, "Our Machines Now Have Knowledge We'll Never Understand," *Wired*, April 18, 2017. Similarly, Fei-Fei Li, a Stanford computer science professor and at the time head of Google Cloud's AI research division, wrote in the *New York Times* that "thanks to the growth of big data, advances in algorithms like neural networks and an abundance of powerful computer hardware, something momentous has occurred: A.I. has gone from an academic niche to the leading differentiator in a wide range of industries, including manufacturing, health care, transportation and retail." Li, "How to Make A.I. Human-Friendly," *New York Times*, March 8, 2018. A very similar "purely technical" narrative was used to explain the popularity of neural networks in the late 1980s, a narrative that Seymour Papert critiqued at the time in "One AI or Many?," in *The Artificial Intelligence Debate: False Starts, Real Foundations*, ed. Stephen Graubard (Cambridge, Mass.: MIT Press, 1988), 241–67. For discussion of the narratives that have been used in the past to explain the rise and fall of neural networks research, see Mikel Olazaran, "A Sociological Study of the Official History of the Perceptrons Controversy," *Social Studies of Science* 26, no. 3 (1996): 611–59.

4. As one example of many, consider the coverage of a scientific journal article that presented a statistical model which the authors claim recognizes emotions better than people: Carlos F. Benitez-Quiroz, Ramprakash Srinivasan, and Aleix M. Martinez, "Facial Color Is an Efficient Mechanism to Visually Transmit Emotion," *Proceedings of the National Academy of Sciences* 115, no. 14 (2018): 3581–86. The article does not reference AI at all, but that is how it was described in the media. See Sophie Kleber, "3 Ways AI Is Getting More Emotional," *Harvard Business Review*, July 31, 2018. The authors present what they call a "machine-learning" algorithm, based on a statistical analysis technique dating back to the early twentieth century, that does not employ neural networks, especially large data, or any recently developed form of parallel computing.

5. For lack of a better term, I will refer to companies such as Google, Microsoft, Facebook, and Amazon as the major platform companies. How to concisely refer to such entities is not obvious. The phrase "tech company" is imprecise and equates "technology" with what is in fact a narrow range of computing practices. I chose "platform" to highlight the role that platform construction and ownership plays in these companies' political power. As Nick Srnicek writes, "Platforms became an efficient way to monopolise,

extract, analyse, and use the increasingly large amounts of data that were being recorded." Nick Srnicek, *Platform Capitalism* (Malden, Mass.: Polity, 2017), 42–43.

6. Glenn Greenwald, *No Place to Hide: Edward Snowden, the NSA, and the US Surveillance State* (New York: Macmillan, 2014).

7. Shoshana Zuboff, "Big Other: Surveillance Capitalism and the Prospects of an Information Civilization," *Journal of Information Technology* 30, no. 1 (2015): 75–89.

8. See the controversy surrounding Cambridge Analytica as reported, for instance, in "Cambridge Analytica Files," *Guardian*, https://www.theguardian.com/news/series/cambridge-analytica-files.

9. Nick Bilton, "Google Buys A.I. Company for Search, Not Robots," *New York Times*, January 28, 2014.

10. David Ignatius, "A Tech Bridge from the Pentagon to Silicon Valley," *Washington Post*, January 25, 2019.

11. See, for example, Nate Silver, *The Signal and the Noise: Why So Many Predictions Fail—but Some Don't* (New York: Penguin, 2012), 264.

12. The Global Artificial Intelligence Conference of 2018 invited participants to "hear from AI pioneers representing: Google, Capital One, Johnson & Johnson, Bloomberg, Facebook, Amazon, McKinsey, SAP, Microsoft, Biogen, Royal Caribbean Cruise Line, Uber, IBM, The Boston Consulting Group, Trulia Teradata, Columbia Sportswear Company etc." It listed five reasons for attending: "Learn how to organize your AI team and toolset so you can increase productivity whilst democratizing the knowledge produced; for those at the start of the AI journey, learn how to construct an effective AI strategy from the ground up; enjoy proactive and organized networking opportunities to build new business relationships and opportunities inspired by others in your field; get to grips with the world's latest and most advanced AI tools and technologies to optimize your testing phase; benchmark your organization's AI initiative amongst your competitors and across different industries."

13. Yarden Katz, "Manufacturing an Artificial Intelligence Revolution," *Social Science Research Network*, November 30, 2017.

14. The media's uncritical embrace of AI was crucial to the recent rebranding. Nonetheless, some mainstream outlets ran articles questioning the enthusiasm about AI. One piece in the *Guardian*, for instance, suggested the discourse on AI is plagued by "magical thinking." See John Naughton, "Magical Thinking About Machine Learning Won't Bring the Reality of AI Any Closer," *Guardian*, August 5, 2018. Such articles, however, merely suggest that AI discourse suffers from too much "hype" and don't challenge

the idea of AI as a coherent and powerful force (instead they ask: Is AI quite as powerful as experts advertise?). Even these articles are a small minority, though, and they appear—in places like the *Guardian*—alongside the kind of AI propaganda discussed throughout this book. See Alex Hern, "Computers Now Better than Humans at Recognising and Sorting Images," *Guardian*, May 13, 2015; Tim Adams, "Artificial Intelligence: 'We're Like Children Playing with a Bomb,'" *Guardian*, June 12, 2016; Ian Sample, "AI Will Create 'Useless Class' of Human, Predicts Bestselling Historian," *Guardian*, May 20, 2016; Ian Sample, "'It's Able to Create Knowledge Itself': Google Unveils AI That Learns on Its Own," *Guardian*, October 18, 2017; Ian Sample, "Artificial Intelligence Risks GM-Style Public Backlash, Experts Warn," *Guardian*, November 1, 2017; Andrew Dickson, "The New Tool in the Art of Spotting Forgeries: Artificial Intelligence," *Guardian*, August 6, 2018; Ian Sample, "Joseph Stiglitz on Artificial Intelligence: 'We're Going Towards a More Divided Society,'" *Guardian*, September 8, 2018; Jess Cartner-Morley, "Do Robots Dream of Prada? How Artificial Intelligence Is Reprogramming Fashion," *Guardian*, September 15, 2018; Stephen Cave, "To Save Us from a Kafkaesque Future, We Must Democratise AI," *Guardian*, January 4, 2019; and Hannah Jane Parkinson, "AI Can Write Just like Me. Brace for the Robot Apocalypse," *Guardian*, February 15, 2019. Moreover, some within the AI expert industry have cynically acknowledged AI's recent rebranding. For example, the AI reporter at *MIT Technology Review*, Karen Hao, circulated one cartoon poking fun at how "AI" was really a rebranding of "machine-learning," which itself was a rebranding of "statistics," and another cartoon that ridicules the arbitrariness in determining whether something is "using AI" (see http://dx.doi.org/10.6084/m9.figshare.1208 4849). Yet such parodies live ephemerally on social media, serving as more bits of "AI content" that amass clicks and views. The ideological nucleus of AI discourse stays intact.

15. As computer scientist and statistician Michael I. Jordan has observed, "Such [re]labeling may come as a surprise to optimization or statistics researchers, who find themselves suddenly called AI researchers." Jordan, "Artificial Intelligence—The Revolution Hasn't Happened Yet," *Harvard Data Science Review*, June 23, 2019. But while Jordan recognizes a rebranding of sorts, he does not question the possibility and coherence of AI nor the political forces capitalizing on its rise. Rather, he argues that the real workhorses behind the recent advances were his own fields of statistics and optimization, which produced "ideas hidden behind the scenes" that "have powered companies such as Google, Netflix, Facebook, and Amazon." As

Jordan writes, "By the turn of the century forward-looking companies such as Amazon were already using ML [machine-learning] throughout their business, solving mission-critical, back-end problems in fraud detection and supply-chain prediction, and building innovative consumer-facing services such as recommendation systems." His main point is that these technical ideas and the disciplines that produced them weren't part of an attempt to "imitate" human intelligence and thus should not be labeled "AI." In a familiar turn, Jordan offers to switch the letters and call it instead "Intelligence Augmentation (IA)."

16. These include conferences such as NIPS (later renamed NeurIPS), which companies such as Google, Microsoft, and IBM have sponsored since as early as 2006. Other conference sponsors include Twitter, Amazon, Apple, and Uber.

17. Sam Shead, "Google I/O: Google Research Becomes Google AI," *Forbes*, May 9, 2018.

18. Alain Supiot, *The Spirit of Philadelphia: Social Justice vs. the Total Market* (New York: Verso, 2012).

19. Philip Mirowski, *Science-Mart: Privatizing American Science* (Cambridge, Mass.: Harvard University Press, 2011), 25.

20. For an analysis of the interest of major platform companies (such as Facebook) in scientific research, see Philip Mirowski, "The Future(s) of Open Science," *Social Studies of Science* 48, no. 2 (2018): 171–203.

21. Kurt Wagner, "Mark Zuckerberg's Philanthropy Organization Is Acquiring a Search and AI Startup Called Meta," *Recode*, January 24, 2017.

22. Antonio Regalado, "Google's AI Explosion in One Chart," *MIT Technology Review*, March 25, 2017.

23. Jeremy Gillula and Daniel Nazer, *Stupid Patent of the Month: Will Patents Slow Artificial Intelligence?*, Electronic Frontier Foundation, September 29, 2017.

24. See U.S. Patents No. 4,670,848 and No. 15,434,558.

25. CBInsights, "Microsoft, Google Lead In AI Patent Activity, While Apple Lags Behind," January 20, 2017, https://www.cbinsights.com/research /google-apple-microsoft-ai-patents/.

26. As the label became popular, the tools produced by the platform companies also started to receive more attention. For example, when Google released its open source library TensorFlow for running neural network models in November 2015, it instantly displaced similar projects in terms of attention and visibility. Some media outlets referred to this as "Google's AI Land Grab." *Wired* magazine gushed that the company had released its "AI engine," which "sits at the heart of its empire." Cade Metz, "Google

Just Open Sourced TensorFlow, Its Artificial Intelligence Engine," *Wired*, November 9, 2015.

27. Jerry Kaplan, *Humans Need Not Apply: A Guide to Wealth and Work in the Age of Artificial Intelligence* (New Haven, Conn.: Yale University Press, 2015), 182.

28. Mark Tegmark, *Life 3.0: Being Human in the Age of Artificial Intelligence* (New York: Knopf, 2017). The book is influential in mainstream discourse on AI. It was a *New York Times* best seller and was reviewed favorably by major newspapers (including in the *Guardian* by historian Yuval Noah Harari, himself a prominent interpreter of AI-driven futures in recent years). Barack Obama named the book as one of his favorite reads of 2018, while Bill Gates and other prominent entrepreneurs have endorsed it as well. See Yuval Noah Harari, "Life 3.0 by Max Tegmark Review—We Are Ignoring the AI Apocalypse," *Guardian*, September 22, 2017; Lanre Bakare, "Barack Obama Reveals His Cultural Highlights of 2018, from Roma to Zadie Smith," *Guardian*, December 28, 2018.

29. Tegmark, *Life 3.0*, 120.

30. Christof Koch, "We'll Need Bigger Brains," *Wall Street Journal*, October 27, 2017, C1.

31. Nick Bostrom, *Superintelligence: Paths, Dangers, Strategies* (Oxford: Oxford University Press, 2016), 66.

32. Norbert Wiener also discussed the view of computers as a form of slave labor in his book *The Human Use of Human Beings* (1950). An *Observer* piece in 1973 endorsed Wiener's contention that "any labor which competes with slave labor must accept the economic conditions of slave labor" and urged readers to turn away from "men" to "the new slave labour instead"—that is, computers.

33. See Tegmark, *Life 3.0*, 118–21. Tegmark's politics become clear not only in his discussion of labor but also in his framing of debates on "autonomous" AI weapons, where he looks to Henry Kissinger for inspiration: "I met Henry Kissinger at a dinner event in 2016, and got the opportunity to ask him about his role in the biological weapons ban. He explained how back when he was the U.S. national security adviser, he'd persuaded President Nixon that a ban would be good for U.S. national security. . . . Since the United States already enjoyed superpower status thanks to its conventional and nuclear forces, it had more to lose than to gain from a worldwide bioweapons arms race with uncertain outcome. In other words, if you're already top dog, then it makes sense to follow the 'maxim' 'If it ain't broke, don't fix it.'" Tegmark repeats here a sanitized view of Kissinger's record.

For a counterview of Kissinger's legacy, see Greg Grandin, *Kissinger's Shadow: The Long Reach of America's Most Controversial Statesman* (New York: Holt, 2015).

34. Nils J. Nilsson, "Artificial Intelligence, Employment, and Income," in *Impacts of Artificial Intelligence*, ed. Robert Trappl (Amsterdam: North Holland, 1986), 103–23. Nilsson builds on the idea of AI as a "mechanical slave" described by the philosopher Margaret Boden, who has an essay in the same collection titled "Impacts of Artificial Intelligence." The two essays have much in common. Boden predicted that in the coming decade AI's "economic impacts will be far-reaching" and "traditional manufacturing and clerical-administrative jobs will be decimated" (69). She adds: "Radical structural changes in society are likely, and the transition phase will not be easy." Ironically, in the same piece Boden called for funds to be devoted to "combatting the ignorance and sensationalism that attends AI today" (75). For a discussion of the proliferation, not reduction, of administrative jobs in capitalist societies and the connection to Keynes's prediction of a diminished work week, see David Graeber, "On the Phenomenon of Bullshit Jobs: A Work Rant," *Strike Magazine* 3 (August 2013).

35. Simon won great acclaim in both AI and economics. Within the latter he is often presented as a "heretical" thinker, despite winning the field's coveted Swedish National Bank's Prize in Economics. See Leonard Silk, "Nobel Winner's Heretical Views," *New York Times*, November 9, 1978. His heresy boils down to this: in contrast to a model of *homo economicus* developed within neoclassical economics—which views people as rational agents pursuing goals with maximal efficiency—Simon conceived of individuals as agents that "satisfice," not maximize, their utility: they find good enough solutions, behaving "rationally" but under constraints. This distinction, important from an economics insider's perspective, is marginal given Simon's major premise—uniting his work in AI and economics—that intelligence is simply the rational pursuit of goals by individual agents. Moreover, Simon's views on broader social issues are hardly out of line with the orthodoxy of the American economics profession. In 1978 the *New York Times* ran an interview with Simon that gave a glimpse into his politics: "Is the system actually in peril and is a revolution dawning? Mr. Simon says that he sees no signs of it. But he adds, before the French Revolution, nobody anticipated it. 'I don't see brittleness in the system,' he says. 'The [labor] unions are no threat. They throw some sand in the machinery, but there has been a decline in blue-collar work and their power is waning. I see no shift in the balance of forces within government.' . . . Mr. Simon

dislikes excessive government intervention in companies and universities and the growing litigiousness of society."

36. Nilsson draws heavily here on the work of another winner of the Swedish National Bank's Prize in Economics, Wassily Leontief. Nilsson subscribes to the idea that technology has always improved human life by generating wealth and concludes that since computing is the most sophisticated of technologies, and AI the apogee of computing, AI would therefore accelerate the technological creation of wealth for everyone. In a radically different analysis, Nicholas Mirzoeff highlighted the ways in which computing systems sustain a vast system of financial debt and thus actually work to limit people's freedoms rather than liberating them from labor. See Nicholas Mirzoeff, "You Are Not A Loan: Debt and New Media," in *New Media, Old Media: A History and Theory Reader,* ed. Wendy H. K. Chun, Anna W. Fisher, and Thomas Keenan (New York: Routledge, 2016), 356–68.

37. Nilsson, "Artificial Intelligence," 119.

38. Nilsson writes: "Even if technology were temporarily slowed in one country, so much the worse for that country; its foreign competitors would soon outrace it and it would have unemployment anyway—unemployment *and* poverty" (114).

39. For example, in 2017 the Berkman Klein Center for Internet & Society at Harvard University and the MIT Media Lab jointly received a $7.6 million grant from a fund created by Reid Hoffman (cofounder of LinkedIn), Pierre Omidyar (cofounder of eBay), William and Flora Hewlett (of Hewlett-Packard Company), and the Knight Foundation to study the "ethics and governance" of AI. Other universities have launched similar initiatives. UC Berkeley, for instance, began a $5.5 million initiative in 2016 to study AI, sponsored through a foundation created by Facebook cofounder Dustin Moskovitz, as well as by the Elon Musk–funded Future of Life foundation. See "Berkeley Launches Center for Human-Compatible Artificial Intelligence," *Philanthropy News Digest,* September 5, 2016. Carnegie Mellon University started its own new AI center, in partnership with Boeing, Uber, IBM, Microsoft, and the Pentagon, among others.

40. On AI and human rights, for instance, see Filippo Raso et al., *Artificial Intelligence & Human Rights: Opportunities & Risks* (Cambridge, Mass: Berkman Klein Center for Internet & Society Research Publication, September 2018). Like most commentary in this space, AI is framed as a coherent and powerful force that can benefit all but also comes with risks. On AI, copyright, and art, see Jessica Fjeld and Mason Kortz, "A Legal Anatomy of AI-Generated Art: Part 1," *Journal of Law and Technology,*

November 21, 2017. Similar reports have been produced about AI and national security, such as a report by Harvard University's Belfer Center that was commissioned by the Pentagon: Gregory C. Allen et al., *Strategic Competition in an Era of Artificial Intelligence*, Artificial Intelligence and International Security (Washington D.C.: Center for New American Security, 2018).

41. Like the Data & Society Center, AI Now Institute was launched with an investment from Microsoft Research. The cofounder of AI Now, K. Crawford, is employed by Microsoft, and up until July 2019 the other cofounder and executive director, M. Whittaker, was employed by Google. Another core team member, S. M. West, was formerly a Google policy fellow, while the cofounder and head of Applied AI at DeepMind, M. Suleyman, serves on AI Now's advisory board. AI Now also receives funding from Google, DeepMind, and Microsoft, though the amounts are undisclosed. The symposium marking the launch of the institute, organized in collaboration with the White House, featured speakers from the corporate world (including Facebook, Intel, and Google's DeepMind), academic social scientists, as well as representatives of the White House and the National Economic Council.

42. As with AI Now, the Berkman Klein Center's "Ethics and Governance of AI" initiative has numerous ties to major platform companies. For instance, the director of the center's AI initiative, T. Hwang, formerly held the "global policy lead" position at Google, and many participants in the Berkman Klein Center are either current or former employees of companies such as Google and Microsoft. MIT, which the Berkman Klein Center has partnered with, is part of numerous corporate partnerships around AI, and former Google CEO Eric Schmidt serves as MIT's advisor on AI matters. Similarly, in 2019 Stanford University announced a center for Human-Centered Artificial Intelligence (HAI) co-led by Fei-Fei Li, a Google advisor. HAI's advisory board includes Eric Schmidt in addition to other Google and Microsoft employees, as well as representatives from venture capital firms and the consulting firm McKinsey. Out of HAI's inaugural group of nineteen "distinguished fellows," five are employed by Google and two by Microsoft.

43. A report by AI Now in 2017 rehearses the usual "technical" explanation for AI's reemergence: "While the concept of artificial intelligence has existed for over sixty years, real-world applications have only accelerated in the last decade due to three concurrent developments: better algorithms, increases in networked computing power and the tech industry's ability to capture and store massive amounts of data." Alex Campolo et al., *AI Now*

2017 Report, AI Now Institute, January 2017, https://www.microsoft.com/en-us/research/publication/ai-now-2017-report/2017. Popular and journalistic accounts of AI tend to enthusiastically endorse think tanks such as AI Now and Data & Society and do not find their enmeshment with corporate and state power problematic; rather, these centers are seen as providing a critical and "balanced view of AI." Meredith Broussard, *Artificial Unintelligence: How Computers Misunderstand the World* (Cambridge, Mass.: MIT Press, 2018), 194–95. Even considerably more critical recent accounts take "AI" without scrutiny, embracing the AI-centric framing advanced by those think tanks.

44. See INCITE!, *The Revolution Will Not Be Funded: Beyond the Non-Profit Industrial Complex* (Durham, N.C.: Duke University Press, 2017), 3. INCITE! describes itself as "a national activist organization of radical feminists of color advancing a movement to end all forms of violence against women, gender non-conforming, and trans people of color through direct action, critical dialogue, and grassroots organizing."

45. New York University, "New Artificial Intelligence Research Institute Launches: First of Its Kind Dedicated to the Study of Social Implications of AI," press release, November 20, 2017, https://engineering.nyu.edu/news/new-artificial-intelligence-research-institute-launches.

46. Patrick Butler, "UN Accuses Blackstone Group of Contributing to Global Housing Crisis," *Guardian*, March 26, 2019.

47. Ryan Grim, "A Top Financier of Trump and McConnell Is a Driving Force Behind Amazon Deforestation," *Intercept*, August 27, 2019.

48. Jon Lee Anderson, "Jair Bolsonaro's Southern Strategy," *New Yorker*, April 1, 2019.

49. See Group of MIT students, faculty, staff and alumni, "Celebrating War Criminals at MIT's 'Ethical' College of Computing," *Tech*, February 14, 2019; Danny McDonald, "MIT Group Calls for University to Cancel Celebration of New College, Apologize for Henry Kissinger Invite," *Boston Globe*, February 18, 2019; Zoe Sheill and Whitney Zhang, "Protesters Gather Against College of Computing Celebration," *Tech*, March 7, 2019. A group at Oxford University has also protested Schwarzman's donation to start the Stephen A. Schwarzman Center for the Humanities at their university, arguing that such a center would be "built with the proceeds of the exploitation and disenfranchisement of vulnerable people across the world." Alayna Lee, Rose Horowitch, and Olivia Tucker, "Schwarzman Donation to Oxford Draws Criticism," *Yale Daily News*, October 1, 2019.

50. A portion of Chomsky's speech is captured in the documentary *MIT: Progressions* (1969). For a partial transcript, see Gabriel Matthew Schivone,

"On Responsibility, War Guilt and Intellectuals," *CounterPunch*, August 3, 2007. For discussion of the 1969 protests at MIT ("Pentagon East"), see Stuart W. Leslie, *The Cold War and American Science: The Military-Industrial-Academic Complex at MIT and Stanford* (New York: Columbia University Press, 1993), chap. 9.

51. la paperson, *A Third University Is Possible* (Minneapolis: University of Minnesota Press, 2017), 32.

52. Remarks by Lee Farris of the Cambridge Residents Alliance (cambridgeresidentsalliance.org) at the "Whose University Is It?" gathering in Cambridge, Massachusetts, February 27, 2019, http://whoseuniversityisit .github.io.

53. See Sarah Leonard and Rebecca Rojer, "Housekeepers Versus Harvard: Feminism for the Age of Trump," *Nation*, March 2017; Sandra Y. L. Korn, "Harvard's Timber Empire," *Harvard Crimson*, April 7, 2014; GRAIN and Rede Social de Justiça e Direitos Humanos, *Harvard's Billion-Dollar Farmland Fiasco*, September 2018.

54. GRAIN and Rede Social de Justiça e Direitos Humanos, 12.

55. GRAIN and Rede Social de Justiça e Direitos Humanos, 6.

56. Kristine E. Guillaume and Jamie D. Halper, "Overseer Resigns Over Harvard's Continued Fossil Fuel Investment," *Harvard Crimson*, May 23, 2018.

57. In 2016 the U.S. Congress created a colonial governing board known as PROMESA to manage Puerto Rico's financial crisis. The board's imposed neoliberal restructuring plan favors payments to the biggest debt holders, which are primarily hedge funds. The major debt holder is Boston-based Baupost Group, run by Seth Klarman, which has about one billion dollars of Puerto Rico's debt. Baupost also manages several universities' endowment funds, which it has invested in the island's debt. PROMESA's plan commits Puerto Rico to forty years of high sales tax in order to pay entities like Baupost, while the board has also ordered the closing of public schools and cutbacks to health care programs and pensions. McKinsey was hired by PROMESA to provide expert advice, even though the firm is invested in the island's debt; see Andrew Rice, "The McKinsey Way to Save an Island," *New York Magazine*, April 17, 2019. For analyses of Puerto Rico's debt, PROMESA, and the connection to U.S. universities, see Kevin Connor and Dennis Abner, "Hedge Funds Win, Puerto Ricans Lose in First Debt Restructuring Deal," *American Prospect*, February 8, 2019; Adriana Colón-Adorno and Alejandro Comas-Short, "Yale Benefits from the Puerto Rican Debt—These Students Are Fighting to End That," *Nation*, March 1, 2019.

3. EPISTEMIC FORGERIES AND GHOSTS IN THE MACHINE

1. Cedric J. Robinson, *Forgeries of Memory and Meaning: Blacks and the Regimes of Race in American Theater and Film Before World War II* (Chapel Hill: University of North Carolina Press, 2007), chap. 1.

2. In his book, Robinson uses the phrase "race science," but here I use "racial science" instead to refer to those sciences that attempt to explicitly define or account for "race" as well as sciences that employ racial imagery, tropes, and concepts more broadly (without necessarily explicitly mentioning "the races").

3. Francis Crick, "Letter to John Edsall on IQ," February 1971.

4. Robinson, *Forgeries of Memory and Meaning*, 62.

5. Toni Morrison, "Unspeakable Things Unspoken: The Afro-American Presence in American Literature," Tanner Lectures on Human Values, 1988.

6. For Licklider's role in sponsoring AI research, see Paul N. Edwards, *The Closed World: Computers and the Politics of Discourse in Cold War America* (Cambridge, Mass.: MIT Press, 1997), chap. 8.

7. Robert W. Taylor, "In Memoriam: JCR Licklider 1915–1990," Digital Systems Research Center, Palo Alto, Calif., 1990.

8. According to one account, Licklider's work on "Man-Computer Symbiosis" was inspired by his involvement with SAGE (Semi-Automatic Ground Environment), the automated weapons system developed at MIT's Lincoln Laboratory: "The SAGE system inspired a few thinkers, including Licklider, to see computing in an entirely new light. SAGE was an early example of what Licklider would later call the 'symbiosis' between humans and machines, where the machine functions as a problem-solving partner. Implied in this symbiotic relationship was the interdependence of humans and computers working in unison as a single system. For instance, in a battle scenario, human operators without computers would be unable to calculate and analyze threats quickly enough to counter an attack. Conversely, computers working alone would be unable to make crucial decisions." Katie Hafner and Matthew Lyon, *Where Wizards Stay up Late: The Origins of the Internet* (New York: Simon and Schuster, 1998), 31.

9. Joseph C. R. Licklider and Robert W. Taylor, "The Computer as a Communication Device," *Science and Technology* 76, no. 2 (1968): 1–3.

10. For discussion of the notion of "freedom" promised by Licklider and other figures in the software world, see Wendy H. K. Chun, *Programmed Visions: Software and Memory* (Cambridge, MA: MIT Press, 2011), chap. 2.

11. In an interview in 1988, Licklider described his efforts to pitch new approaches to "command and control" to the CIA and NSA. See Licklider's oral history interview, Charles Babbage Institute, University of Minnesota, 1988, 35–40. With his training as a psychologist, Licklider also oversaw ARPA's Behavioral Sciences Program, which participated in a counterinsurgency research effort in Thailand in the 1960s. ARPA established a research center in Bangkok that collected anthropometric data about local populations and sought to develop ways to suppress potential counterinsurgencies, not just in Thailand but around the world. See Annie Jacobsen, *The Pentagon's Brain: An Uncensored History of DARPA, America's Top-Secret Military Research Agency* (Boston: Little, Brown, 2015), chap. 9; and Advanced Research Projects Agency, *Activities of the Research and Development Center—Thailand*, Report No. 167324, December 29, 1971.

12. Alison Adam, *Artificial Knowing: Gender and the Thinking Machine* (New York: Routledge, 2006), 37, 93.

13. Allen Newell and Herbert A. Simon, *Human Problem Solving* (Englewood Cliffs, N.J.: Prentice-Hall, 1972), 3–4.

14. I owe this succinct formulation to Joan Richards.

15. Peter Norvig, *Paradigms of Artificial Intelligence Programming: Case Studies in Common LISP* (Burlington, Mass.: Morgan Kaufmann, 1992), 119. Another AI practitioner, Drew McDermott, wrote in 1976: "Remember GPS? By now, 'GPS' is a colorless term denoting a particularly stupid program to solve puzzles. But it originally meant 'General Problem Solver,' which caused everybody a lot of needless excitement and distraction." McDermott, "Artificial Intelligence Meets Natural Stupidity," *ACM SIGART Bulletin* 57 (1976): 4–9.

16. Daniel Crevier, *AI: The Tumultuous History of the Search for Artificial Intelligence* (New York: Basic Books, 1993), 341.

17. A *Foreign Affairs* article from 2016 provides a typical example: "By studying lots of examples, identifying relevant patterns, and applying them to new examples, computers have been able to achieve human and superhuman levels of performance in a range of tasks: recognizing street signs, parsing human speech, identifying credit fraud, modeling how materials will behave under different conditions, and more." Andrew McAfee and Erik Brynjolfsson, "Human Work in the Robotic Future," *Foreign Affairs*, June 13, 2016. See also the "Deep Image" system and its media coverage: Ren Wu et al., "Deep Image: Scaling up Image Recognition," ArXiv Preprint ArXiv:1501.02876, July 8, 2015; Alex Hern, "Computers Now Better than Humans at Recognising and Sorting Images," *Guardian*, May 13, 2015.

On "emotions," see Sophie Kleber, "3 Ways AI Is Getting More Emotional," *Harvard Business Review*, July 31, 2018.

18. Arun Vishwanath, "When a Robot Writes Your News, What Happens to Democracy?," CNN, February 27, 2018.

19. Matt Karolian, "AI Improves Publishing," *NiemanLab*, December 16, 2016.

20. Hannah Jane Parkinson, "AI Can Write Just like Me. Brace for the Robot Apocalypse," *Guardian*, February 15, 2019.

21. Ahmed Alkhateeb, "Can Scientific Discovery Be Automated?," *Atlantic*, April 25, 2017.

22. Mark O'Connell, "Why Silicon Valley Billionaires Are Prepping for the Apocalypse in New Zealand," *Guardian*, February 15, 2018.

23. Matt McFarland, "Elon Musk: 'With Artificial Intelligence We Are Summoning the Demon,'" *Washington Post*, October 24, 2014.

24. Glenn Greenwald, "Glenn Greenwald: As Bezos Protests Invasion of His Privacy, Amazon Builds Global Surveillance State," *Democracy Now!*, February 11, 2019.

25. Max Tegmark, "Let's Aspire to More than Making Ourselves Obsolete," in *Possible Minds: 25 Ways of Looking at AI*, ed. John Brockman (New York: Penguin, 2019), 80.

26. DeepMind has developed two major systems that play Go: AlphaGo and its successor AlphaGo Zero. I will simply refer to "AlphaGo" since my comments apply to both systems.

27. DeepMind, "AlphaGo Zero: Discovering New Knowledge," October 18, 2017, https://www.youtube.com/watch?v=WXHFqTvfFSw.

28. Brenden M. Lake et al., "Building Machines That Learn and Think Like People," *Behavioral and Brain Sciences* 40, no. E253 (2016): 1–101.

29. Lake et al., 8.

30. DeepMind, "AlphaGo Zero."

31. Microsoft COCO is described in Tsung-Yi Lin et al., "Microsoft COCO: Common Objects in Context," in *Proceedings of the European Conference on Computer Vision*, 2014, 740–55. For a similar data set, the "Caltech" objects, see Fei-Fei Li, Rob Fergus, and Pietro Perona, "One-Shot Learning of Object Categories," *IEEE Transactions on Pattern Analysis and Machine Intelligence* 28, no. 4 (2006): 594–611.

32. Brian Wallis, "Black Bodies, White Science: Louis Agassiz's Slave Daguerreotypes," *American Art* 9, no. 2 (1995): 39–61.

33. Anh Nguyen, Jason Yosinski, and Jeff Clune, "Deep Neural Networks Are Easily Fooled: High Confidence Predictions for Unrecognizable Images," in *Proceedings of the IEEE Conference on Computer Vision and Pattern Recognition*, 2015, 427–36.

34. Oriol Vinyals et al., "Show and Tell: A Neural Image Caption Generator," in *Proceedings of the IEEE Conference on Computer Vision and Pattern Recognition*, 2015, 3156–64.

35. The incident occurred during a protest in the village of Nabi Saleh in the West Bank in the summer of 2015. See "A Perfect Picture of the Occupation," editorial, *Haaretz*, August 31, 2015.

36. See Lin et al., "Microsoft COCO." Other image captions were taken from various people's accounts on the image-sharing platform Flickr. See Vicente Ordonez, Girish Kulkarni, and Tamara L. Berg, "Im2text: Describing Images Using 1 Million Captioned Photographs," in *Advances in Neural Information Processing Systems* (Cambridge, Mass.: MIT Press, 2011), 1143–51.

37. Lilly Irani, "Difference and Dependence Among Digital Workers: The Case of Amazon Mechanical Turk," *South Atlantic Quarterly* 114, no. 1 (2015): 225–34.

38. Irani, 228.

39. Vinyals et al., "Show and Tell."

40. Xiaoliang Ling et al., "Model Ensemble for Click Prediction in Bing Search Ads," in *Proceedings of the 26th International Conference on World Wide Web Companion*, 2017, 689–98.

41. Philip Mirowski, *Machine Dreams: Economics Becomes a Cyborg Science* (Cambridge: Cambridge University Press, 2002); Philip Mirowski, *Science-Mart: Privatizing American Science* (Cambridge, Mass.: Harvard University Press, 2011).

42. Hayek writes, "A pre-formation of an order or pattern in a brain or mind is . . . an inferior method of securing an order." Friedrich A. Hayek, *The Fatal Conceit: The Errors of Socialism*, Collected Works of F. A. Hayek (Chicago: University of Chicago Press, 1991), 79.

43. Hayek, 78.

44. David Weinberger, "Our Machines Now Have Knowledge We'll Never Understand," *Wired*, April 18, 2017.

45. Steven Strogatz, "One Giant Step for a Chess-Playing Machine," *New York Times*, December 26, 2018.

46. This behaviorist core was made explicit by *Nature* magazine's coverage of DeepMind's reinforcement-learning system. According to the magazine, a primary challenge for such systems is "avoiding 'superstitious behavior' in which statistical associations may be misinterpreted as causal." Bernhard Schölkopf, "Artificial Intelligence: Learning to See and Act," *Nature* 518, no. 7540 (2015): 486–87. "Superstitious behavior" here is a reference to B. F. Skinner's famous paper from 1948 in which he claimed that pigeons

are fooled into "superstitiously" believing that their past behavior won them food (reinforcement) even when their behavior was not causally linked to reward—though other behaviorist psychologists have disputed Skinner's interpretation. See John E. R. Staddon, "The 'Superstition' Experiment: A Reversible Figure," *Journal of Experimental Psychology: General* 121, no. 3 (1992): 270–72. Also note that reinforcement learning as a field encompasses multiple modeling approaches, including ones where the agents form internal representations that a behaviorist such as Skinner might have rejected as "mentalistic." But the important point of the rebranded AI's narratives is that "intelligence" can be achieved through reinforcement; how the "intelligent" agent is internally structured is less relevant. The prominence of this behaviorist principle contradicts the popular narrative that the so-called cognitive revolution that began in the 1950s vanquished behaviorism. Behaviorist psychologist Staddon has described how the use of computer simulation helped promote cognitive psychology (and cognitive science) over behaviorism: "The digital computer meant that theories—of mental life, perception, syntax or whatever—could be *simulated*, made up into a working *computer model.* . . . Not only did computation offer power, it also offered respectability. . . . The ability to simulate mentalistic theories with quantitative precision conferred a Good Science Seal of Approval on cognitive psychology. No longer need cognitive psychologists feel embarrassed by hardheaded behaviorists. Philosophical objections to the study of subjective experience remained unanswered, but no matter: Computers could remember, perceive, even understand. The possibilities appeared boundless." John R. Staddon, *The New Behaviorism* (London: Taylor & Francis, 2014), 150–51 (italics in original). Nonetheless, cognitive psychology following the "revolution" shares more with behaviorism than many cognitive psychologists or behaviorists like to admit. Thomas H. Leahey has suggested that "The coming of cognitive psychology is best regarded, not as the revolutionary creation of a new paradigm slaying the older one of behaviorism, but as the appearance of a new form of behavioralism based on a new technology, the computer." Leahey, "The Mythical Revolutions of American Psychology," *American Psychologist* 47, no. 2 (1992): 308–18.

47. Like every stream of computing that at some point appeared under the umbrella of "AI," reinforcement learning has been developed in other fields and under different labels. The most popular reinforcement learning textbook was published in the late 1990s; see Richard S. Sutton and Andrew G. Barto, *Reinforcement Learning: An Introduction* (Cambridge, Mass.: MIT Press, 1998). Yet the rebranded AI's narratives present it as an utterly new

development. *MIT Technology Review*, for example, featured "reinforcement learning" in its list of "breakthrough technologies" in 2014.

48. B. F. Skinner, *Reflections on Behaviorism and Society* (Englewood Cliffs, N.J.: Prentice-Hall, 1978).

49. Joseph Weizenbaum has criticized Skinner's position along these lines. He quotes Skinner's claim—"In the behavioristic view, man can now control his own destiny because he knows what must be done and how to do it"—and writes, "That last sentence cannot be read as meaning anything other than, 'I, B. F. Skinner, know what must be done and how to do it.'" Weizenbaum, *Computer Power and Human Reason: From Judgment to Calculation* (New York: Freeman, 1976), 245. Noam Chomsky has also provided an influential critique of Skinner's program and its political ramifications, see Chomsky, "A Review of B. F. Skinner's Verbal Behavior," *Language* 35, no. 1 (1959): 26–58; Chomsky, "Psychology and Ideology," *Cognition* 1, no. 1 (1972): 11–46. Chomsky's technical arguments were echoed in later critiques of neural networks that pointed out the similarities between behaviorism and connectionism. See Jerry A. Fodor and Zenon W. Pylyshyn, "Connectionism and Cognitive Architecture: A Critical Analysis," *Cognition* 28, no. 1–2 (1988): 3–71.

50. Skinner, *Reflections on Behaviorism and Society*, 15.

51. As Shoshana Zuboff has argued, the behaviorist frame aligns closely with the ideology of the major platform companies. These platforms are used to delegate "rewards and punishments of a new kind of invisible hand," making it possible to modify "the behaviors of persons and things for profit and control." Zuboff, "Big Other: Surveillance Capitalism and the Prospects of an Information Civilization," *Journal of Information Technology* 30, no. 1 (2015): 75–89.

52. For examples of the fascination with "explainable AI," see Weinberger, "Our Machines Now Have Knowledge"; Finale Doshi-Velez et al., *Accountability of AI Under the Law: The Role of Explanation* (Cambridge, Mass.: Berkman Klein Center for Internet & Society Research Publication, 2017); David Weinberger, "Don't Make AI Stupid in the Name of Transparency," *Wired*, January 28, 2018. According to a brochure for an O'Reilly conference on AI in New York City in 2017, "explainable AI is a hot new topic in the field, with the goal of having AI not only provide answers and solve problems, but to also provide a model of the reasoning used. Most machine learning systems . . . have been traditionally viewed as a 'black box'—training and input go in one end and answers/solutions come out the other. Researchers weren't really interested in HOW the black boxes got their answers, only that they could. However, now that

AI and machine learning systems are becoming more mainstream, people are (rightly) concerned about whether or not these systems can be trusted to make important decisions."

53. As Weizenbaum notes: "*Most existing programs, and especially the largest and most important ones, are not theory-based.* . . . These gigantic computer systems have usually been put together (one cannot always use the word 'designed') by teams of programmers, whose work is often spread over many years. By the time these systems come into use, most of the original programmers have left or turned their attention to other pursuits. It is precisely when such systems begin to be used that their inner workings can no longer be understood by any single person or by a small team of individuals." Weizenbaum, *Computer Power and Human Reason*, 232 (italics in original).

54. The IBM software engineer and project manager Fred P. Brooks famously described the so-called Mythical Man-Month: the recurring lesson that software projects cannot be saved or sped up by hiring more programmers. Part of the reason, Brooks pointed out, is the medium. A piece of software might have started out as an orderly abstraction in a programmer's mind, but its eventual behavior is revealed as a physically realized system only through interactions with users. The computing medium thus continually constrains and surprises programmers. See Brooks, *The Mythical Man-Month, Anniversary Edition: Essays On Software Engineering, Portable Documents* (London: Pearson Education, 1995).

55. This is Weizenbaum's analogy for large software, building on Marvin Minsky: "A large program is, to use an analogy of which Minsky is also fond, an intricately connected network of courts of law, that is, of subroutines, to which evidence is transmitted by other subroutines. These courts weigh (evaluate) the data given them and then transmit their judgments to still other courts. The verdicts rendered by these courts may, indeed, often do, involve decisions about what court has 'jurisdiction' over the intermediate results then being manipulated. The programmer thus cannot even know the path of decisionmaking within his own program, let alone what intermediate or final results it will produce. Program formulation is thus rather more like the creation of a bureaucracy than like the construction of a machine of the kind Lord Kelvin may have understood." Weizenbaum, *Computer Power and Human Reason*, 234.

56. On how the procedure used to train multilayered neural networks matters, see Stuart Geman, Elie Bienenstock, and René Doursat, "Neural Networks and the Bias/Variance Dilemma," *Neural Computation* 4, no. 1 (1992): 1–58.

57. This is especially problematic when we consider, for instance, that many neural network models are instantiations of established (but currently less flashy) statistical methods, such as various forms of regression. AI commentators aren't concerned with the "indecipherability" of regression, though, even as systems that use familiar forms of regression get rebranded as "AI."
58. Finale Doshi-Velez and Mason Kortz, "A.I. Is More Powerful than Ever. How Do We Hold It Accountable?," *Washington Post*, March 20, 2018.
59. Weinberger, "Don't Make AI Stupid in the Name of Transparency."
60. Ruth Perry and Lisa Greber, "Women and Computers: An Introduction," *Signs: Journal of Women in Culture and Society* 16, no. 1 (1990): 74–101.

4. ADAPTATION, NOT ABOLITION

1. Cheryl I. Harris, "Whiteness as Property," *Harvard Law Review* 106, no. 8 (1993): 1707–91; George Lipsitz, *The Possessive Investment in Whiteness: How White People Profit from Identity Politics* (Philadelphia: Temple University Press, 2009), chaps. 1–2.
2. Robin D. G. Kelley, *Freedom Dreams: The Black Radical Imagination* (Boston: Beacon Press, 2002), 9.
3. Mitch Smith, "In Wisconsin, a Backlash Against Using Data to Foretell Defendants' Futures," *New York Times*, June 22, 2016.
4. Nicholas Diakopoulos, *Algorithmic Accountability Reporting: On the Investigation of Black Boxes*, Tow Center for Digital Journalism, Columbia University, 2014.
5. Alex S. Vitale, *The End of Policing* (New York: Verso Books, 2018), chap. 9.
6. Immigrant Defense Project, Mijente, and National Immigration Project of the National Lawyers Guild, *Who's Behind Ice? The Tech and Data Companies Fueling Deportations*, August 2018.
7. U.S. Department of Homeland Security, "Secure Communities," 2019, https://www.ice.gov/secure-communities.
8. Immigrant Defense Project et al., *Who's Behind Ice?*.
9. Daisuke Wakabayashi and Scott Shane, "Google Will Not Renew Pentagon Contract That Upset Employees," *New York Times*, June 1, 2019; Rachel Lerman, "Microsoft President Brad Smith Defends Company's Work with U.S. Military, Bid for Pentagon Contract," *Seattle Times*, October 26, 2018.
10. Lerman, "Microsoft President Brad Smith."
11. Author interview with Jacinta González, November 13, 2018.
12. Kimberlé W. Crenshaw, "From Private Violence to Mass Incarceration: Thinking Intersectionally about Women, Race, and Social Control," *UCLA Law Review* 59 (2011): 1418–72.

13. Sam Roberts, "U.C.L.A. Center on Police-Community Ties Will Move to John Jay College," *New York Times*, March 21, 2016.

14. Data & Society also partnered with the Police Executive Research Forum (PERF), whose mission is "reducing police use of force; developing community policing and problem-oriented policing; using technologies to deliver police services to the community; and evaluating crime reduction strategies."

15. Vitale, *The End of Policing*.

16. As Robin D. G. Kelley noted, "The colonial relationship that originally structured the police presence remains virtually unchanged. As occupying armies with almost no organic connection to the neighborhoods to which they are assigned, these big-city police forces operate no differently from the imperial forces of yesterday: every colonial subject is suspect. . . . The police work for the state or the city, and their job is to keep an entire criminalized population in check, to contain the chaos of the ghetto within its walls, and to make sure the most unruly subjects stay in line. They operate in a permanent state of war." Kelley, "Slangin' Rocks . . . Palestinian Style: Dispatches from the Occupied Zones of North America," in *Police Brutality: An Anthology*, ed. Jill Nelson (New York: Norton, 2000), 49.

17. Vitale, *The End of Policing*, 34.

18. George Padmore, *The Life and Struggles of Negro Toilers* (Hollywood, Calif.: Sun Dance Press, 1931), 49.

19. In addition to companies such as Microsoft and Google's DeepMind, AI Now's sponsors include the Partnership on AI (PAI), a consortium of companies (such as Amazon, Google, and Facebook) and not-for-profits that seeks "Fair, Transparent, and Accountable AI." Like the other major initiatives we have encountered, PAI is committed to the notion of AI as a coherent and transformative force ("AI offers great potential for promoting the public good, for example in the realms of education, housing, public health, and sustainability"), and to the idea that AI can benefit everyone if it is developed through collaboration between private industry, government, not-for-profits, and academia.

20. Rashida Richardson, Jason Schultz, and Kate Crawford, "Dirty Data, Bad Predictions: How Civil Rights Violations Impact Police Data, Predictive Policing Systems, and Justice," *New York University Law Review Online*, April 2019.

21. Randy Rieland, "Artificial Intelligence Is Now Used to Predict Crime. But Is It Biased?," *Smithsonian*, March 5, 2018.

22. The report states: "Our research demonstrates the risks and consequences associated with overreliance on unaccountable and potentially biased data

to address sensitive issues like public safety." Richardson, Schultz, and Crawford, "Dirty Data, Bad Predictions."

23. Dillon Reisman et al., *Algorithmic Impact Assessments: A Practical Framework for Public Agency Accountability*, AI Now Institute, April 2018.

24. Peter Dizikes, "AI, the Law, and Our Future," *MIT Computer Science and Artificial Intelligence Laboratory News*, January 18, 2019.

25. Robyn Caplan, Alex Rosenblat, and danah boyd, "Open Data, the Criminal Justice System, and the Police Data Initiative," *Data & Civil Rights* (October 2015): 1–13.

26. Angela Y. Davis, *Are Prisons Obsolete?*, Open Media Series (New York: Seven Stories Press, 2003), 16.

27. This turn to abstraction recurs within the history of the prison as an institution. As Davis observed, in the eighteenth century some saw the creation of penitentiaries as a "reform"—an alternative to methods of corporeal and capital punishment—and "sentencing time" became the unit for measuring punishment. The "prison sentence," Davis writes, "which is always computed in terms of time, is related to abstract quantification, evoking the rise of science and what is often referred to as the Age of Reason." This transition, she notes, coincided with the rise of industrial capitalism and the embrace of working time as the unit of labor. An abstraction (unit of time) has thus served the exploitation of labor both inside and outside prison. In the United States, the two have been deeply entwined through the transition from chattel slavery to the convict lease system and the creation of the prison-industrial complex. The time spent serving a sentence is directly related to time laboring and hence to the profits extracted, whether in the convict lease system or the current prison-industrial complex. These continuities and the dependence of capitalism on bondage labor are erased in the critical experts' framing of predictive policing. See Davis, *Are Prisons Obsolete?*, 44–47.

28. Author interview with Hamid Khan, March 27, 2019.

29. Stop LAPD Spying Coalition, "Before the Bullet Hits the Body: Dismantling Predictive Policing in Los Angeles," May 8, 2018.

30. Stop LAPD Spying Coalition, "Before the Bullet Hits the Body."

31. Hamid Khan, "Abolish Risk Assessment," Rustbelt Abolition Radio, February 28, 2019.

32. Stop LAPD Spying Coalition, "Before the Bullet Hits the Body."

33. This line of work treats crime as a natural phenomenon, innate to human societies. This aligns with frequent talk in the media of crime as an "epidemic." Indeed, various academics have applied models from epidemiology to data collected by police departments in order to analyze crime, further

contributing to the view that crime is an organic phenomenon driven by individual decisions (and relations among individuals in a "network"). See, for instance, an article on gun violence in Chicago, coauthored by Yale academics, that appeared in the *Journal of American Medical Association Internal Medicine*: Ben Green, Thibaut Horel, and Andrew V. Papachristos, "Modeling Contagion Through Social Networks to Explain and Predict Gunshot Violence in Chicago, 2006 to 2014," *JAMA Internal Medicine* 177, no. 3 (2017): 326–33. When Yale University's press office covered the article, they described it as showing that "gun violence is a 'contagious' social epidemic" and even led the piece with a photograph of a broken window. See Bess Connolly, "Yale Study Finds That Gun Violence Is a 'Contagious' Social Epidemic," *Yale News*, January 4, 2017.

34. The coalition clearly recognizes that individuals from aggrieved communities can still be part of policing—that there's a difference between individuals and the system they fit into. As the report puts it, "Among our populous, there are people who know police officers personally; they are mothers and fathers, sisters and brothers, neighbors and lovers. Thus, the personal connection the state has created results in a statement such as 'not all cops are bad.' But we're not focusing on individual police; rather, we're looking at the culture of policing and its effects. The state is violent towards Black, Brown, and poor bodies and the police are agents of the state; therefore, police reproduce state violence towards these communities even when they are from these very same communities." Stop LAPD Spying Coalition, "Before the Bullet Hits the Body."

35. As Khan told me during our interview, "The space has been occupied by academics, quite frankly, you being an academic, and the complicity of academia needs to be lifted here."

36. Author interview with Hamid Khan.

37. Khan was referring to the report on predictive policing by AI Now. His remark on the hijacking of "abolition" is reminiscent of how the term "decolonization" has been co-opted for a variety of initiatives and used only metaphorically, with no concern for rematriation of land (or really anything pertaining to land and sovereignty in many cases). See Eve Tuck and K. Wayne Yang, "Decolonization Is Not a Metaphor," *Decolonization: Indigeneity, Education & Society* 1, no. 1 (2012): 1–40.

38. An abolitionist agenda, as Angela Y. Davis describes it, would contest the relationships and ideologies that sustain the prison-industrial complex, and seek "a constellation of alternative strategies and institutions, with the ultimate aim of removing the prison from the social and ideological landscapes of our society," including notions of justice based on "strategies of

reparation, rather than retribution." Davis, *Are Prisons Obsolete?*, 107–14. Indeed, it is not impossible to imagine alternatives to the carceral system, as Robin Kelley does: "I would go so far as to propose the complete dismantling of police departments (and consequently the entire criminal justice system) as we know it. Perhaps we might return to the long-standing radical proposal for community-based policing. Imagine institutions for public safety structured along nonmilitary lines and run by elected community boards! I am not simply proposing that community members be employed to do the work of policing; rather, I am suggesting that the very job itself be reinvented. New institutions of public safety would require radically new modes of training. Employees and volunteers would have to attend intensive workshops on race, gender, sexuality, domestic abuse, rape, violence, and inequality, among other things, and the institutions of public safety would have to reflect the racial and ethnic makeup of the communities they serve and to maintain an equal gender balance in all areas of work. They would be required to reside in the neighborhood in which they work and to conduct a thorough study of that neighborhood in all of its historical, social, economic, and psychological dimensions—a little like writing an honors thesis before graduating from the 'academy of public safety.'" Kelley, "Slangin' Rocks," 51.

39. The conference featured speakers from academia as well as Google, Microsoft, the Microsoft-backed think tank Data & Society, the World Bank, NBC News, and the U.S. Department of Justice. Several Palantir employees were also originally scheduled to speak.

40. See Mijente's petition, "UC Berkeley: Cut your ties to Palantir!," https://action.mijente.net/petitions/uc-berkeley-cut-your-ties-to-palantir; and Marisa Franco, "Palantir Has No Place at Berkeley: They Help Tear Immigrant Families Apart," *Guardian*, May 31, 2019.

41. See Mijente's "#TakeBackTech" website, mijente.net/takebacktech/#156632 1508952-b8a795a4-1667.

42. Rodriguez writes: "The Left's investment in the essential political logic of civil society—specifically, the inherent legitimacy of racist state violence in upholding a white freedom, social 'peace,' and 'law and order' that is fundamentally designed to maintain brutal inequalities in the putative free world—is *symbiotic with (and not oppositional to)* the policing and incarceration of marginalized, racially pathologized communities, as well as the state's *ongoing absorption* of organized dissent through the non-profit structure." Dylan Rodriguez, "The Political Logic of the Non-Profit Industrial Complex," in *The Revolution Will Not Be Funded: Beyond the Non-Profit Industrial Complex*, ed. INCITE! (Durham, N.C.: Duke University Press, 2017), 23 (italics in original).

43. AI Now, for example, has criticized Amazon in an exhibit called *The Anatomy of an AI System*. See James Vincent, "This Beautiful Map Shows Everything That Powers an Amazon Echo, from Data Mines to Lakes of Lithium," *Verge*, September 9, 2018. The critique is narrow and the label "AI" is applied uncritically, as to be expected, but even this level of scrutiny is not applied to AI Now's major benefactors such as Microsoft.

44. Aaron Gregg and Jay Greene, "Pentagon Awards Controversial $10 Billion Cloud Computing Deal to Microsoft, Spurning Amazon," *Washington Post*, October 25, 2019.

45. See Olivia Solon, "Why Did Microsoft Fund an Israeli Firm That Surveils West Bank Palestinians?," *NBC News*, 2019. The Israeli company Microsoft has invested in is AnyVision, whose tagline is "Making AI Accessible to the World." AnyVision has also partnered with Nvidia, among other companies, "to achieve high-speed, real-time face recognition from surveillance video streams."

46. Jean Baudrillard, *Simulacra and Simulation*, trans. Sheila Faria Glaser (Ann Arbor: University of Michigan Press, 1994), 16.

5. ARTIFICIAL WHITENESS

1. Max Tegmark, *Life 3.0: Being Human in the Age of Artificial Intelligence* (New York: Knopf, 2017), 119.

2. Toni Morrison, *Playing in the Dark: Whiteness and the Literary Imagination*, William E. Massey, Sr., Lectures in the History of American Civilization (New York: Vintage Books, 1993), 63.

3. Richard Barbrook and Andy Cameron, "The Californian Ideology," *Science as Culture* 6, no. 1 (1996): 44–72.

4. Tegmark, *Life 3.0*.

5. Jürgen Schmidhuber, "True Artificial Intelligence Will Change Everything," Keynote lecture at European Communication Summit, July 7, 2016.

6. Tegmark, *Life 3.0*, 240, 246.

7. Kyle Wiggers, "Google Will Open an AI Center in Ghana Later This Year, Its First in Africa," *VentureBeat*, June 13, 2018.

8. Victor Asemota, "'Ghana Is the Future of Africa': Why Google Built an AI Lab in Accra," CNN, July 15, 2018.

9. Jemima Pierre notes: "Though the White population in Ghana is mostly transient, and White positionality is hardly rigid, Whiteness has retained its undisputed, if contested, power of position. . . . Whiteness continues to have currency in this nominally Black postcolonial African nation,

revealing a clear discourse of race that is articulated through practices that both reflect global economic, political, and cultural hierarchies, and that reinforce White privilege on the local level." Pierre explains that this requires us to "distinguish between Whiteness—historically as ideology, trope, and cultural practice—and actual racialized White bodies" and recognize that "race (in this case, Whiteness) articulates with racialized-as-White bodies, all the while moving beyond such bodies and expressing itself in other representations of itself—such as culture, aesthetics, wealth, and so on." Pierre, *The Predicament of Blackness: Postcolonial Ghana and the Politics of Race* (Chicago: University of Chicago Press, 2012), 72. The rhetoric surrounding Google's AI laboratory in Accra thus exemplifies the transatlantic grip of whiteness that Pierre brings to light.

10. Ziauddin Sardar, "alt.civilizations.faq: Cyberspace as the Darker Side of the West," in *The Cybercultures Reader*, ed. David Bell and Barbara M. Kennedy (New York: Routledge, 2000).

11. Some researchers working in the field of ALife considered that label, like "AI," to be a "stroke of advertising genius," going so far as to state that without the label there would be no field. And as with AI, other scientists thought, "What an ill-defined subject, Artificial Life. A silly name. We live in an age of soundbites." Stefan Helmreich, *Silicon Second Nature: Culturing Artificial Life in a Digital World* (Berkeley: University of California Press, 2000), 9.

12. Stefan Helmreich has insightfully explored the imagery of colonization (and the biblical creation stories that often come along with it) in the work of artificial life researchers. See Helmreich, 92–96, 113–22.

13. Quoted in David F. Noble, *The Religion of Technology: The Divinity of Man and the Spirit of Invention* (New York: Knopf, 1997), 171. The context was Rucker's call for more to enlist in the study of cellular automata and help realize this "manifest destiny." See Rudy Rucker, "Cellular Automata," in *Seek! Selected Nonfiction* (Philadelphia: Running Press, 1999), 64–84.

14. Helmreich notes that "genetic difference, coded here [in a computing system called PolyWorld that uses genetic algorithms], is to be handled carefully, with populations kept pure of contamination from others. In the universes of Artificial Life, sexual recombination, which produces new combinations of traits, must be kept within boundaries, lest lineages lose their vigor. The shadow of eugenics haunts selection stories in genetic algorithms." Helmreich, *Silicon Second Nature*, 155–56. Helmreich also points out that metaphors of heterosexual reproduction are repeatedly used to describe the "mating" of artificial organisms. This is despite the fact that artificial organisms are generally represented as "bags" of genes (in the

form of bit strings) and sexual differences in reproduction are not modeled (146–54).

15. See chapter 1.
16. See chapter 3.
17. Nell Irvin Painter, *The History of White People* (New York: Norton, 2010), 37.
18. For an analysis of Blumenbach's account of race, see Painter, chap. 6. Contradictions also plagued the work of later race theorists. For example, at the end of the nineteenth century William Z. Ripley, an American economics professor, had set out to scientifically map European races (of which he concluded there were three) in order to classify immigrants arriving to the United States and, as Painter noted, appeared to "have been blinded by the magnitude of his task, aiming as he did to reconcile a welter of conflicting racial classifications that could not be reconciled" (214). For the organization of races referenced by Du Bois, see W. E. B. Du Bois, *The Conservation of Races* (American Negro Academy Washington, D.C., 1897).
19. Cedric J. Robinson described, for instance, the anthropometric studies produced by the U.S. Sanitary Commission (USSC), a body authorized by Abraham Lincoln in 1861 and tasked with "studying the physical and moral condition of Federal troops." The USSC found many anthropometric "differences" between black and white soldiers: "The Sanitary Commission found that the Black male body was more anthropoid, that is, apelike, than the white body. This was already the generally accepted opinion among these scientists and their colleagues. . . . Comparisons of head size, weight, and height permitted the commission to conclude that not only were Blacks inferior to whites but that mulattos were inferior to their 'originals.' Clearly, race-mixing was a dead-end." Robinson, *Forgeries of Memory and Meaning: Blacks and the Regimes of Race in American Theater and Film Before World War II* (Chapel Hill: University of North Carolina Press, 2007), 67–68.
20. When I refer to societies or institutions structured by "white supremacy," I follow Cheryl I. Harris's definition, which names "a political, economic, and cultural system in which whites overwhelmingly control power and material resources, conscious and unconscious ideas of white superiority and entitlement are widespread, and relations of white dominance and non-white subordination are daily reenacted across a broad array of institutions and social settings." Harris, "Whiteness as Property," *Harvard Law Review* 106, no. 8 (1993): 1714–91.
21. Matthew Frye Jacobson, *Whiteness of a Different Color* (Cambridge, Mass.: Harvard University Press, 1999), 38.

22. Khaled A. Beydoun, "Boxed in: Reclassification of Arab Americans on the US Census as Progress or Peril," *Loyola University Chicago Law Journal* 47 (2015): 693–759.
23. See Thomas F. Gossett, *Race: The History of an Idea in America*, Race and American Culture (Oxford: Oxford University Press, 1997), 30; Robinson, *Forgeries of Memory and Meaning*, 31–37; Theodore W. Allen, *The Invention of the White Race*, Vol. 2: *The Origin of Racial Oppression in Anglo-America* (New York: Verso Books, 2012), chap. 10.
24. As Theodore W. Allen has noted, an important distinction between "African American" and "European American" bond laborers was drawn in 1640, when the Virginia General Court sentenced John Punch (an African) to a lifetime of bond-servitude but gave a lesser sentence to the two bond laborers (one Dutch and the other a Scot) who fled with him. Allen concludes, "Whether the decision in this instance was a 'thinking' or an 'unthinking' one, the court by citing John Punch's 'being a negro' in justification of his life sentence was resorting to mere bench law, devoid of reference to English or Virginia precedent." Allen, *Invention of the White Race*, 179.
25. In 1691 fines and potential jail sentences were imposed on "white" women who give birth to a "mulatto" child. Similarly, Virginia's "Act Concerning Servants and Slaves" (1705) increased the indenture of a "mulatto" child born to a white woman and punished with a jail sentence and a fine any white person who married a black partner.
26. The U.S. government used the notion of blood quantum inconsistently to try to dispossess Native Americans and promote acceptance of capitalist notions of property. As Melissa L. Meyer has argued, crafters of U.S. Indian policy "believed that, despite their irredeemable hybrid stock, those of mixed descent would serve as a 'civilizing' force and pave the way for the success of assimilation programs. . . . The reasoning was carried to absurd extremes until even land policies rested on a foundation of 'blood.' People of mixed descent, in general, had greater opportunity to acquire plots of land than native people. 'Half-breeds' or 'mixed bloods' were supposed to sever their tribal ties when they accepted land scrip, but they often did not. Their tendency toward biculturalism also meant that they were more likely to accept the commodification of land, to understand the workings of the market, and to be among the first to claim further allotments of land and distributions of tribal funds." Meyer, "American Indian Blood Quantum Requirements: Blood Is Thicker than Family," in *Over the Edge: Remapping the American West*, ed. Valerie J. Matsumoto and Blake Allmendinger (Berkeley: University of California Press, 1999), 222. And in the

nineteenth century, as Terry P. Wilson notes, blood quantum requirements were applied inconsistently (or left "indefinite") in order to serve the government's interests: "When the acculturation-minded government was pressing for individual parceling of tribally held land, the signatures of mixed bloods were sought to satisfy the three-fourths approval of tribal adult males prerequisite to such distribution. On these occasions the government pushed for mixed bloods to be considered full members of the tribe. . . . Contrarily, when strong antiacculturationist or antigovernment stances by tribes have been partially instigated by mixed bloods or when the government has wanted to cut expenditures for Native Americans, U.S. policymakers have tried to categorize as non-Indian those with lesser blood quantum. At such times the Indian Office generally has urged the disassociation from the tribe of those possessing less than a one-half blood quantum." Wilson, "Blood Quantum: Native American Mixed Bloods," in *Racially Mixed People in America*, ed. Maria P. P. Root (Newbury Park, Calif: Sage, 1992), 120–21. By the early twentieth century, Wilson notes, simple blood quantum was sometimes replaced by anthropometric measurements (of hair, skin and feet), devised by anthropologists employed by the federal government, to assess "full blood" Indian identity. For the significance of blood quantum, see also Jack D. Forbes, "Blood Quantum: A Relic of Racism and Termination," *People's Voice*, November 2000, 1–2.

27. This pattern in which the articulation of whiteness is shaped by both economic interests and struggles against oppression is documented in studies of racial capitalism, settler-colonialism, and the social construction of race. For examples, see Ruth Frankenberg, *White Women, Race Matters: The Social Construction of Whiteness*, Gender, Racism, Ethnicity (Minneapolis: University of Minnesota Press, 1993), 72–77; Robinson, *Forgeries of Memory and Meaning*, 31–37; Jacobson, *Whiteness of a Different Color*; George Lipsitz, *The Possessive Investment in Whiteness: How White People Profit from Identity Politics* (Philadelphia: Temple University Press, 2009), chap. 1; Ignatiev, Noel, *How the Irish Became White* (United Kingdom: Routledge, 2009); Gerald Horne, *The Counter-Revolution of 1776: Slave Resistance and the Origins of the United States of America* (New York: NYU Press, 2016), chap. 4; Gerald Horne, *The Apocalypse of Settler Colonialism: The Roots of Slavery, White Supremacy, and Capitalism in 17th Century North America and the Caribbean* (New York: Monthly Review Press, 2018), chap. 7; and Charles W. Mills, *Blackness Visible: Essays on Philosophy and Race* (Ithaca, N.Y.: Cornell University Press, 2015), chaps. 3–4. Horne, for instance, describes the efforts to create "cross-class, Pan-European" whiteness in the seventeenth and eighteenth centuries in order to maintain

slavery and colonial rule. A primary aim was to build a "white" coalition large enough to suppress African and indigenous uprisings in the European colonies, sometimes by granting limited (and temporary) privileges to groups discriminated against on European soil, such as Jews or Irish people. This led to the typical contradictions of racial categories, as Horne notes: "It was as if the elite did not interrogate 'whiteness,' then no one else would either, and the inherent frailty of this unstable category would somehow magically disappear." Horne, *Counter-Revolution of 1776*, 152. Theodore Allen has described the transition in colonial America from a racial system based on different European "races" or "stocks" to one based on whiteness. See Allen, *Invention of the White Race*, chaps. 7–10.

28. Mills, *Blackness Visible*, 77.

29. See Harris, "Whiteness as Property." Harris's notes bear many gifts.

30. Embedded in all these is the right, on which whiteness is based, to exclude others. Harris traces the origin of this right to the way the English colonists treated the indigenous peoples in America, and the manner in which the incipient legal regime privileged European notions of property acquisition (by conquest) over indigenous conceptions of land and shared living.

31. As Harris notes, "property" is defined broadly within Anglo-American law, extending far beyond physical assets to could include professional degrees and more abstract entities such as individual reputations and expectations. This broad understanding of property is crucial to protecting white supremacy. See Harris, 1724–35.

32. In one Supreme Court case cited by Harris (1769), the court reasoned that standardized test scores and grade point averages constitute "merit," ignoring the ways in which such scores are intertwined with race and class (as well as the history by which such tests came to be part of admissions criteria).

33. See Morrison, *Playing in the Dark*, 59. This does not mean that the notion of "race" has no significance or meaning; quite the opposite. Morrison has commented on the ironic turn in the academic discourse on "race," which can mask the very realness of this constructed concept: "For three hundred years black Americans insisted that 'race' was no usefully distinguishing factor in human relationships. During those same three centuries every academic discipline, including theology, history, and natural science, insisted 'race' was *the* determining factor in human development. When blacks discovered they had shaped or become a culturally formed race, and that it had specific and revered difference, suddenly they were told there is no such thing as 'race,' biological or cultural, that matters and that genuinely intellectual exchange cannot accommodate it." Toni Morrison,

"Unspeakable Things Unspoken: The Afro-American Presence in American Literature," Tanner Lectures on Human Values, 1988. Pointing to the ways by which concepts like "race" were constructed doesn't make the consequences any less real.

34. G. Flood, "Don't Call It AI, Call It the Intelligent System," *Software Futures STFT* 4, no. 11 (1995).

35. Boots Riley, *Sorry to Bother You*, Script, 2017, 15.

36. Robin D. G. Kelley, "Sorry, Not Sorry," *Boston Review*, September 13, 2018.

37. Stefano A. Cerri, "The Intersection of AI and Education: Investing in Thought-Intensive Endeavors," in *Impacts of Artificial Intelligence*, ed. Robert Trappl (Amsterdam: North Holland, 1986), 86.

38. New York University, "New Artificial Intelligence Research Institute Launches: First of Its Kind Dedicated to the Study of Social Implications of AI," press release, November 20, 2017.

39. Tegmark, *Life 3.0*, 119.

40. Tegmark, 105.

41. Filippo Raso et al., *Artificial Intelligence & Human Rights: Opportunities & Risks*, Cambridge, Mass: Berkman Klein Center for Internet & Society Research Publication, September 2018.

42. Raso et al.

43. U.K. Department for Business, Energy & Industrial Strategy and Department for Digital, Culture, Media & Sport, *AI Sector Deal*, policy paper, April 26, 2018, https://www.gov.uk/government/publications/artificial-intelligence-sector-deal/ai-sector-deal.

44. Tegmark, *Life 3.0*, 121.

45. Daniel Crevier, *AI: The Tumultuous History of the Search for Artificial Intelligence* (New York: Basic Books, 1993), 340.

46. Lipsitz, *The Possessive Investment in Whiteness*.

47. Robin DiAngelo, "White Fragility," *International Journal of Critical Pedagogy* 3, no. 3 (2011): 54–70.

48. On how prominent practitioners and AI's triumphalist historians reacted to Dreyfus, see Pamela McCorduck, *Machines Who Think: A Personal Inquiry Into the History and Prospects of Artificial Intelligence* (New York: Freeman, 1979), 196–203. Major figures within AI presented critics of their endeavor as irrational and personally hostile. Edward A. Feigenbaum and McCorduck wrote of AI's critics: " 'Charlatans' has been a favorite epithet, as if AI people knew what they were up to couldn't possibly work, but they were willfully defrauding their supporting agencies of money and the public of its peace of mind." Feigenbaum and McCorduck, *The Fifth Generation: Artificial Intelligence and Japan's Computer Challenge to the World* (Boston: Addison-Wesley, 1983), 32.

49. Black in AI, https://blackinai.github.io/.

50. Sandra Harding, *Whose Science? Whose Knowledge? Thinking from Women's Lives* (Ithaca, N.Y.: Cornell University Press, 1991), 41.

51. Rediet Abebe, "Why AI Needs Diversity," *Forbes*, November 29, 2018.

52. The issue also contained a report written "in partnership with Intel" titled "How Are Companies Leveraging AI Today?"

53. For background on MIT Media Lab's politics, culture, and funding, see Lawrence Hunter, "Gadgets For Utopia," *New York Times*, 1987; Will Boisvert, "Future Schlock: Creating the Crap of Tomorrow at the MIT Media Lab," *Baffler* 19 (March 2012); Jonathan Cohn, "Female Labor and Digital Media: Pattie Maes, Postfeminism, and the Birth of Social Networking Technologies," *Camera Obscura: Feminism, Culture, and Media Studies* 28, no. 2 (83) (2013): 151–75; Grif Peterson and Yarden Katz, "Elite Universities Are Selling Themselves—and Look Who's Buying," *Guardian*, March 30, 2018; Nell Gluckman, "Hype vs. Reality at the MIT Media Lab," *Chronicle of Higher Education*, September 11, 2019; and Yarden Katz and Grif Peterson, "Liberal Outrage and White Supremacy: The Case of Epstein," *Tech*, October 3, 2019.

54. See Tamara Best, "How Breaking the Rules Could Win You $250,000," *New York Times*, March 9, 2017; MIT Media Lab, "Defiance: Disobedience for the Good of All," *MIT News*, July 25, 2017.

55. Ford Foundation, *Fighting the "Coded Gaze": How We Make Technology Benefit All*, November 13, 2018.

56. As Donna Haraway notes, the famous transcription of Truth's speech was written in "the white abolitionist's imagined idiolect of The Slave, the supposedly archetypical black plantation slave of the South." Yet Sojourner Truth "was not southern. She was born in New York and owned by a Dutchman. As a young girl, she was sold with some sheep to a Yankee farmer who beat her for not understanding English. Sojourner Truth as an adult almost certainly spoke an Afro-Dutch English peculiar to a region that was once New Amsterdam." Haraway, "Ecce Homo, Ain't (Ar'n't) I A Woman, and Inappropriated Others: The Human in a Post-Humanist Landscape," in *The Haraway Reader* (New York: Routledge, 2004), 58–59. For readings of Sojourner Truth that try to imagine her voice and Afro-Dutch accent, see the Sojourner Truth Project, http://thesojournertruthproject.com.

57. Joy Buolamwini, "AI, Ain't I A Woman?," 2018, https://www.youtube.com/watch?v=QxuyfWoVV98.

58. Joy Buolamwini and Timnit Gebru, "Gender Shades: Intersectional Accuracy Disparities in Commercial Gender Classification," in *Proceedings of Machine Learning Research, Conference on Fairness, Accountability and Transparency* 81 (2018): 1–15.

59. The poem also attributes great powers to AI. The very title "AI, Ain't I A Woman?" suggests that AI can be talked to, and pleaded with, as if it had agency.

60. See, for instance, Anne Fausto-Sterling's analyses of sex and gender, which are informed by developmental and dynamic systems theory: Fausto-Sterling, *Sexing the Body: Gender Politics and the Construction of Sexuality* (New York: Basic Books, 2000); Anne Fausto-Sterling, "Gender/Sex, Sexual Orientation, and Identity Are in the Body: How Did They Get There?," *Journal of Sex Research* 56, no. 4–5 (2019): 529–55. Fausto-Sterling argues for "the study of gender/sex development as a continuously evolving (both intra- and intergenerationally) set of habits resulting from ongoing interactions between the child and other humans and objects in their world. Gender/sex (from infancy to adulthood) would be understood to sediment gradually in the body, seeming to arise 'naturally,' but in fact being a biosocial sediment built up over a lifetime" (534).

61. Buolamwini writes of the diversity problem in the corporate world, pointing out that "less than 2% of employees in technical roles at Facebook and Google are black." She writes: "It's becoming clear just how important it is to have broader representation in the design, development, deployment, and governance of AI. The underrepresentation of women and people of color in technology, and the under-sampling of these groups in the data that shapes AI, has led to the creation of technology that is optimized for a small portion of the world." Buolamwini concludes: "There is still time to shift towards building ethical and inclusive AI systems that respect our human dignity and rights. By working to reduce the exclusion overhead and enabling marginalized communities to engage in the development and governance of AI, we can work toward creating systems that embrace full spectrum inclusion." Joy Buolamwini, "Artificial Intelligence Has a Problem with Gender and Racial Bias. Here's How to Solve It," *Time*, February 2019.

62. This is another example of how facial recognition systems are being used, as Lisa Nakamura observed, to "operationalize and instrumentalize race." Lisa Nakamura, *Digitizing Race: Visual Cultures of the Internet* (Minneapolis: University of Minnesota Press, 2008), 209. What stands out to me in the case of Gender Shades and related projects is the "radical" agenda that this instrumentalization of race supposedly serves.

63. Angela Y. Davis, *Are Prisons Obsolete?*, Open Media Series (New York: Seven Stories Press, 2003), 77.

64. Apart from their alliances with academia, various platform companies have appropriated imagery from social justice movements. Fred Turner describes how, when used by Facebook, "images of Dolores Huerta and Black Lives

Matter marchers have been hollowed of the hard work of movement organizing. On Facebook's walls they suggest that the company is so powerful
that it can render political dissent into just another mode of self-expression.
They make it harder to see the ways in which Facebook's power continues to
depend on the same kinds of contracts and secrecy that characterized the
corporate giants of the industrial era. At the same time, they remind us
that Facebook's success depends on a steady campaign to characterize the
needs of the firm and the needs of the public as one in the same." Turner,
"The Arts at Facebook: An Aesthetic Infrastructure for Surveillance
Capitalism," *Poetics* 67 (2018): 53–62.

65. See Jack Nicas, "Atlanta Asks Google Whether It Targeted Black Homeless People," *New York Times*, October 4, 2019. Apple has made similar
statements after being questioned on whether the facial recognition system on its mobile devices is going to be "racist." Al Franken, then a U.S.
senator, asked: "What steps did Apple take to ensure its system was trained
on a diverse set of faces, in terms of race, gender, and age? How is Apple
protecting against racial, gender, or age bias in Face ID?" Apple responded
that it used "a representative group of people accounting for gender, age,
ethnicity, and other factors. We augmented the studies as needed to provide
a high degree of accuracy for a diverse range of users." Kate Conger, "How
Apple Says It Prevented Face ID from Being Racist," *Gizmodo*, October 16, 2017. Recent discussions of these issues are typically framed around
Buolamwini's claim that "AI-based" facial recognition used by these
companies is racially biased.

66. Amitai Ziv, "This Israeli Face-Recognition Startup Is Secretly Tracking
Palestinians," *Haaretz*, July 15, 2019.

67. Nabil Hassein, "Against Black Inclusion in Facial Recognition," *Digital
Talking Drum*, August 15, 2017. Regarding Buolamwini's call for "inclusion," Ruha Benjamin similarly notes: "While inclusion and accuracy are
worthy goals in the abstract, given the encoding of long-standing racism
in discriminatory design, what does it mean to be included and hence more
accurately identifiable, in an unjust set of social relations? . . . Inclusion in
this context is more akin to possession, as in Fanon's plea that the 'tool
never possess the man,' where possession alerts us to the way freedom is
constrained." Benjamin, *Race After Technology: Abolitionist Tools for the New
Jim Code* (New York: Wiley, 2019), 124.

68. Frantz Fanon, *Black Skin, White Masks*, Get Political (New York: Grove
Press, 2008), 96.

69. While I don't claim that AI is unique in all these ways, I think its historical
trajectory does offer something that, even if not singular, is at least peculiar.
I am hard pressed to find many other concepts that are intimately linked to

286 &D 5. ARTIFICIAL WHITENESS

the production of models of self, that shuttle in and out of mainstream discourse—with great gusto and an unrelenting stream of propaganda—over the span of decades, and that can flexibly nestle at the top of the agendas of both Pentagon officials and those who consider themselves social justice activists following in the footsteps of Frantz Fanon and Ida B. Wells.

70. I share Tara McPherson's perspective that the political history of the United States—concerning matters of race, gender, and civil rights—should be considered together with the development of computing, rather than seen as a "parallel" and disconnected story, and that abstract constructions from the computing world (in McPherson's case, the design principles of the Unix operating system) can reinforce white privilege. In particular, McPherson has argued that the modular mindset promoted by computing practitioners and the broad treatment of computing as an autonomous technological domain reinforce the idea that the politics of race and gender are specialized concerns that have no bearing on "technical" spheres like the world of computing—a notion that, if accepted, would help protect structures of white supremacy. See McPherson, "US Operating Systems at Mid-Century: The Intertwining of Race and UNIX," in *Race After the Internet*, ed. Lisa Nakamura and Peter A. Chow-White (New York: Routledge, 2013), 27–43.

6. DISSENTING VISIONS

1. Sigrid Schmalzer, Alyssa Botelho, and Daniel S. Chard, *Science for the People: Documents from America's Movement of Radical Scientists* (Amherst: University of Massachusetts Press, 2018).

2. For instance, Britt Rusert has described some of the ways in which African Americans in antebellum America engaged, critiqued, and subverted their day's scientific enterprise and questioned the authority of the laboratory. See Rusert, *Fugitive Science: Empiricism and Freedom in Early African American Culture* (New York: NYU Press, 2017).

3. la paperson, *A Third University Is Possible* (Minneapolis: University of Minnesota Press, 2017), 24.

4. For historical background on situated perspectives in AI and cognitive science and their overlap with systems theory and cybernetics, see William J. Clancey, "Scientific Antecedents of Situated Cognition," in *The Cambridge Handbook of Situated Cognition*, ed. Philip Robbins and Murat Aydede, Cambridge Handbooks in Psychology (Cambridge: Cambridge University Press, 2009), 11–34.

5. Alison Adam, *Artificial Knowing: Gender and the Thinking Machine* (New York: Routledge, 2006), 157.

6. For a critical discussion of the problematic distinction between "analytic" and "Continental" philosophy, see Adi Ophir, "How to Take Aim at the Heart of the Present and Remain Analytic," *International Journal of Philosophical Studies* 9, no. 3 (2001): 401–15.

7. I say unfairly because, contrary to many caricatures of his work, Descartes was actually very much concerned with the body, even if, as Silvia Federici has pointed out, his treatment of the body was ultimately in the service of denigrating it—and making it wholly subservient to reason. For a discussion of how this aspect of Descartes's philosophy fits within the historical development of capitalist production, see Federici, *Caliban and the Witch.* (New York: Autonomedia, 2004), 138–55.

8. Merleau-Ponty also thought that science in general was too susceptible to trends: "Today more than ever, science is sensitive to intellectual fashions. When a model has succeeded in one order of problems, it is tried out everywhere else. Currently, our embryology and biology are full of *gradients.* Just how these differ from what the classical tradition called 'order' or 'totality' is not at all clear. This question, however, is not and must not be asked. The gradient is a net we throw out to sea, without knowing what it will haul in. Or yet, it is the slender branch upon which unforeseeable crystallizations will form." Maurice Merleau-Ponty, "Eye and Mind," in *The Merleau-Ponty Reader,* ed. T. Toadvine and L. Lawlor, Northwestern University Studies (Evanston, Ill.: Northwestern University Press, 2007), 351–52. For Merleau-Ponty, this fashion of developmental biology showed how scientific fields are more interested in their own internal, artificial models than in the lived human experience.

9. There are important differences between Heidegger's and Merleau-Ponty's approaches. For a concise discussion in the context of AI and situated cognition, see Lewis A. Loren and Eric S. Dietrich, "Phenomenology and Situated Action," in *Papers from the 1996 Fall Symposium on Embodied Cognition and Action,* Technical Report FS-96-02 (Menlo Park, Calif: AAAI, 1996), 78–81.

10. Hubert L. Dreyfus, *What Computers Still Can't Do: A Critique of Artificial Reason* (Cambridge, Mass.: MIT Press, 1992), 37.

11. An article by Dreyfus that appeared several decades later also reads like an in-principle case against AI. See Hubert L. Dreyfus, "Why Heideggerian AI Failed and How Fixing It Would Require Making It More Heideggerian," *Philosophical Psychology* 20, no. 2 (2007): 247–68.

12. Dreyfus's abstract critique invites an obvious rejoinder from AI practitioners, who can simply say that not yet having a satisfactory logical description of all the relevant contexts of "being" doesn't mean that such a description is unattainable (and that Dreyfus has not given mathematical proof that the task is impossible). After Dreyfus's initial work, though, more AI practitioners have offered (far narrower) critiques of the logic-based approach within AI. For instance, Drew McDermott, riffing on Immanuel Kant, sketched his own "Critique of Pure Reason" in which he criticizes the "logicist" program of formalizing knowledge purely using first-order logic. See McDermott, "A Critique of Pure Reason," in *The Philosophy of Artificial Intelligence*, ed. Margaret A. Boden, Oxford Readings in Philosophy (Oxford: Oxford University Press, 1990), 206–30.

13. Dreyfus notes: "Artificial Intelligence workers who feel that some concrete results are better than none, and that we should not abandon work on artificial intelligence until the day we are in a position to construct such artificial men, cannot be refuted. The long reign of alchemy has shown that any research which has had an early success can always be justified and continued by those who prefer adventure to patience." Dreyfus, *What Computers Still Can't Do*, 304.

14. Hubert L. Dreyfus, *Alchemy and Artificial Intelligence*, Report No. P-3244 (Santa Monica, Calif.: RAND Corporation, 1965).

15. Stuart E. Dreyfus and Hubert L. Dreyfus, *The Scope, Limits, and Training Implications of Three Models of Aircraft Pilot Emergency Response Behavior*, Report No. ORC-79-2 (Berkeley: Operations Research Center, University of California, February 1979), 32.

16. For acrimonious exchanges between prominent AI practitioners and Dreyfus, especially after Dreyfus was beaten in chess by a computer program, see Pamela McCorduck, *Machines Who Think: A Personal Inquiry Into the History and Prospects of Artificial Intelligence*, University of Pittsburgh Publication (New York: Freeman, 1979), chap. 9.

17. That was Edward Feigenbaum's assessment; see McCorduck, 197.

18. As Jean-Pierre Dupuy points out, cyberneticians did not necessarily equate "thinking" with disembodied manipulation of symbols on a digital computer, as many cognitive scientists have. This is because, first, those kinds of computers did not exist at the time early cyberneticians were writing, and second, cybernetics operated with a different notion of "machine" that is not identical to a digital computer. See Dupuy, *On the Origins of Cognitive Science: The Mechanization of the Mind*, trans. M. B. DeBevoise (Cambridge, Mass.: MIT Press, 2009), 5.

19. In my interview with him on June 1, 2018, Winograd said that he and coauthor Fernando Flores, unlike many other AI practitioners, took Hubert Dreyfus's critique of AI seriously.

20. Interview with Terry Winograd.

21. Eden Medina, *Cybernetic Revolutionaries: Technology and Politics in Allende's Chile* (Cambridge, Mass.: MIT Press, 2011).

22. Winograd and Flores write, "Our intention is to provide an opportunity for the reader to develop a new orientation." Their "larger goal is to clarify the background of understanding in which the discourse about computers and technology takes place, and to grasp its broader implications. . . . In this quest, progress is not made by finding the 'right answers,' but by asking meaningful questions—ones that evoke an openness to new ways of being. We invite the readers to create with us an openness that can alter our collective vision of how computer technology will develop in the coming decades." Terry Winograd and Fernando Flores, *Understanding Computers and Cognition: A New Foundation for Design* (Norwood, N.J.: Ablex, 1986), 8, 13.

23. Interview with Terry Winograd.

24. Humberto R. Maturana, *Biology of Cognition*, Biological Computer Laboratory, Department of Electrical Engineering (Urbana: University of Illinois, 1970). For Maturana's telling of the history of this maxim, see Humberto Maturana, "Autopoiesis, Structural Coupling and Cognition: A History of These and Other Notions in the Biology of Cognition," *Cybernetics & Human Knowing* 9, no. 3–4 (2002): 5–34.

25. Maturana and Varela distinguish between "medium" and "environment," and technically what I mean here is "medium," but this distinction does not bear on our discussion.

26. As Maturana put it: "We need, therefore, no longer speak of the flow of information but instead, when observing an organism in its environment, ask ourselves how the strange structural coupling between the activities of the nervous system, the body of the organism, and the external circumstances functions in detail." Humberto R. Maturana, *From Being to Doing: The Origins of the Biology of Cognition*, ed. Bernhard Poerksen (London: Karnac Books, 2004), 65.

27. Humberto R. Maturana and Francisco J. Varela, *The Tree of Knowledge*, rev. ed. (Boulder, Colo: Shambhala Press, 1998), 248.

28. Lucy Suchman, "Do Categories Have Politics? The Language/Action Perspective Reconsidered," in *Proceedings of the Third European Conference on Computer-Supported Cooperative Work 13–17 September 1993*, Milan, Italy, 1–14.

29. The company, Action Technologies, was listed as Flores's affiliation in *Understanding Computers and Cognition*.

30. Eden Medina has argued that "by the end of the 1990s, Flores and Beer had switched places. Flores had morphed into a wealthy international consultant driven by the conviction that organization, communication, and action were all central to making businesses successful. Meanwhile, Beer had become increasingly interested in societal problems and changing the world for the better." See Medina, *Cybernetic Revolutionaries*, 232–33.

31. It is important to note, however, that Winograd and Flores's position is in some respects more radical than Suchman's, who in her critique of the pair offers a familiar liberal view of "technology." Suchman writes: "In their concern with the hegemony of received perspectives, Winograd and Flores come close to agreeing with the old adage that AI as presently constituted is equivalent to the tree-climber who believes that by that route he is moving closer to the moon. . . . But the failures of AI, in principle at least, can be as valuable as its successes. That is to say, while research in AI may not get us to an artificial intelligence soon, or even ever, in principle it can still contribute to our understanding of human intelligence, through its efforts to get closer." Suchman suggests that AI's "failures" can be "instructive" if practitioners show an "intellectual honesty" concerning "the frustrations and downright failures of their efforts, as well as their successes," and if one adopts "a clear distinction between the basis for evaluating technology, and the basis for evaluating long-term research. With respect to technology, we need to question whether or not, given the state of the art, AI holds the best hope for appropriate and useful technologies in a given domain. With respect to long-term research, we need to consider that it is the exploration that is the payoff, including understanding what isn't working and why, rather than any foreseeable applications." Suchman says the direction of the AI field "should be elucidating, tentative, and open always to radical redirection." Suchman, "Do Categories Have Politics?," 229. Consider the premises of this view: (1) "artificial intelligence" is a coherent and desirable thing (indeed, to achieve it would be a "success" like reaching the moon); (2) it is a "technology" and as such has many applications, which should be evaluated on a pragmatic case-by-case basis; (3) AI practitioners get to define the "successes" and "failures" of this technology (which are apparently clear when the goal of realizing "AI" is considered universally desirable); (4) AI practitioners can cultivate more critical stances as individuals, which would lead to better technologies for "us"; and (5) collaboration and dialogue with practitioners would enable this unspecified "we" to better decide how and when such a technology is best

applied. In Suchman's framing, essentially everything about AI, from the way it is normally conceptualized to its institutional structure, remains intact.

32. Agre writes: "I went into AI because I actually thought that it was a way to learn about people and their lives. It is, it turns out, but only in reverse: the more one pushes against AI's internal logic, the more one appreciates the profound difference between human beings and any sort of computers that we can even imagine." Agre then decided to start "listening to the technology as it refuses to do the things it is advertised to do." Philip E. Agre, "How Bad Philosophy Lives Through Our Computers," *Red Rock Eater News*, December 30, 2000.

33. Agre describes the failures of the project to make an "embodied" robot that makes breakfast, discovering that this required an understanding of how people use their hands: "I made several studies of people picking up telephones, holding forks, and otherwise exercising their fingers. It quickly became apparent that people were taking advantage of every single property of their hands, including the exact degree of 'stickiness' and 'stretchiness' of their skin—neither of which was even remotely amenable to known computational methods or implementable in known materials on robots." Agre then turned to the neurophysiology of hands for inspiration, at which point "the thought of implementing any of this on a real robot was hopelessly impractical. . . . I wrote a series of programs that simulated the movements of human hands, whereupon I discovered that the impossible-to-compute interactions between the skin of people's hands and the tools and materials of breakfast-making were still impossible to compute, and therefore impossible to simulate." He concluded that the project was doomed to fail because the simplifications needed for computational simulation "distort the reality to make it fit with the computational methods, which in turn are badly wrong-headed. . . . I despaired because I saw what was going on: all of the traditional AI assumptions that I was trying to reject were creeping back into my project. My breakfast-making 'robot' no longer had a body in any meaningful sense." Agre, "How Bad Philosophy Lives Through Our Computers."

34. Agre offered his advice through "how-to's" (manuals that are familiar to users of free software and the GNU/Linux operating system): "How-to's are produced by institutions to the same degree that anything is, and the long tradition of business how-to's is easily explicable in terms of the incentives and forms of imagination that business culture has created. The books that management consultants write to advertise their services generally take just this form: identifying some of the fundamental forces that

already operate on businesses, claiming to analyze them and their consequences more systematically than others have, and spelling out the decision frameworks that all businesses should use to align themselves more completely with those forces going forward. And my own how-to's have something of the same character: they advise individuals to move back and forth between identifying emerging themes in their field and building professional networks around those themes. Building a network deepens the epistemic conditions for identifying emerging themes; identifying those themes creates the conditions in turn for building networks of individuals who appreciate their significance and have something to say about them. Someone who fully understands this advice and gets practice following it will achieve a profound and hopefully unsettling understanding of the nature of social forces and their manifestation in people's lives and careers. In effect the how-to's, mine and others', advise people to become the wind, or in another metaphor to become channels for the messages that history is urging on us." Philip E. Agre, "In Defense of How-to's," *Red Rock Eater News*, December 13, 2001.

35. Maturana and Varela, *The Tree of Knowledge*, 247, 246.
36. Martin Luther King, Jr., "Beyond Vietnam: A Time to Break Silence," speech, Riverside Church, New York, April 4, 1967.
37. Maturana and Varela, *The Tree of Knowledge*, 249.
38. In an interview, Maturana was asked: "Could the rift that I sense between you and Francisco Varela have to do with different styles of thinking? Varela is very keen to translate ideas into a mathematical language, to formalise them, whereas you have always been very critical of such an interest in formalization," to which Maturana responded: "This is definitely a crucial point. I have always been a biologist but he [Varela] has been, I would say, more of a mathematician." Maturana, *From Being to Doing*, 164.
39. Milan Zeleny, "Self-Organization of Living Systems: A Formal Model of Autopoiesis," *International Journal of General System* 4, no. 1 (1977): 13–28.
40. Milan Zeleny, "Machine/Organism Dichotomy and Free-Market Economics: Crisis or Transformation?," *Human Systems Management* 29, no. 4 (2010): 191–204.
41. Zeleny wrote: "Human societies, and any other societies of autopoietic components, can maintain their cohesiveness and unity through the 'rules of conduct' that are spontaneously generated by the autopoiesis of the components. . . . Hayek emphasized that the order of social events, though it is the result of human action, has not been entirely created by men deliberately arranging the elements in a preconceived pattern. If the forces or rules that bring about such spontaneous orders are understood, then such

knowledge could be used to produce orders that are far more complex than those attempted by deliberately arranging all the activities of a complex society." Zeleny, "Self-Organization of Living Systems," 25–27. While Zeleny states this is not meant to be "an argument against planning," his work fits rather squarely in the neoliberal epistemic frame that sees markets as powerful, decentralized information-processors.

42. Milan Zeleny, "Crisis and Transformation: On the Corso and Ricorso of Human Systems," *Human Systems Management* 31, no. 1 (2012): 49–63.

43. Fred Turner describes how individuals such as Stewart Brand (of *Whole Earth Catalog* fame) brought together people from the corporate world, academia, the military, and the media around themes of self-organization, cybernetic control, networks, and distributed learning: "The notion of distributed learning, in which individuals learn together as elements in a system, was simultaneously congenial to Shell executives ('because that's pretty much how they do their administration'), to cyberneticians such as Francisco Varela (because it seemed to describe his notion of 'awakening systems'), to computer engineers like Danny Hillis (because it was a conceptual element of massively parallel computing), and to Brand's own 'access to tools' approach to life." Turner, *From Counterculture to Cyberculture: Stewart Brand, the Whole Earth Network, and the Rise of Digital Utopianism* (Chicago: University of Chicago Press, 2010), 183. The meetings Brand convened eventually led to the formation of the Global Business Network (GBN). In addition to AI practitioners and biologists, GBN's orbit included social scientists such as Sherry Turkle and Mary Catherine Bateson and the writer Kevin Kelly (who later became editor of *Wired* magazine). Turner writes that Brand's gatherings "offered participants a chance to imagine themselves as members of a mobile elite, able to glimpse in the natural and economic systems around them the invisible laws according to which all things functioned." The concept of networks played multiple roles here: as a metaphor for the biological world, for the synthetic world (electronic circuits and interacting computing devices), as well as for the social activities of the participants.

44. Cooper has argued that Gaia, and related frameworks where organisms are viewed as complex, self-organizing systems, can end up supporting neoliberal visions of life: "The political and ecological consequences of biosphere and complexity science are becoming difficult to ignore. Such theories may well have their origins in essentially revolutionary histories of the earth, but in the current context they are more likely to lend themselves to a distinctly neoliberal antienvironmentalism." Whether this aligns with these theorists' intentions, Cooper writes, is less relevant "since in

294 ɔ 6. DISSENTING VISIONS

the absence of any substantive critique of political economy, any philosophy of *life as such* runs the risk of celebrating *life as it is*." Melinda E. Cooper, *Life as Surplus: Biotechnology and Capitalism in the Neoliberal Era*, In Vivo: The Cultural Mediations of Biomedical Science (Seattle: University of Washington Press, 2011), 41–42. Although Cooper's analyses are remarkably insightful, her account of neoliberalism as a relatively recent hijacking of biological life misses racial capitalism, as Alys Eve Weinbaum has recently argued. See Weinbaum, *The Afterlife of Reproductive Slavery: Biocapitalism and Black Feminism's Philosophy of History* (Durham, N.C.: Duke University Press, 2019), 41–43.

45. Maturana disliked the way autopoiesis was being applied by social scientists. He described his reaction after attending a meeting on the relevance of autopoiesis to social systems, held at the London School of Economics, as follows: "At the end, I was asked to say a few concluding words. I said: 'For three days I have been listening to your ideas and exchanges, and I want to put the following question to you now: What are the features of a social system that would justify choosing as the topic of this conference the problem whether a social system could be classified as autopoietic or not?' . . . Applying the concept of autopoiesis to explain social phenomena will cause them to vanish from your field of vision because your whole attention will be absorbed by the concept of autopoiesis." See Maturana, *From Being to Doing*, 104–6.

46. This notion is closely related to Maturana and Varela's idea of a consensual domain, brought forth as a product of the organism's autopoietic structure and its medium.

47. Francisco J. Varela, Evan Thompson, and Eleanor Rosch, *The Embodied Mind: Cognitive Science and Human Experience* (Cambridge, Mass.: MIT Press, 2017), 245.

48. As VTR write: "It is, rather, that we must achieve an understanding of groundlessness as a middle way by working from our own cultural premises. These premises are largely determined by science, for we live in a scientific culture. We have therefore chosen to follow Nishitani's [Keiji Nishitani, former student of Martin Heidegger] lead by building a bridge between cognitive science and mindfulness/awareness as a specific practice that embodies an open-ended approach to experience. Furthermore, since we cannot embody groundlessness in a scientific culture without reconceptualizing science itself as beyond the need of foundations, we have followed through the inner logic of research in cognitive science to develop the enactive approach. This approach should serve to demonstrate that a commitment to science need not include as a premise a commitment to objectivism or to subjectivism." Varela, Thompson, and Rosch, 242–43.

49. With one potential exception: "Lakoff" is ambiguous. It could refer to Robin Lakoff or George Lakoff.

50. Varela, Thompson, and Rosch, 207.

51. Many have argued that "embodiment" as a concept does not necessarily require having a physical body (and certainly not a human body), but for much of the work in situated robotics, this more nuanced conception of embodiment is less relevant as physical robots are actually being built—notably for use by the military.

52. But as H. R. Ekbia noted, Brooks's treatment of AI has changed dramatically with time, in a way that probably depended on the popularity of his own approach with the field's patrons. Brooks went from rhetorically asking, in the early 1990s, "Have you ever seen an AI failure?" (and rehashing, according to Ekbia, parts of Hubert Dreyfus's critique), to declaring a decade later, "There's this stupid myth out there that AI has failed." As Ekbia observes, "When Brooks's own approach . . . had moved into the limelight, he seems to have changed his opinion altogether, arguing [in 2002] that 'AI is everywhere.'" Ekbia, *Artificial Dreams: The Quest for Non-Biological Intelligence* (Cambridge: Cambridge University Press, 2008), 283–84. Ekbia's account is supported by the change of recent years: as deep learning became hugely popular since the rebranding of AI in the 2010s, Brooks switched back into critic mode, writing articles with titles such as "The Seven Deadly Sins of AI Predictions." See Rodney Brooks, "The Seven Deadly Sins of AI Predictions," *MIT Technology Review*, October 6, 2017.

53. The Roomba does not have a stable, centralized internal representation of its world, according to Brooks: "If some part of them failed, if one of the drive wheels failed for instance, they just continued on blissfully unaware of their failure, and in this case ran around in a circle. They had no awareness of self, and no awareness that they were cleaning, or 'feeding,' in any sense; no sense or internal representation of agency. If they fed a lot, their bin full sensor would say they were 'satiated,' but there was no connection between those two events inside the robot in any way, whether physically or in software. No adaptation of behavior based on past experience." Rodney Brooks, "What Is It Like to Be a Robot?," *Rodney Brooks Blog: Robots, AI, and Other Stuff,* 2017.

54. Lucy Suchman, "Situational Awareness: Deadly Bioconvergence at the Boundaries of Bodies and Machines," *MediaTropes Test Journal* 5 no. 1 (2015): 1–24.

55. iRobot has since migrated its war-related operations into another company called Endeavor Robotics. See Caroline Lester, "What Happens When Your Bomb-Defusing Robot Becomes a Weapon," *Atlantic*, 2018. In

2017–2018 the U.S. Army gave Endeavor Robotics several contracts, amounting to hundreds of millions of dollars, to develop military robots. See Justin Bachman, "The U.S. Army Is Turning to Robot Soldiers," *Bloomberg*, May 18, 2018.

56. See Brian M. Yamauchi, "PackBot: A Versatile Platform for Military Robotics," in *Proceedings of SPIE 5422, Unmanned Ground Vehicle Technology VI*, September 2, 2004, 228–38. NASA has described a line of Pack-Bots as follows: "PackBot EOD is a rugged, lightweight robot designed to conduct explosive ordnance disposal, HAZMAT, search-and-surveillance, hostage rescue, and other vital law enforcement tasks for bomb squads, SWAT teams, military units, and other authorities seeking to meet the security challenges of the 21st century." Note that iRobot's products have been tested by the military since the 1990s; see Lester, "What Happens When Your Bomb-Defusing Robot Becomes a Weapon."

57. David Miller, *Tell Me Lies: Propaganda and Media Distortion in the Attack on Iraq* (London: Pluto Press, 2004).

58. The PackBots "platform" enables different manufacturers to create various add-ons, like the rapid-fire machine gun "Metal Storm." See Lester, "What Happens When Your Bomb-Defusing Robot Becomes a Weapon."

59. Tiziana Terranova, *Network Culture: Cultural Politics for the Information Age* (London: Pluto Press, 2004), 130.

60. Andrew Pickering has argued that frameworks such as cellular automata (and the ways of thinking he associates with them) offer a "nonmodern ontology" and a radically different paradigm from that of modern scientific practice (as exemplified by fields like physics). He argues for the inclusion of courses on decentralized computing and robotics (e.g., cellular automata and robotics as practiced by Rodney Brooks). He writes that he "would be prepared to argue for one such course as a requirement [at universities] for all freshmen, whatever their field." Pickering concludes that he is "very attracted to this idea of systematically introducing students to a nonmodern ontology, beginning at an early age. If done right, it could easily produce a generation that would automatically say 'wait a minute' when presented with the next high-modernist project of enframing, who would immediately see the point of Latour's 'politics of nature,' and who would, moreover, be in just the right position to come up with new projects that center on revealing rather than enframing. I would enjoy sharing a world with people like that." Pickering, *The Cybernetic Brain: Sketches of Another Future* (Chicago: University of Chicago Press, 2010), 402. Stefan Helmreich offers a counterpoint to the view (shared by Pickering and Terranova) that things like cellular automata constitute a "nonmodern" (or

"postmodern") departure from dominant scientific thinking. Helmreich writes that artificial life—a field largely framed around the computational frameworks and ontologies that Pickering and Terranova are hopeful about—in fact "holds fast to modernist ideas about the unity of science and the world." While Helmreich says "the practice of simulation pulls it along a postmodern trajectory that threatens/promises to undermine these foundations," he concludes that artificial life "may not be postmodern so much as 'metamodern' or 'hypermodern.'" Helmreich, *Silicon Second Nature: Culturing Artificial Life in a Digital World* (Berkeley: University of California Press, 2000), 235–36.

61. Like Pickering and Terranova, Manuel DeLanda sees great liberatory potential in decentralized, biologically inspired computation. In his book *War in the Age of Intelligent Machines* (1991), DeLanda claims that Pandemonium, a decentralized computational model developed by Oliver Selfridge, constitutes the "only path to real Artificial Intelligence" (a concept that DeLanda invokes uncritically). DeLanda says that the military is resistant to this form of computation since it threatens hierarchical notions of command-and-control, but that "the Pandemonium . . . is a technology that should be adopted by the military on purely pragmatic grounds." But he states that before the military gets to it, Pandemonium could pave to way to "truly liberating paths." DeLanda, *War in the Age of Intelligent Machines* (New York: Zone Books, 1991), 230–31.

62. Hayek quoted in Paul Van Riper and Robert H. Scales, Jr., "Preparing for War in the 21st Century," in *Future Warfare: Anthology*, ed. Robert H. Scales (Carlisle, Penn.: Strategic Studies Institute, 2000).

63. For footage of the exercise, including an interview with Van Riper, see "USA—Wall Street Marines" segment aired on ABC, April 29, 1996. See also Seth Schiesel, "Marines Polish Command Skills, Switching Places with Traders," *New York Times*, December 16, 1996.

64. Andrew Ilachinski, *Artificial War: Multiagent-Based Simulation of Combat* (Singapore: World Scientific, 2004), x.

65. Ilachinski, xiii, xiv.

66. Ilachinski writes: "The epiphany that finally sparked my realization that there is a deep connection between complexity and combat . . . was this: if combat—on a real battlefield—is viewed from a 'birds-eye' [*sic*] perspective so that only the overall patterns of behavior are observed, and the motions of individual soldiers are indistinguishably blurred into the background (i.e., if combat is viewed wholistically, as a single gestalt-like dynamic pattern), then *combat is essentially equivalent to the cellular automata 'toy universes'*" (xiv; italics in original).

67. Barton Gellman and Thomas E. Ricks, "Images of Past Wars May Not Fit Present Foe," *Washington Post*, September 16, 2001.

68. For background on the U.S. Defense Department's war games and simulations, see Tim Lenoir and Henry Lowood, "Theaters of War: The Military-Entertainment Complex," in *Collection, Laboratory, Theater: Scenes of Knowledge in the 17th Century*, ed. Helmar Schramm, Ludger Schwarte, and Lazardzig Jan (New York: Walter de Gruyter, 2002), 427–56; and Annie Jacobsen, *The Pentagon's Brain: An Uncensored History of DARPA, America's Top-Secret Military Research Agency* (Boston: Little, Brown, 2015), chap. 14.

69. In an interview with Fox News in 2004, Van Riper said "when the war started, and I saw about half of the number of units on the ground . . . what I think happened is at the very senior leadership in civilian you have those, and we're talking now not only the secretary but the deputy secretary, who are not professionally schooled. They don't understand war."

70. Gil Ariely, "Operational Knowledge Management in the Military," in *Encyclopedia of Knowledge Management*, 2d ed. (Hershey, Penn.: IGI Global, 2011), 1250–60.

71. Peter Galison, "Computer Simulations and the Trading Zone," in *The Disunity of Science: Boundaries, Contexts, and Power*, ed. Peter L. Galison and David J. Stump (Stanford, Calif.: Stanford University Press, 1996), 118–56.

72. Roger Stahl, *Militainment, Inc.: War, Media, and Popular Culture* (New York: Routledge, 2009), 109.

73. Stahl, 97.

74. ICT's platforms have also been used outside military and gaming settings. Along with the University of Southern California's Shoah Foundation, ICT developed the virtual characters used in "Dimensions in Testimony," a project that seeks to preserve, in virtual form, testimonies of Jewish survivors of the Nazi holocaust.

75. This environment is taken from a promotional video by ICT, "USC Institute for Creative Technologies, Overview: USC Institute for Creative Technologies," July 10, 2014, https://www.youtube.com/watch?v=K45PL CgrzfM. ICT has developed several projects for "immersive" battlefield training, such as the Soldier/Squad Virtual Trainer (S/SVT), which is meant to provide "synthetic environment immersion, the replication of complex environments, and tactical/psychological conditioning" for soldiers in "bloodless battle." According to ICT's promotional materials, such semivirtual environments are desirable because they "allow us [U.S. military] to train, rehearse, and fight with the same weapon systems. . . . It saves money and makes that training much more realistic."

76. Patrick Kenny et al., "Building Interactive Virtual Humans for Training Environments," in *Proceedings of i/Itsec*, no. 174 (2007): 911–16.

77. In one such system, called ELECT-BILAT, "students assume the role of a U.S. Army officer who needs to conduct a series of bi-lateral engagements or meetings with local leaders to achieve the mission objectives." Randall W. Hill et al., "Enhanced Learning Environments with Creative Technologies (Elect) Bilateral Negotiation (Bilat) System," U.S. Patent Application 12/261,299, filed May 14, 2009. ICT's virtual characters have also been used to create computerized therapists, as well as to train soldiers in interrogation techniques. "Embodiment" of a sort is central here. ICT's virtual therapist system, for instance, tracks the gestures, speech, and eye movements (among other features) of the person interacting with it. The virtual characters are created based on detailed analyses of these facets of human behavior.

78. Vadim Bulitko et al., "Modeling Culturally and Emotionally Affected Behavior," in *Proceedings of the Fourth Artificial Intelligence and Interactive Digital Entertainment Conference* (Stanford, Calif.: AAAI, 2008), 10–15.

79. When I interviewed Jonathan Gratch, a member of ICT and professor at the University of Southern California who has worked on integrating cultural and emotional aspects into military training systems, he stressed the importance of situated and embodied perspectives. I asked him whether he sees tensions between approaches within cognitive science and AI that emphasize symbolic representations and those that take a more embodied, situated view. He replied, "I'm very sympathetic to the Heideggerian situated view." He also noted the limitations of current efforts to build systems in accord with the "situated view." ICT's "virtual humans," he said, are "pretty superficial with regard to having a body," and "even work in robotics, I would say, is somewhat superficial in how it tries to link mental and bodily processes." For Gratch, the embodied and situated elements of cognition are of great importance, and he expressed the need to incorporate these more fully into his own work: "What emotion is doing, emotion is reprogramming your body to prepare for certain contingencies and that reprogramming itself then feedbacks to your perception of what is possible in the moment, and that kind of rich loop between cognition, action, and sensing, I feel like we don't have sophisticated enough machines to do that. I actually spent the fall [semester] trying to read some Heidegger and Dreyfus, they talk about that kind of stuff, particularly Dreyfus, and how it relates to work by Phil Agre [AI practitioner] and Lucy Suchman [anthropologist and science and technology studies scholar]. I think that work is right and I want to do that kind of work and I still don't know

how to do that well." Author interview with Jonathan Gratch, October 18, 2018.

80. For examples of these integrations, see Kenny et al., "Building Interactive Virtual Humans."

81. In fact, Soar's developers have stated that the agents they build already have a kind of "situatedness" to them. See John E. Laird and Paul S. Rosenbloom, "The Evolution of the Soar Cognitive Architecture," in *Mind Matters: A Tribute to Allen Newell*, ed. David Steier and Tom M. Mitchell, Carnegie Mellon Symposia on Cognition (New York: Psychology Press, 1996), 1–50.

82. Jack D. Forbes, *Columbus and Other Cannibals: The Wétiko Disease of Exploitation, Imperialism, and Terrorism* (New York: Seven Stories Press, 2008), 181–82. Forbes also goes on to challenge several entrenched ideas from evolutionary and developmental biology: "Who was my mother? An egg? Who was my father, a little animal called a sperm? But where did this egg and this sperm come from? They grew inside a woman and inside a man, but they had their own life-paths distinct from those of the man and the woman. Their bodies, that flesh, my ancestor, grew inside of them and what was it? It was the earth, it was the sky, it was the sun, it was the plants and animals. We are very lucky to have so many wonderful mothers and fathers."

83. Humberto R. Maturana and Ximena P. Dávila, "The Biology of Knowing and the Biology of Loving: Education as Viewed from the Biological Matrix of Human Existence," *Prelac* 2 (2006): 30–39.

7. A GENERATIVE REFUSAL

1. What these streams are missing is essentially the commitment to "unlearning" the imperial institutions and practices that Ariella Aïsha Azoulay has urged for. This is a commitment to challenge what Azoulay calls the "onto-epistemic premises" of imperialism. See Azoulay, *Potential History: Unlearning Imperialism* (New York: Verso Books, 2019).

2. In his study of debt and new media, Nicholas Mirzoeff similarly argues: "The goal of this work is not to say that new media studies needs a subfield on debt but to investigate how new media sustains the debt system with the goal of finding a politics of debt and debt refusal." Mirzoeff, "You Are Not A Loan: Debt and New Media," in *New Media, Old Media: A History and Theory Reader*, ed. Wendy H. K. Chun, Anna W. Fisher, and Thomas Keenan (New York: Routledge, 2016), 346. The same attitude applies in our context. Moreover, there is the danger of further fueling what Joy James has diagnosed as an "addiction" to white

supremacy: "The addict's trap. To embrace or reject WS [white suprem-acy] . . . all require a concentration of energy, nerve, and mind on 'white-ness.'" James, "The Academic Addict: Mainlining (& Kicking) White Supremacy (WS)," in *What White Looks Like: African-American Philoso-phers on the Whiteness Question*, ed. George Yancy (New York: Routledge, 2004), 264.

3. George Lipsitz, *The Possessive Investment in Whiteness: How White People Profit from Identity Politics* (Philadelphia: Temple University Press, 2009), xiii.

4. Sandy Grande, "Refusing the University," in *Toward What Justice? Describ-ing Diverse Dreams of Justice in Education*, ed. E. Tuck and K. W. Yang (Abingdon, UK: Taylor & Francis, 2018), 247.

5. Audra Simpson, *Mohawk Interruptus: Political Life Across the Borders of Set-tler States* (Durham, N.C.: Duke University Press, 2014), 194.

6. Grande, "Refusing the University," 47.

7. Stefano Harney and Fred Moten, *The Undercommons: Fugitive Planning & Black Study* (London: Minor Compositions, 2013), 26.

8. As Harney and Moten write, "To be a critical academic in the university is to be against the university, and to be against the university is always to recognize it and be recognized by it" (31). Grande similarly frames refusal of the university as distinct from a politics of recognition. For Grande, refusal is "the un-demand, the un-desire to be either *of* or *in* the univer-sity." Grande, "Refusing the University," 62.

9. Harney and Moten write: "The subversive intellectual came under false pretenses, with bad documents, out of love. Her labor is as necessary as it is unwelcome. The university needs what she bears but cannot bear what she brings." Harney and Moten, *The Undercommons*, 26. Thus, "like the colonial police force recruited unwittingly from guerrilla neighborhoods, university labor may harbor refugees, fugitives, renegades, and castaways. But there are good reasons for the university to be confident that such ele-ments will be exposed or forced underground."

10. A parallel path is to find a radically different way to pursue something like the sciences of thought and action without being blind to the imperial and capitalist structures in which such inquiry unfolds; chapter 6 suggests there is something to be salvaged from prior attempts. Perhaps these old gears could be repurposed into building what la paperson calls "decolonizing operations." la paperson, *A Third University Is Possible* (Minneapolis: Uni-versity of Minnesota Press, 2017), 24. I don't really know how to do that, but maybe you do.

11. Harney and Moten, *The Undercommons*, 35.

12. Herman Melville, *Moby-Dick, Or, The Whale*, Modern Library Classics (1851; New York: Penguin, 2000), 282.

13. Toni Morrison, "Unspeakable Things Unspoken: The Afro-American Presence in American Literature," Tanner Lectures on Human Values, 1988, 142.

14. Melville, *Moby-Dick,* 282.

15. Morrison, "Unspeakable Things Unspoken," 141–42.

16. Melville, *Moby-Dick,* 190.

17. Melville, 707, 709.

18. I am hearing here Grande's call for a "radical and ongoing reflexivity about who we are and how we situate ourselves in the world. This includes but is not limited to a refusal of the cycle of individualized inducements— particularly, the awards, appointments, and grants that require complicity or allegiance to institutions that continue to oppress and dispossess. It is also a call to refuse the perceived imperative to self-promote, to brand one's work and body. This includes all the personal webpages, incessant Facebook updates, and Twitter feeds featuring our latest accomplishments, publications, grants, rewards, etc. etc. Just. Make. It. Stop." Grande adds, "The journey is not about self . . . it is about the disruption and dismantling of those structures and processes that create hierarchies of individual worth and labor." Grande, "Refusing the University," 61.

BIBLIOGRAPHY

Abebe, Rediet. "Why AI Needs Diversity." *Forbes*, November 29, 2018.

Adam, Alison. *Artificial Knowing: Gender and the Thinking Machine*. New York: Routledge, 2006.

Adams, Tim. "Artificial Intelligence: 'We're Like Children Playing with a Bomb.'" *Guardian*, June 12, 2016.

Advanced Research Projects Agency. *Activities of the Research and Development Center—Thailand*. Report No. 167324, December 29, 1971.

Agre, Philip E. "How Bad Philosophy Lives Through Our Computers." *Red Rock Eater News*, December 30, 2000.

——. "In Defense of How-to's." *Red Rock Eater News*, December 13, 2001.

——. "Toward a Critical Technical Practice: Lessons Learned in Trying to Reform AI." In *Social Science, Technical Systems, and Cooperative Work: Beyond the Great Divide*, ed. G. Bowker, S. L. Star, L. Gasser, and W. Turner. Abingdon, UK: Taylor & Francis, 1997.

Alkhateeb, Ahmed. "Can Scientific Discovery Be Automated?" *Atlantic*, April 25, 2017.

Allen, Gregory C., Michael C. Horowitz, Elsa Kania, and Paul Scharre. *Strategic Competition in an Era of Artificial Intelligence*. Artificial Intelligence and International Security. Washington D.C.: Center for New American Security, 2018.

Allen, Theodore W. *The Invention of the White Race*. Vol. 2: *The Origin of Racial Oppression in Anglo-America*. 1997. New York: Verso Books, 2014.

Anderson, Jon Lee. "Jair Bolsonaro's Southern Strategy." *New Yorker*, April 1, 2019.

Ariely, Gil. "Operational Knowledge Management in the Military." In *Encyclopedia of Knowledge Management*. 2d ed., 1250–60. Hershey, Penn.: IGI Global, 2011.

Arkin, Ronald C. *A Robotocist's Perspective on Lethal Autonomous Weapon Systems.* United Nations Office of Disarmament Affairs (UNODA) Occasional Papers, 2018, 35–47.

Asemota, Victor. "'Ghana Is the Future of Africa': Why Google Built an AI Lab in Accra." CNN, July 15, 2018.

Association for Computing Machinery (ACM). "1971 A. M. Turing Award Citation for John McCarthy."

Atherton, Kelsey D. "Are Killer Robots the Future of War? Parsing the Facts on Autonomous Weapons." *New York Times*, November 15, 2018.

Auslin, Michael. "Can the Pentagon Win the AI Arms Race?" *Foreign Affairs*, October 19, 2018.

Azoulay, Ariella Aïsha. *Potential History: Unlearning Imperialism.* New York: Verso Books, 2019.

Bachman, Justin. "The U.S. Army Is Turning to Robot Soldiers." Bloomberg, May 18, 2018.

Bakare, Lanre. "Barack Obama Reveals His Cultural Highlights of 2018, from Roma to Zadie Smith." *Guardian*, December 28, 2018.

Baldwin, James. "Stranger in the Village." In *Notes of a Native Son*, 159–75. Boston: Beacon Press, 1955.

Barbrook, Richard, and Andy Cameron. "The Californian Ideology." *Science as Culture* 6, no. 1 (1996): 44–72.

Barhat, Vikram. "China Is Determined to Steal A.I. Crown from US and Nothing, Not Even a Trade War, Will Stop It." CNBC, May 4, 2018.

Baudrillard, Jean. *Simulacra and Simulation.* Trans. Sheila Faria Glaser. Ann Arbor: University of Michigan Press, 1994.

Bell, Trudy E. "The Teams and The Players." In *Next-Generation Computers*, ed. Edward A. Torrero, 13–14. Spectrum Series, Institute of Electrical and Electronics Engineers, 1985.

Benitez-Quiroz, Carlos F., Ramprakash Srinivasan, and Aleix M. Martinez. "Facial Color Is an Efficient Mechanism to Visually Transmit Emotion." *Proceedings of the National Academy of Sciences* 115, no. 14 (2018): 3581–86.

Benjamin, Ruha. *Race After Technology: Abolitionist Tools for the New Jim Code.* New York: Wiley, 2019.

Best, Tamara. "How Breaking the Rules Could Win You $250,000." *New York Times*, March 9, 2017.

Beydoun, Khaled A. "Boxed in: Reclassification of Arab Americans on the US Census as Progress or Peril." *Loyola University Chicago Law Journal* 47 (2015): 693.

Bilton, Nick. "Google Buys A.I. Company for Search, Not Robots." *New York Times*, January 28, 2014.

Black in AI. https://blackinai.github.io/.

Boden, Margaret. "Impacts of Artificial Intelligence." In *Impacts of Artificial Intelligence*, ed. Robert Trappl, 64–77. Amsterdam: North Holland, 1986.

Boffey, Philip M., "Software Seen as Obstacle in Developing 'Star Wars.'" *New York Times*, September 16, 1986.

Boisvert, Will. "Future Schlock: Creating the Crap of Tomorrow at the MIT Media Lab." *Baffler* 19 (March 2012).

Bostrom, Nick. *Superintelligence: Paths, Dangers, Strategies*. Oxford: Oxford University Press, 2016.

Brooks, Fred P. *The Mythical Man-Month. Anniversary Edition: Essays on Software Engineering, Portable Documents*. London: Pearson Education, 1995.

Brooks, Rodney. "The Seven Deadly Sins of AI Predictions." *MIT Technology Review*, October 6, 2017.

——. "What Is It Like to Be a Robot?" *Rodney Brooks Blog: Robots, AI, and Other Stuff*. March 18, 2017.

Brooks, Rodney A., Bruce G. Buchanan, Douglas B. Lenat, David M. McKeown, and J. D. Fletcher. *Panel Review of the Semi-Automated Forces*. Alexandria, Va.: Institute for Defense Analyses, September 1989.

Broussard, Meredith. *Artificial Unintelligence: How Computers Misunderstand the World*. Cambridge, Mass.: MIT Press, 2018.

Brown, Wendy. *Undoing the Demos: Neoliberalism's Stealth Revolution*. New York: Zone Books, 2015.

Bulitko, Vadim, Steve Solomon, Jonathan Gratch, and Michael Van Lent. "Modeling Culturally and Emotionally Affected Behavior." In *Proceedings of the Fourth Artificial Intelligence and Interactive Digital Entertainment Conference*, 10–15. Stanford, Calif.: AAAI, 2008.

Bulkeley, William. "Bright Outlook for Artificial Intelligence Yields to Slow Growth and Big Cutbacks." *Wall Street Journal*, July 5, 1990.

Bundy, Alan. "What Kind of Field Is AI?" In *The Foundations of Artificial Intelligence: A Sourcebook*, ed. Derek Partridge and Yorick Wilks. Cambridge: Cambridge University Press, 1990.

Buolamwini, Joy. "AI, Ain't I A Woman?," June 28, 2018. https://www.youtube.com/watch?v=QxuyfWoVV98.

——. "Artificial Intelligence Has a Problem with Gender and Racial Bias. Here's How to Solve It." *Time*, February 2019.

Buolamwini, Joy, and Timnit Gebru. "Gender Shades: Intersectional Accuracy Disparities in Commercial Gender Classification." In *Proceedings of Machine Learning Research, Conference on Fairness, Accountability and Transparency* 81 (2018): 1–15.

Butler, Patrick. "UN Accuses Blackstone Group of Contributing to Global Housing Crisis." *Guardian*, March 26, 2019.

Campolo, Alex, Madelyn Sanfilippo, Meredith Whittaker, and Kate Crawford. *AI Now 2017 Report*. AI Now Institute, January 2017. https://www.microsoft .com/en-us/research/publication/ai-now-2017-report/.

Caplan, Robyn, Alex Rosenblat, and danah boyd. "Open Data the Criminal Justice System and the Police Data Initiative." *Data & Civil Rights* (October 2015): 1–13.

Cartner-Morley, Jess. "Do Robots Dream of Prada? How Artificial Intelligence Is Reprogramming Fashion." *Guardian*, September 15, 2018.

Cave, Stephen. "To Save Us From a Kafkaesque Future, We Must Democratise AI." *Guardian*, January 4, 2019.

CBInsights. "Microsoft, Google Lead in AI Patent Activity, While Apple Lags Behind." January 20, 2017. https://www.cbinsights.com/research/google -apple-microsoft-ai-patents/.

Cerri, Stefano A. "The Intersection of AI and Education: Investing in Thought-Intensive Endeavors." In *Impacts of Artificial Intelligence*, ed. Robert Trappl, 78–88. Amsterdam: North Holland, 1986.

Chapman, Robert L., John L. Kennedy, Allen Newell, and William C. Biel. "The Systems Research Laboratory's Air Defense Experiments." *Management Science* 5, no. 3 (1959): 250–69.

Chomsky, Noam. "Psychology and Ideology." *Cognition* 1, no. 1 (1972): 11–46.

——. "A Review of B. F. Skinner's Verbal Behavior." *Language* 35, no. 1 (1959): 26–58.

Chun, Wendy H. K. "Introduction: Race and/as Technology; Or, How to Do Things to Race." *Camera Obscura: Feminism, Culture, and Media Studies* 70, no. 1 (24) (2009).

——. *Programmed Visions: Software and Memory*. Cambridge, Mass.: MIT Press, 2011.

Clancey, William J. "Scientific Antecedents of Situated Cognition." In *The Cambridge Handbook of Situated Cognition*, ed. Philip Robbins and Murat Aydede, 11–34. Cambridge Handbooks in Psychology. Cambridge: Cambridge University Press, 2009.

Coats, Pamela K. "Why Expert Systems Fail." *Financial Management* 17, no. 3 (1988): 77–86.

Cohn, Jonathan. "Female Labor and Digital Media: Pattie Maes, Postfeminism, and the Birth of Social Networking Technologies." *Camera Obscura: Feminism, Culture, and Media Studies* 28, no. 2 (83) (2013): 151–75.

Colón-Adorno, Adriana, and Alejandro Comas-Short. "Yale Benefits from the Puerto Rican Debt—These Students Are Fighting to End That." *Nation*, March 1, 2019.

Connolly, Bess. "Yale Study Finds That Gun Violence Is a 'Contagious' Social Epidemic." *Yale News*, January 4, 2017.

Connor, Kevin, and Dennis Abner. "Hedge Funds Win, Puerto Ricans Lose in First Debt Restructuring Deal." *American Prospect*, February 8, 2019.

Conway, Flo, and Jim Siegelman. *Dark Hero of the Information Age: In Search of Norbert Wiener—Father of Cybernetics*. New York: Basic Books, 2005.

Cooper, Melinda E. *Life as Surplus: Biotechnology and Capitalism in the Neoliberal Era*. Vivo: The Cultural Mediations of Biomedical Science. Seattle: University of Washington Press, 2011.

Crenshaw, Kimberlé W. "From Private Violence to Mass Incarceration: Thinking Intersectionally about Women, Race, and Social Control." *UCLA Law Review* 59 (2011): 1418.

Crevier, Daniel. *AI: The Tumultuous History of the Search for Artificial Intelligence*. New York: Basic Books, 1993.

Crick, Francis. "Letter to John Edsall on IQ." February 1971.

Currier, Cora, and Henrik Moltke. "Spies in the Sky: Israeli Drone Feeds Hacked by British and American Intelligence." *Intercept*, 2016.

Davis, Angela Y. *Are Prisons Obsolete?* Open Media Series. New York: Seven Stories Press, 2003.

DeepMind. "AlphaGo Zero: Discovering New Knowledge." October 18, 2017. https://www.youtube.com/watch?v=WXHFqTvfFSw.

Defense Advanced Research Projects Agency. "DARPA Artificial Intelligence Grants Records, 1963–2017 (Case No. 19-F-0077)." March 15, 2019.

DeLanda, Manuel. *War in the Age of Intelligent Machines*. New York: Zone Books, 1991.

Diakopoulos, Nicholas. *Algorithmic Accountability Reporting: On the Investigation of Black Boxes*. Tow Center for Digital Journalism, Columbia University, 2014.

DiAngelo, Robin. "White Fragility." *International Journal of Critical Pedagogy* 3, no. 3 (2011).

Dickson, Andrew. "The New Tool in the Art of Spotting Forgeries: Artificial Intelligence." *Guardian*, August 6, 2018.

Dickson, Paul. *The Electronic Battlefield*. Bloomington: Indiana University Press, 1976.

Dietrich, Eric. "Programs in the Search for Intelligent Machines: The Mistaken Foundations of AI." In *The Foundations of Artificial Intelligence: A Sourcebook*, ed. Derek Partridge and Yorick Wilks. Cambridge: Cambridge University Press, 1990.

Dizikes, Peter. "AI, the Law, and Our Future." *MIT Computer Science and Artificial Intelligence Laboratory News*, January 18, 2019.

Domingos, Pedro. *The Master Algorithm: How the Quest for the Ultimate Learning Machine Will Remake Our World*. New York: Basic Books, 2015.

Doshi-Velez, Finale, and Mason Kortz. "A.I. Is More Powerful than Ever. How Do We Hold It Accountable?" *Washington Post*, March 20, 2018.

Doshi-Velez, Finale, Mason Kortz, Ryan Budish, Chris Bavitz, Sam J. Gershman, David O'Brien, et al. *Accountability of AI Under the Law: The Role of Explanation.* Cambridge, Mass.: Berkman Klein Center for Internet & Society Research Publication, 2017.

Dreyfus, Hubert L. *Alchemy and Artificial Intelligence.* Report No. P-3244. Santa Monica, Calif.: RAND Corporation, 1965.

——. *What Computers Still Can't Do: A Critique of Artificial Reason.* 1972. Cambridge, Mass.: MIT Press, 1992.

——. "Why Heideggerian AI Failed and How Fixing It Would Require Making It More Heideggerian." *Philosophical Psychology* 20, no. 2 (2007): 247–68.

Dreyfus, Stuart E., and Hubert L. Dreyfus. *The Scope, Limits, and Training Implications of Three Models of Aircraft Pilot Emergency Response Behavior.* Report No. ORC-79-2. Berkeley: Operations Research Center, University of California, February 1979.

Du Bois, W. E. B. *The Conservation of Races.* Washington, D.C.: American Negro Academy, 1897.

Dupuy, Jean-Pierre. *On the Origins of Cognitive Science: The Mechanization of the Mind.* Trans. M. B. DeBevoise. Cambridge, Mass.: MIT Press, 2009.

Edwards, Paul N. *The Closed World: Computers and the Politics of Discourse in Cold War America.* Cambridge, Mass.: MIT Press, 1997.

Ekbia, H. R. *Artificial Dreams: The Quest for Non-Biological Intelligence.* Cambridge: Cambridge University Press, 2008.

Fanon, Frantz. *Black Skin, White Masks.* New York: Grove Press, 2008.

Fausto-Sterling, Anne. "Gender/Sex, Sexual Orientation, and Identity Are in the Body: How Did They Get There?" *Journal of Sex Research* 56, no. 4–5 (2019): 529–55.

——. *Sexing the Body: Gender Politics and the Construction of Sexuality.* New York: Basic Books, 2000.

Federici, Silvia. *Caliban and the Witch.* New York: Autonomedia, 2004.

Feigenbaum, Edward A. *Knowledge Engineering: The Applied Side of Artificial Intelligence.* Stanford, Calif.: Stanford University, 1980.

Feigenbaum, Edward A., and Pamela McCorduck. *The Fifth Generation: Artificial Intelligence and Japan's Computer Challenge to the World.* Boston: Addison-Wesley, 1983.

Finkelstein, Norman G. "Middle East Watch and the Gulf War." *Z Magazine*, September 1992, 15–19.

Fischetti, Mark A. "A Review of Progress at MCC: Although Its Current Objectives Do Not Include 'Beating Japan,' This US Organization Is Positioned to Help Industry Do So." *IEEE Spectrum* 23, no. 3 (1986): 76–82.

——. "The United States." *IEEE Spectrum* 20, no. 11 (1983): 51–69.

Fjeld, Jessica, and Mason Kortz. "A Legal Anatomy of AI-Generated Art: Part 1." *Journal of Law and Technology*, November 21, 2017.

Fleck, James. "Development and Establishment in Artificial Intelligence." In *Scientific Establishments and Hierarchies*, ed. N. Elias, H. Martins, and R. Whitley, 169–217. New York: Springer, 1982.

Flood, G. "Don't Call It AI, Call It the Intelligent System." *Software Futures STFT* 4, no. 11 (1995).

Fodor, Jerry A., and Zenon W. Pylyshyn. "Connectionism and Cognitive Architecture: A Critical Analysis." *Cognition* 28, no. 1–2 (1988): 3–71.

Forbes, Jack D. "Blood Quantum: A Relic of Racism and Termination." *People's Voice*, November 2000, 1–2.

——. *Columbus and Other Cannibals: The Wétiko Disease of Exploitation, Imperialism, and Terrorism.* New York: Seven Stories Press, 2008.

Ford Foundation. *Fighting the "Coded Gaze": How We Make Technology Benefit All.* November 13, 2018.

Foucault, Michel. *The Birth of Biopolitics.* 1979. New York: Palgrave Macmillan, 2008.

Franco, Marisa. "Palantir Has No Place at Berkeley: They Help Tear Immigrant Families Apart." *Guardian*, May 31, 2019.

Frankenberg, Ruth. *White Women, Race Matters: The Social Construction of Whiteness.* Gender, Racism, Ethnicity. Minneapolis: University of Minnesota Press, 1993.

Galison, Peter. "Computer Simulations and the Trading Zone." In *The Disunity of Science: Boundaries, Contexts, and Power*, ed. Peter L. Galison and David J. Stump, 118–56. Stanford, Calif.: Stanford University Press, 1996.

——. "The Ontology of the Enemy: Norbert Wiener and the Cybernetic Vision." *Critical Inquiry* 21, no. 1 (1994): 228–66.

Gellman, Barton, and Thomas E. Ricks. "Images of Past Wars May Not Fit Present Foe." *Washington Post*, September 16, 2001.

Geman, Stuart, Elie Bienenstock, and René Doursat. "Neural Networks and the Bias/Variance Dilemma." *Neural Computation* 4, no. 1 (1992): 1–58.

Gillula, Jeremy, and Daniel Nazer. *Stupid Patent of the Month: Will Patents Slow Artificial Intelligence?* Electronic Frontier Foundation, September 29, 2017.

Gluckman, Nell. "Hype vs. Reality at the MIT Media Lab." *Chronicle of Higher Education*, September 11, 2019.

Gonzaléz, Jacinta. Interview by author, November 13, 2018.

Gossett, Thomas F. *Race: The History of an Idea in America.* Race and American Culture. 1963. Oxford: Oxford University Press, 1997.

Graeber, David. "On the Phenomenon of Bullshit Jobs: A Work Rant." *Strike Magazine* 3 (August 2013).

———. *Toward An Anthropological Theory of Value: The False Coin of Our Own Dreams.* New York: Palgrave, 2001.

GRAIN and Rede Social de Justiça e Direitos Humanos. *Harvard's Billion-Dollar Farmland Fiasco.* September 2018.

Grande, Sandy. "Refusing the University." In *Toward What Justice? Describing Diverse Dreams of Justice in Education,* ed. E. Tuck and K. W. Yang. Abingdon, UK: Taylor & Francis, 2018.

Grandin, Greg. *Kissinger's Shadow: The Long Reach of America's Most Controversial Statesman.* New York: Holt, 2015.

Gratch, Jonathan. Interview by author, October 18, 2018.

Green, Ben, Thibaut Horel, and Andrew V. Papachristos. "Modeling Contagion Through Social Networks to Explain and Predict Gunshot Violence in Chicago, 2006 to 2014." *JAMA Internal Medicine* 177, no. 3 (2017): 326–33.

Greenwald, Glenn. "Glenn Greenwald: As Bezos Protests Invasion of His Privacy, Amazon Builds Global Surveillance State." *Democracy Now!,* February 11, 2019.

———. *No Place to Hide: Edward Snowden, the NSA, and the US Surveillance State.* New York: Macmillan, 2014.

Gregg, Aaron, and Jay Greene. "Pentagon Awards Controversial $10 Billion Cloud Computing Deal to Microsoft, Spurning Amazon." *Washington Post,* October 25, 2019.

Grim, Ryan. "A Top Financier of Trump and McConnell Is a Driving Force Behind Amazon Deforestation." *Intercept,* August 27, 2019.

Group of MIT students, faculty, staff, and alumni. "Celebrating War Criminals at MIT's 'Ethical' College of Computing." *Tech,* February 14, 2019.

Guillaume, Kristine E., and Jamie D. Halper. "Overseer Resigns Over Harvard's Continued Fossil Fuel Investment." *Harvard Crimson,* May 23, 2018.

Haaretz. "A Perfect Picture of the Occupation." Editorial, August 31, 2015.

Hafner, Katie, and Matthew Lyon. *Where Wizards Stay Up Late: The Origins of the Internet.* New York: Simon and Schuster, 1998.

Hambling, David. "Armed Russian Robocops to Defend Missile Bases." *New Scientist,* April 23, 2014.

Harari, Yuval Noah. "Life 3.0 by Max Tegmark Review—We Are Ignoring the AI Apocalypse." *Guardian,* September 22, 2017.

Haraway, Donna. "Ecce Homo, Ain't (Ar'n't) I a Woman, and Inappropriated Others: The Human in a Post-Humanist Landscape." In *The Haraway Reader,* 49–61. New York: Routledge, 2004.

Harding, Sandra. *Whose Science? Whose Knowledge? Thinking from Women's Lives.* Ithaca, N.Y.: Cornell University Press, 1991.

Harney, Stefano, and Fred Moten. *The Undercommons: Fugitive Planning & Black Study*. London: Minor Compositions, 2013.

Harris, Cheryl I. "Whiteness as Property." *Harvard Law Review* 106, no. 8 (1993): 1707–91.

Hart, Peter E. *Artificial Intelligence*. Technical Note No. 126. Menlo Park, Calif.: Stanford Research Institute, February 1976.

Hart, Peter E., and Richard O Duda. *PROSPECTOR—A Computer Based Consultation System for Mineral Exploration*. Technical Note No. 155. Menlo Park, Calif.: SRI International, October, 1977.

Harwell, Drew. "Defense Department Pledges Billions Toward Artificial Intelligence Research." *Washington Post*, September 7, 2018.

Hassein, Nabil. "Against Black Inclusion in Facial Recognition." *Digital Talking Drum*, August 15, 2017.

Hayek, Friedrich A. *The Fatal Conceit: The Errors of Socialism*. Collected Works of F. A. Hayek. Chicago: University of Chicago Press, 1991.

Heckerman, David. "Bayesian Networks for Data Mining." *Data Mining and Knowledge Discovery* 1, no. 1 (1997): 79–119.

Hedberg, Sara Reese. "DART: Revolutionizing Logistics Planning." *IEEE Intelligent Systems* 17, no. 3 (2002): 81–83.

——. "Is AI Going Mainstream as Last? A Look Inside Microsoft Research." *IEEE Intelligent Systems and Their Applications* 13, no. 2 (1998): 21–25.

Helmreich, Stefan. *Silicon Second Nature: Culturing Artificial Life in a Digital World*. Berkeley: University of California Press, 2000.

Hern, Alex. "Computers Now Better than Humans at Recognising and Sorting Images." *Guardian*, May 13, 2015.

Hicks, Marie. "Why Tech's Gender Problem Is Nothing New." *Guardian*, October 12, 2018.

Hill, Randall W., David Hendrie, Eric Forbell, and Julia M. Kim. "Enhanced Learning Environments with Creative Technologies (Elect) Bilateral Negotiation (Bilat) System." U.S. Patent Application 12/261,299, filed May 14, 2009.

Horne, Gerald. *The Apocalypse of Settler Colonialism: The Roots of Slavery, White Supremacy, and Capitalism in 17th Century North America and the Caribbean*. New York: Monthly Review Press, 2018.

——. *The Counter-Revolution of 1776: Slave Resistance and the Origins of the United States of America*. New York: NYU Press, 2016.

Horowitz, Michael C. "Artificial Intelligence, International Competition, and the Balance of Power." *Texas National Security Review* 1, no. 3 (2018).

Hunter, Lawrence. "Gadgets for Utopia." *New York Times*, September 27, 1987.

Ignatiev, Noel. *How the Irish Became White*. 1995. New York: Routledge, 2009.

Ignatius, David. "A Tech Bridge from the Pentagon to Silicon Valley." *Washington Post*, January 25, 2019.

——. "China's Application of AI Should Be a Sputnik Moment for the U.S. But Will It Be?" *Washington Post*, November 7, 2018.

——. "The Chinese Threat That an Aircraft Carrier Can't Stop." *Washington Post*, August 7, 2018.

Ilachinski, Andrew. *Artificial War: Multiagent-Based Simulation of Combat*. Singapore: World Scientific, 2004.

Immigrant Defense Project, Mijente, and National Immigration Project of the National Lawyers Guild. *Who's Behind ICE? The Tech and Data Companies Fueling Deportations*. August 2018.

INCITE!. *The Revolution Will Not Be Funded: Beyond the Non-Profit Industrial Complex*. Durham, N.C.: Duke University Press, 2017.

Irani, Lilly. "Difference and Dependence Among Digital Workers: The Case of Amazon Mechanical Turk." *South Atlantic Quarterly* 114, no. 1 (2015): 225–34.

Jacobsen, Annie. *The Pentagon's Brain: An Uncensored History of DARPA, America's Top-Secret Military Research Agency*. Boston: Little, Brown, 2015.

Jacobson, Matthew Frye. *Whiteness of a Different Color*. Cambridge, Mass.: Harvard University Press, 1999.

James, Joy. "The Academic Addict: Mainlining (& Kicking) White Supremacy (WS)." In *What White Looks Like: African-American Philosophers on the Whiteness Question*, ed. George Yancy, 263–68. New York: Routledge, 2004.

Johnson, George. "Artificial Brain Again Seen as a Guide to the Mind." *New York Times*, August 16, 1988.

——. "Japan Plans Computer to Mimic Human Brain." *New York Times*, August 25, 1992.

Jordan, Michael I. "Artificial Intelligence—The Revolution Hasn't Happened Yet." *Harvard Data Science Review*, June 23, 2019.

Kaplan, Jerry. *Humans Need Not Apply: A Guide to Wealth and Work in the Age of Artificial Intelligence*. New Haven, Conn.: Yale University Press, 2015.

Karolian, Matt. "AI Improves Publishing." *NiemanLab*, December 16, 2016.

Katz, Yarden. "Manufacturing an Artificial Intelligence Revolution." *Social Science Research Network*, November 30, 2017.

Katz, Yarden, and Grif Peterson. "Liberal Outrage and White Supremacy: The Case of Epstein." *Tech*, October 3, 2019.

Kelley, Robin D. G. *Freedom Dreams: The Black Radical Imagination*. Boston: Beacon Press, 2002.

——. "Slangin' Rocks . . . Palestinian Style: Dispatches from the Occupied Zones of North America." In *Police Brutality: An Anthology*, ed. Jill Nelson, 21–59. New York: Norton, 2000.

———. "Sorry, Not Sorry." *Boston Review*, September 13, 2018.

Kenny, Patrick, Arno Hartholt, Jonathan Gratch, William Swartout, David Traum, Stacy Marsella, et al. "Building Interactive Virtual Humans for Training Environments." In *Proceedings of i/Itsec*, no. 174 (2007): 911–16.

Khan, Hamid. "Abolish Risk Assessment." Rustbelt Abolition Radio, February 28, 2019.

———. Interview by author. March 27, 2019.

Kharpal, Arjun. "Stephen Hawking Says A.I. Could Be 'Worst Event in the History of Our Civilization.'" CNBC, November 6, 2017.

King, Martin Luther, Jr. "Beyond Vietnam: A Time to Break Silence." Speech, Riverside Church, New York, April 4, 1967.

Kissinger, Henry A. "How the Enlightenment Ends." *Atlantic*, June 15, 2018.

Kleber, Sophie. "3 Ways AI Is Getting More Emotional." *Harvard Business Review*, July 31, 2018.

Knight, Will. "China Has Never Had a Real Chip Industry. Making AI Chips Could Change That." *MIT Technology Review*, December 14, 2018.

Koch, Christof. "We'll Need Bigger Brains." *Wall Street Journal*, October 27, 2017.

Korn, Sandra Y. L. "Harvard's Timber Empire." *Harvard Crimson*, April 7, 2014.

Laird, John E., and Randolph M. Jones. "Building Advanced Autonomous AI Systems for Large Scale Real Time Simulations." Paper presented to Computer Games Development Conference, Long Beach, Calif., 1998.

Laird, John E., and Paul S. Rosenbloom. "The Evolution of the Soar Cognitive Architecture." In *Mind Matters: A Tribute to Allen Newell*, ed. David Steier and Tom M. Mitchell, 1–50. Carnegie Mellon Symposia on Cognition. New York: Psychology Press, 1996.

———. "In Pursuit of Mind: The Research of Allen Newell." *AI Magazine* 13, no. 4 (1992): 17–45.

Laird, John E., and Michael Van Lent. "Human-Level AI's Killer Application: Interactive Computer Games." *AI Magazine* 22, no. 2 (2001): 15.

Lake, Brenden M., Tomer D. Ullman, Joshua B. Tenenbaum, and Samuel J. Gershman. "Building Machines That Learn and Think Like People." *Behavioral and Brain Sciences* 40, no. E253 (2016): 1–101.

la paperson. *A Third University Is Possible*. Minneapolis: University of Minnesota Press, 2017.

Leahey, Thomas H. "The Mythical Revolutions of American Psychology." *American Psychologist* 47, no. 2 (1992): 308–18.

Lee, Alayna, Rose Horowitch, and Olivia Tucker. "Schwarzman Donation to Oxford Draws Criticism." *Yale Daily News*, October 1, 2019.

Lenoir, Tim, and Henry Lowood. "Theaters of War: The Military-Entertainment Complex." In *Collection, Laboratory, Theater: Scenes of Knowledge in the*

17th Century, ed. Helmar Schramm, Ludger Schwarte, and Jan Lazardzig, 427–56. New York: de Gruyter, 2002.

Leonard, Sarah, and Rebecca Rojer. "Housekeepers Versus Harvard: Feminism for the Age of Trump." *Nation*, March 2017.

Lerman, Rachel. "Microsoft President Brad Smith Defends Company's Work with U.S. Military, Bid for Pentagon Contract." *Seattle Times*, October 26, 2018.

Leslie, Stuart W. *The Cold War and American Science: The Military-Industrial-Academic Complex at MIT and Stanford*. New York: Columbia University Press, 1993.

Lester, Caroline. "What Happens When Your Bomb-Defusing Robot Becomes a Weapon." *Atlantic*, April 26, 2018.

Li, Fei-Fei. "How to Make A.I. Human-Friendly." *New York Times*, March 8, 2018.

Li, Fei-Fei, Rob Fergus, and Pietro Perona. "One-Shot Learning of Object Categories." *IEEE Transactions on Pattern Analysis and Machine Intelligence* 28, no. 4 (2006): 594–611.

Licklider, Joseph C. R. Oral history interview. Minneapolis: Charles Babbage Institute, University of Minnesota, 1988.

Licklider, Joseph C. R., and Robert W Taylor. "The Computer as a Communication Device." *Science and Technology* 76, no. 2 (1968): 1–3.

Lighthill, James. *A Report on Artificial Intelligence*. London: UK Science and Engineering Research Council, 1973.

Lin, Tsung-Yi, Michael Maire, Serge Belongie, James Hays, Pietro Perona, Deva Ramanan, Piotr Dollár, and C. Lawrence Zitnick. "Microsoft COCO: Common Objects in Context." In *Proceedings of the European Conference on Computer Vision*, 2014, 740–55.

Lindsay, Robert K., Bruce G. Buchanan, Edward A. Feigenbaum, and Joshua Lederberg. "DENDRAL: A Case Study of the First Expert System for Scientific Hypothesis Formation." *Artificial Intelligence* 61, no. 2 (1993): 209–61.

Ling, Xiaoliang, Weiwei Deng, Chen Gu, Hucheng Zhou, Cui Li, and Feng Sun. "Model Ensemble for Click Prediction in Bing Search Ads." In *Proceedings of the 26th International Conference on World Wide Web Companion*, 2017, 689–98.

Lipsitz, George. *The Possessive Investment in Whiteness: How White People Profit from Identity Politics*. Philadelphia: Temple University Press, 2009.

Loren, Lewis A., and Eric S. Dietrich. "Phenomenology and Situated Action." In *Papers from the 1996 Fall Symposium on Embodied Cognition and Action*, Technical Report FS-96-02, 78–81. Menlo Park, Calif., AAAI, 1996.

Maturana, Humberto R. "Autopoiesis, Structural Coupling and Cognition: A History of These and Other Notions in the Biology of Cognition." *Cybernetics & Human Knowing* 9, no. 3–4 (2002): 5–34.

———. *Biology of Cognition*. Biological Computer Laboratory, Department of Electrical Engineering. Urbana: University of Illinois, 1970.

———. *From Being to Doing: The Origins of the Biology of Cognition*, ed. Bernhard Poerksen. London: Karnac Books, 2004.

Maturana, Humberto R., and Ximena P. Dávila. "The Biology of Knowing and the Biology of Loving: Education as Viewed from the Biological Matrix of Human Existence." *Prelac* 2 (2006): 30–39.

Maturana, Humberto R., and Francisco J. Varela. *The Tree of Knowledge*, rev. ed. Boulder, Colo.: Shambhala Press, 1998.

McAfee, Andrew, and Erik Brynjolfsson. "Human Work in the Robotic Future." *Foreign Affairs*, June 13, 2016.

McCarthy, John. *Defending AI Research: A Collection of Essays and Reviews*. Stanford, Calif.: CSLI Publications, 1996.

McClintock, Anne. *Imperial Leather: Race, Gender, and Sexuality in the Colonial Contest*. New York: Routledge, 2013.

McCorduck, Pamela. *Machines Who Think: A Personal Inquiry Into the History and Prospects of Artificial Intelligence*. New York: New York: Freeman, 1979.

———. "Selling Concept of 'Fifth Generation' Book to Publishers." Letter, January 19, 1982. In Edward A. Feigenbaum Papers, 1950–2007, Stanford University, SC0340, Accession 2005-101, Box 37, Folder 5.

McDermott, Drew. "Artificial Intelligence Meets Natural Stupidity." *ACM SIGART Bulletin* 57 (1976): 4–9.

———. "A Critique of Pure Reason." In *The Philosophy of Artificial Intelligence*, ed. Margaret A. Boden, 206–30. Oxford Readings in Philosophy. Oxford: Oxford University Press, 1990.

McDonald, Danny. "MIT Group Calls for University to Cancel Celebration of New College, Apologize for Henry Kissinger Invite." *Boston Globe*, February 18, 2019.

McFarland, Matt. "Elon Musk: 'With Artificial Intelligence We Are Summoning the Demon.'" *Washington Post*, October 24, 2014.

McPherson, Tara. "US Operating Systems at Mid-Century: The Intertwining of Race and UNIX." In *Race After the Internet*, ed. Lisa Nakamura and Peter A. Chow-White, 27–43. New York: Routledge, 2012.

Medina, Eden. *Cybernetic Revolutionaries: Technology and Politics in Allende's Chile*. Cambridge, Mass.: MIT Press, 2011.

Melville, Herman. *Moby-Dick, Or, The Whale*. Modern Library Classics. 1851. New York: Penguin, 2000.

Merleau-Ponty, Maurice. "Eye and Mind." In *The Merleau-Ponty Reader*, ed.
    T. Toadvine and L. Lawlor. Northwestern University Studies. Evanston, Ill.:
    Northwestern University Press, 2007.
Metz, Cade. "Google Just Open Sourced TensorFlow, Its Artificial Intelligence
    Engine." *Wired*, November 9, 2015.
Meyer, David. "Vladimir Putin Says Whoever Leads in Artificial Intelligence
    Will Rule the World." *Fortune*, September 4, 2017.
Meyer, Melissa L. "American Indian Blood Quantum Requirements: Blood Is
    Thicker than Family." In *Over the Edge: Remapping the American West*, ed. Valerie
    J. Matsumoto and Blake Allmendinger, 231–44. Berkeley: University of
    California Press, 1999.
Miller, David. *Tell Me Lies: Propaganda and Media Distortion in the Attack on Iraq.*
    London: Pluto Press, 2004.
Mills, Charles W. *Blackness Visible: Essays on Philosophy and Race.* Ithaca, N.Y.:
    Cornell University Press, 2015.
Mirowski, Philip. "The Future(s) of Open Science." *Social Studies of Science* 48,
    no. 2 (2018): 171–203.
——. *Machine Dreams: Economics Becomes a Cyborg Science.* Cambridge: Cam-
    bridge University Press, 2002.
——. *Science-Mart: Privatizing American Science.* Cambridge, Mass.: Harvard
    University Press, 2011.
Mirzoeff, Nicholas. "You Are Not A Loan: Debt and New Media." In *New
    Media, Old Media: A History and Theory Reader*, ed. Wendy H. K. Chun,
    Anna W. Fisher, and Thomas Keenan, 356–68. New York: Routledge, 2016.
MIT Media Lab. "Defiance: Disobedience for the Good of All." *MIT News*,
    July 25, 2017.
Moor, James. "The Dartmouth College Artificial Intelligence Conference: The
    Next Fifty Years." *AI Magazine* 27, no. 4 (2006): 87.
Morrison, Toni. *Playing in the Dark: Whiteness and the Literary Imagination.* Wil-
    liam E. Massey, Sr., Lectures in the History of American Civilization. New
    York: Vintage Books, 1993.
——. "Unspeakable Things Unspoken: The Afro-American Presence in Ameri-
    can Literature." Tanner Lectures on Human Values, 1988.
Müller, A., and K. H. Müller, eds. *An Unfinished Revolution? Heinz Von Foerster
    and the Biological Computer Laboratory, BCL, 1958–1976.* Complexity, Design,
    Society. Vienna: Edition Echoraum, 2007.
Murphy, Kevin Patrick. "Dynamic Bayesian Networks: Representation, Inference
    and Learning." Ph.D. dissertation, University of California, Berkeley, 2002.
Museum of Modern Art (MoMA). *MoMA R&D: AI—Artificial Imperfection.*
    New York: MOMA, 2018.

Naughton, John. "Magical Thinking About Machine Learning Won't Bring the Reality of AI Any Closer." *Guardian*, August 5, 2018.

Nakamura, Lisa. *Digitizing Race: Visual Cultures of the Internet*. Minneapolis: University of Minnesota Press, 2008.

Needham, R M. "Is There Anything Special About AI?" In *The Foundations of Artificial Intelligence: A Sourcebook*, ed. Derek Partridge and Yorick Wilks. Cambridge: Cambridge University Press, 1990.

Nesbit, Jeff. "We All May Be Dead in 2050." *U.S. News & World Report*, October 29, 2015.

Newell, Allen. "AAAI President's Message." *AI Magazine* 1, no. 1 (1980): 1–4.

——. "Newell Comments Concerning Roadmap of DARPA Funding of AI." Letter, November 3, 1975. In Edward A. Feigenbaum Papers, 1950–2007, Stanford University, SC0340, Accession 2005–101, Box 6, Folder 11.

——. "You Can't Play 20 Questions with Nature and Win: Projective Comments on the Papers of This Symposium." In *Visual Information Processing*, ed. William G. Chase, 283–308. New York: Academic Press, 1973.

Newell, Allen, John C. Shaw, and Herbert. A. Simon. *Report on a General Problem-Solving Program*. Memo P-1584. Santa Monica, Calif: RAND Corporation, December 1958.

Newell, Allen, and Herbert A. Simon. "Computer Science as Empirical Inquiry: Symbols and Search." *Communications of the ACM*, no. 3 (1976): 113–26.

——. *Human Problem Solving*. Englewood Cliffs, N.J.: Prentice-Hall, 1972.

New York University. "New Artificial Intelligence Research Institute Launches: First of Its Kind Dedicated to the Study of Social Implications of AI." Press release, November 20, 2017, https://engineering.nyu.edu/news/new-artificial-intelligence-research-institute-launches.

Nguyen, Anh, Jason Yosinski, and Jeff Clune. "Deep Neural Networks Are Easily Fooled: High Confidence Predictions for Unrecognizable Images." In *Proceedings of the IEEE Conference on Computer Vision and Pattern Recognition*, 2015, 427–36.

Nicas, Jack. "Atlanta Asks Google Whether It Targeted Black Homeless People." *New York Times*, October 4, 2019.

Nilsson, Nils J. "Artificial Intelligence: Employment, and Income." In *Impacts of Artificial Intelligence*, ed. Robert Trappl, 103–23. Amsterdam: North Holland, 1986.

——. *Artificial Intelligence—Research and Applications*. Vol. 2. Menlo Park, Calif.: Stanford Research Institute, May 1975.

——. *A Mobile Automaton: An Application of Artificial Intelligence Techniques*. Menlo Park, Calif.: Stanford Research Institute, 1969.

——. *The Quest for Artificial Intelligence*. Cambridge: Cambridge University Press, 2009.

Noble, David F. *The Religion of Technology: The Divinity of Man and the Spirit of Invention* New York: Knopf, 1997.

Norvig, Peter. *Paradigms of Artificial Intelligence Programming: Case Studies in Common LISP*. Burlington, Mass.: Morgan Kaufmann, 1992.

O'Connell, Mark. "Why Silicon Valley Billionaires Are Prepping for the Apocalypse in New Zealand." *Guardian*, February 15, 2018.

Olazaran, Mikel. "A Sociological Study of the Official History of the Perceptrons Controversy." *Social Studies of Science* 26, no. 3 (1996): 611–59.

Ophir, Adi. "How to Take Aim at the Heart of the Present and Remain Analytic." *International Journal of Philosophical Studies* 9, no. 3 (2001): 401–15.

Ordonez, Vicente, Girish Kulkarni, and Tamara L. Berg. "Im2text: Describing Images Using 1 Million Captioned Photographs." In *Advances in Neural Information Processing Systems*, 1143–51. Cambridge, Mass.: MIT Press, 2011.

Padmore, George. *The Life and Struggles of Negro Toilers*. Hollywood, Calif.: Sun Dance Press, 1931.

Painter, Nell Irvin. *The History of White People*. New York: Norton, 2010.

Papert, Seymour. "One AI or Many?" In *The Artificial Intelligence Debate: False Starts, Real Foundations*, ed. Stephen Graubard, 241–67. Cambridge. Mass.: MIT Press, 1988.

——. "The Summer Vision Project." Vision Memo No. 100. Cambridge, Mass.: MIT Artificial Intelligence Group, 1966.

Parker, Emily. "How Two AI Superpowers—the U.S. and China—Battle for Supremacy in the Field." *Washington Post*, November 2, 2018.

Parkinson, Hannah Jane. "AI Can Write Just like Me. Brace for the Robot Apocalypse." *Guardian*, February 15, 2019.

Perry, Ruth, and Lisa Greber. "Women and Computers: An Introduction." *Signs: Journal of Women in Culture and Society* 16, no. 1 (1990): 74–101.

Peterson, Grif, and Yarden Katz. "Elite Universities Are Selling Themselves—and Look Who's Buying." *Guardian*, March 30, 2018.

Pfeffer, Anshel, "WikiLeaks: IDF Uses Drones to Assassinate Gaza Militants." *Haaretz*, September 2, 2011.

Philanthropy News Digest. "Berkeley Launches Center for Human-Compatible Artificial Intelligence." September 5, 2016.

Pickering, Andrew. *The Cybernetic Brain: Sketches of Another Future*. Chicago: University of Chicago Press, 2010.

Pierre, Jemima. *The Predicament of Blackness: Postcolonial Ghana and the Politics of Race*. Chicago: University of Chicago Press, 2012.

Pollack, Andrew. "'Fifth Generation' Became Japan's Lost Generation." *New York Times*, June 5, 1992.

Rajaraman, V. "John McCarthy—Father of Artificial Intelligence." *Resonance* 19, no. 3 (2014): 198–207.

Raso, Filippo, Hannah Hilligoss, Vivek Krishnamurthy, Christopher Bavitz, and Levin Yerin Kim. *Artificial Intelligence & Human Rights: Opportunities & Risks.* Cambridge, Mass.: Berkman Klein Center for Internet & Society Research Publication. September 2018.

Regalado, Antonio. "Google's AI Explosion in One Chart." *MIT Technology Review*, March 25, 2017.

Reisman, Dillon, Jason Schultz, Kate Crawford, and Meredith Whittaker. *Algorithmic Impact Assessments: A Practical Framework for Public Agency Accountability.* AI Now Institute, April 2018.

Rice, Andrew. "The McKinsey Way to Save an Island." *New York Magazine*, April 17, 2019.

Richardson, Rashida, Jason Schultz, and Kate Crawford. "Dirty Data, Bad Predictions: How Civil Rights Violations Impact Police Data, Predictive Policing Systems, and Justice." *New York University Law Review Online*, April 2019.

Rieland, Randy. "Artificial Intelligence Is Now Used to Predict Crime. But Is It Biased?" *Smithsonian*, March 5, 2018.

Riley, Boots. *Sorry to Bother You.* Script. 2017.

Roberts, Sam. "U.C.L.A. Center on Police-Community Ties Will Move to John Jay College." *New York Times*, March 21, 2016.

Robinson, Cedric J. *Forgeries of Memory and Meaning: Blacks and the Regimes of Race in American Theater and Film Before World War II.* Chapel Hill: University of North Carolina Press, 2007.

Rodriguez, Dylan. "The Political Logic of the Non-Profit Industrial Complex." In *The Revolution Will Not Be Funded: Beyond the Non-Profit Industrial Complex*, ed. INCITE!, 21–40. Durham, N.C.: Duke University Press, 2017.

Roland, Alex, and Philip Shiman. *Strategic Computing: DARPA and the Quest for Machine Intelligence, 1983–1993.* Cambridge, Mass.: MIT Press, 2002.

Rosenberg, Ronald. "AI Alley's Longest Winter." *Boston Globe*, December 18, 1988.

Rota, Gian Carlo. *The End of Objectivity. The Legacy of Phenomenology. Lectures at MIT*, 174. Cambridge, Mass.: MIT Mathematics Department, 1991.

Rucker, Rudy. *Seek! Selected Nonfiction.* Philadelphia: Running Press, 1999.

Rusert, Britt. *Fugitive Science: Empiricism and Freedom in Early African American Culture.* New York: NYU Press, 2017.

Russell, Stuart, and Peter Norvig. *Artificial Intelligence: A Modern Approach*, 2d ed. Englewood Cliffs, N.J.: Prentice Hall, 2002.

Said, Edward W. *Culture and Imperialism.* 1993. New York: Vintage Books, 2012.

——. *Orientalism.* 1978. New York: Vintage Books, 2014.

Sample, Ian. "AI Will Create 'Useless Class' of Human, Predicts Bestselling Historian." *Guardian*, May 20, 2016.

——. "It's Able to Create Knowledge Itself': Google Unveils AI That Learns on Its Own." *Guardian*, October 18, 2017.

——. "Artificial Intelligence Risks GM-Style Public Backlash, Experts Warn." *Guardian*, November 1, 2017.

——. "Joseph Stiglitz on Artificial Intelligence: 'We're Going Towards a More Divided Society.'" *Guardian*, September 8, 2018.

Sardar, Ziauddin. "alt. bivilizations. faq Cyberspace as the Darker Side of the West." In *The Cyberculture Reader*, ed. David Bell and Barbara M. Kennedy, 732–52. New York: Routledge, 2000.

Schiesel, Seth. "Marines Polish Command Skills, Switching Places with Traders." *New York Times*, December 16, 1996.

Schivone, Gabriel Matthew. "On Responsibility, War Guilt and Intellectuals." *CounterPunch*, August 3, 2007.

Schmalzer, Sigrid, Daniel S. Chard, and Alyssa Botelho. *Science for the People: Documents from America's Movement of Radical Scientists*. Science/Technology/ Culture Series. Amherst: University of Massachusetts Press, 2018.

Schmidhuber, Jürgen. "True Artificial Intelligence Will Change Everything." Keynote lecture at European Communication Summit, July 7, 2016.

Schölkopf, Bernhard. "Artificial Intelligence: Learning to See and Act." *Nature* 518, no. 7540 (2015): 486–87.

Shead, Sam. "Google I/O: Google Research Becomes Google AI." *Forbes*, May 9, 2018.

Sheill, Zoe, and Whitney Zhang. "Protesters Gather Against College of Computing Celebration." *Tech*, March 7, 2019.

Shubik, Martin. "Bibliography on Simulation, Gaming, Artificial Intelligence and Allied Topics." *Journal of the American Statistical Association* 55, no. 292 (1960): 736–51.

Silk, Leonard. "Nobel Winner's Heretical Views." *New York Times*, November 9, 1978.

Silver, Nate. *The Signal and the Noise: Why So Many Predictions Fail—but Some Don't*. New York: Penguin Press, 2012.

Simon, Herbert A., and Allen Newell. "Heuristic Problem Solving: The Next Advance in Operations Research." *Operations Research* 6, no. 1 (1958): 1–10.

Simpson, Audra. *Mohawk Interruptus: Political Life Across the Borders of Settler States*. Durham, N.C.: Duke University Press, 2014.

Singju Post. "Artificial Intelligence Is the New Electricity." January 23, 2018.

Skinner, B. F. *Reflections on Behaviorism and Society*. Englewood Cliffs, N.J.: Prentice-Hall, 1978.

Slyomovics, Susan. "French Restitution, German Compensation: Algerian Jews and Vichy's Financial Legacy." *Journal of North African Studies* 17, no. 5 (2012): 881–901.

Smith, Mitch. "In Wisconsin, a Backlash Against Using Data to Foretell Defendants' Futures." *New York Times*, June 22, 2016.

Solomon, Shoshanna. "Military Sees Surge in AI Use, but Not Yet for Critical Missions." *Times of Israel*, October 29, 2018.

Solon, Olivia. "Why Did Microsoft Fund an Israeli Firm That Surveils West Bank Palestinians?" *NBC News*, October 28, 2019.

Springer, Paul J. *Military Robots and Drones: A Reference Handbook*. Contemporary World Issues. Santa Barbara, Calif.: ABC-CLIO, 2013.

Squires, Judith. "Fabulous Feminist Futures and the Lure of Cyberculture." In *The Cyberculture Reader*, ed. David Bell and Barbara M. Kennedy, 360–73. New York: Routledge, 2000.

Srnicek, Nick. *Platform Capitalism*. Malden, Mass.: Polity Press, 2017.

Staddon, John E. R. *The New Behaviorism*. London: Taylor & Francis, 2014.

——. "The 'Superstition' Experiment: A Reversible Figure." *Journal of Experimental Psychology: General* 121, no. 3 (1992): 270–72.

Stahl, Roger. *Militainment, Inc.: War, Media, and Popular Culture*. New York: Routledge, 2009.

Stewart, Phil. "U.S. Weighs Restricting Chinese Investment in Artificial Intelligence." *Reuters*, June 13, 2017.

Stockton, William. "Creating Computers That Think." *New York Times Magazine*, December 7, 1980.

Stop LAPD Spying Coalition. "Before the Bullet Hits the Body: Dismantling Predictive Policing in Los Angeles." May 8, 2018.

Strogatz, Steven. "One Giant Step for a Chess-Playing Machine." *New York Times*, December 26, 2018.

Suchman, Lucy. "Do Categories Have Politics? The Language/Action Perspective Reconsidered." In *Proceedings of the Third European Conference on Computer-Supported Cooperative Work 13–17 September 1993*, Milan, Italy, 1–14.

——. "Situational Awareness: Deadly Bioconvergence at the Boundaries of Bodies and Machines." *MediaTropes Test Journal* 5, no. 1 (2015): 1–24.

Suchman, Lucy, Lilly Irani, and Peter Asaro. "Google's March to the Business of War Must Be Stopped." *Guardian*, May 16, 2018.

Supiot, Alain. *The Spirit of Philadelphia: Social Justice vs. the Total Market*. New York: Verso, 2012.

Sutton, Richard S., and Andrew G. Barto. *Reinforcement Learning: An Introduction*. Cambridge, Mass.: MIT Press, 1998.

Taylor, Robert W. "In Memoriam: JCR Licklider 1915–1990." Digital Systems Research Center, Palo Alto, Calif., 1990.

Tegmark, Max. "Let's Aspire to More than Making Ourselves Obsolete." In *Possible Minds: 25 Ways of Looking at AI*, ed. John Brockman. New York: Penguin, 2019.

——. *Life 3.0: Being Human in the Age of Artificial Intelligence*. New York: Knopf, 2017.

Terranova, Tiziana. *Network Culture: Cultural Politics for the Information Age*. London: Pluto Press, 2004.

Tetley, W. H. "The Role of Computers in Air Defense." In *Papers and Discussions Presented at the December 3–5, 1958, Eastern Joint Computer Conference: Modern Computers: Objectives, Designs, Applications*, 15–18. 1958.

Thompson, Nicholas. "Emmanuel Macron Talks to WIRED About France's AI Strategy." *Wired*, March 31, 2018.

Torrero, Edward A. *Next-Generation Computers*. Spectrum Series. New York: Institute of Electrical and Electronics Engineers, 1985.

Trappl, Robert, ed. *Impacts of Artificial Intelligence*. Amsterdam: North Holland, 1986.

Tuck, Eve, and K. Wayne Yang. "Decolonization Is Not a Metaphor." *Decolonization: Indigeneity, Education & Society* 1, no. 1 (2012): 1–40.

Turner, Fred. "The Arts at Facebook: An Aesthetic Infrastructure for Surveillance Capitalism." *Poetics* 67 (2018): 53–62.

——. *From Counterculture to Cyberculture: Stewart Brand, the Whole Earth Network, and the Rise of Digital Utopianism*. Chicago: University of Chicago Press, 2010.

United Kingdom. Department for Business, Energy & Industrial Strategy and Department for Digital, Culture, Media & Sport. *AI Sector Deal*. Policy paper, April 26, 2018. https://www.gov.uk/government/publications/artificial-intelligence-sector-deal/ai-sector-deal.

United States. Department of Commerce, Office of Industrial Resource Administration. *Critical Technology Assessment of the U.S. Artificial Intelligence Sector*. August 1994.

United States. Department of Homeland Security. "Secure Communities." 2019. https://www.ice.gov/secure-communities.

Van Riper, Paul, and Robert H. Scales, Jr. "Preparing for War in the 21st Century." In *Future Warfare: Anthology*, ed. Robert H. Scales. Carlisle, Penn.: Strategic Studies Institute, 2000.

Varela, Francisco J., Evan Thompson, and Eleanor Rosch. *The Embodied Mind: Cognitive Science and Human Experience*. 1991. Cambridge, Mass.: MIT Press, 2017.

Vincent, James. "This Beautiful Map Shows Everything That Powers an Amazon Echo, from Data Mines to Lakes of Lithium." *Verge*, September 9, 2018.

Vinyals, Oriol, Alexander Toshev, Samy Bengio, and Dumitru Erhan. "Show and Tell: A Neural Image Caption Generator." In *Proceedings of the IEEE Conference on Computer Vision and Pattern Recognition*, 3156–64. 2015.

Vishwanath, Arun. "When a Robot Writes Your News, What Happens to Democracy?" CNN, February 27, 2018.

Vitale, Alex S. *The End of Policing.* New York: Verso Books, 2018.

Wagner, Kurt. "Mark Zuckerberg's Philanthropy Organization Is Acquiring a Search and AI Startup Called Meta." *Recode,* January 24, 2017.

Wakabayashi, Daisuke, and Scott Shane. "Google Will Not Renew Pentagon Contract That Upset Employees." *New York Times,* June 1, 2019.

Wallis, Brian. "Black Bodies, White Science: Louis Agassiz's Slave Daguerreotypes." *American Art* 9, no. 2 (1995): 39–61.

Weinbaum, Alys Eve. *The Afterlife of Reproductive Slavery: Biocapitalism and Black Feminism's Philosophy of History.* Durham, N.C.: Duke University Press, 2019.

Weinberger, David. "Don't Make AI Stupid in the Name of Transparency." *Wired,* January 28, 2018.

——. "Our Machines Now Have Knowledge We'll Never Understand." *Wired,* April 18, 2017.

Weizenbaum, Joseph. *Computer Power and Human Reason: From Judgment to Calculation.* New York: Freeman, 1976.

——. "Computers in Uniform: A Good Fit?" *Science for the People* 17, no. 1 (1985): 26–29.

Weschler, Lawrence. *And How Are You, Dr. Sacks? A Biographical Memoir of Oliver Sacks.* New York: Farrar, Straus and Giroux, 2019.

Wiggers, Kyle. "Google Will Open an AI Center in Ghana Later This Year, Its First in Africa." *VentureBeat,* June 13, 2018.

Wilson, Terry P. "Blood Quantum: Native American Mixed Bloods." In *Racially Mixed People in America,* ed. Maria P. P. Root. Newbury Park, Calif: Sage, 1992.

Winograd, Terry. Interview by author. June 1, 2018.

——. *Strategic Computing Research and the Universities.* Report No. STAN-CS-87-1160. Stanford, Calif.: Department of Computer Science, Stanford University, March 1987.

Winograd, Terry, and Fernando Flores. *Understanding Computers and Cognition: A New Foundation for Design.* Norwood, N.J.: Ablex, 1986.

Winston, Patrick H. Oral history interview. Minneapolis: Charles Babbage Institute, University of Minnesota, 1990.

Wu, Ren, Shengen Yan, Yi Shan, Qingqing Dang, and Gang Sun. "Deep Image: Scaling up Image Recognition." ArXiv Preprint ArXiv:1501.02876, July 8, 2015.

Yamauchi, Brian M. "PackBot: A Versatile Platform for Military Robotics." In *Proceedings of SPIE 5422, Unmanned Ground Vehicle Technology VI,* September 2, 2004.

Yerkes, Robert Mearns. "Psychological Examining in the United States Army." In *Readings in the History of Psychology*, ed. Wayne Dennis, 528–40. New York: Appleton-Century-Crofts, 1948.

Yoon, B. L. "DARPA Artificial Neural Network Technology Program." In *1991 International Symposium on VLSI Technology, Systems, and Applications*, 61–63. 1991.

Zeleny, Milan. "Crisis and Transformation: On the Corso and Ricorso of Human Systems." *Human Systems Management* 31, no. 1 (2012): 49–63.

——. "Machine/Organism Dichotomy and Free-Market Economics: Crisis or Transformation?" *Human Systems Management* 29, no. 4 (2010): 191–204.

——. "Self-Organization of Living Systems: A Formal Model of Autopoiesis." *International Journal of General System* 4, no. 1 (1977): 13–28.

Ziv, Amitai. "This Israeli Face-Recognition Startup Is Secretly Tracking Palestinians." *Haaretz*, July 15, 2019.

Zuboff, Shoshana. "Big Other: Surveillance Capitalism and the Prospects of an Information Civilization." *Journal of Information Technology* 30, no. 1 (2015): 75–89.

INDEX

apartheid, 114

Apple, 68, 71, 74, 285n65

Armer, Paul, 244n37

army, 44, 133, 219, 251n104, 295n55, 299n77

Arpaio, Joe, 179

artificial intelligence (AI):
alternatives to, 11, 14, 185–88, 203–10; autonomy of, 52–53, 58–59, 247n72; coining of term, 3, 22–23, 241nn8–9; dissenting views of, 33–34, 44–48, 193–94; expert industry around, 2–3, 9–10, 66–74; as a foil for neoliberalism, 70–78, 119–22, 166, 226–27; "hype" about, 33, 208, 238n17, 255n14; and models of the self, 5–7, 10, 27–32, 154, 157, 165–67; as a site of imperial struggle, 60–61; individual and institutional investment in, 7–11, 20, 79–81, 154, 167–72, 182, 229; militaristic frame of, 35–38, 45–47, 50–59, 245n44; nebulous and shifting character of, 2–3, 5–6, 10, 22–27, 33–38, 42, 45, 52–55, 63–70, 154–55, 164–67; springs and winters of, 4, 48; sponsorship of, 24–26, 59; rebranding of, 12, 65–70, 80–81; relation to psychology and biology, 5, 21; "technical" narratives about, 2–4, 66–68, 261n43; as a technology of whiteness, 8–11, 155, 172, 181–82

artificial life (ALife): and bio-inspired computing, 210,

296n60; and racial narratives, 159, 277n12–14; relation to AI, 159, 277n11

Artificial War, 212–13

ARPA, 24, 96, 249n85; and Behavioral Sciences Program, 98, 265n11

Association for the Advancement of Artificial Intelligence (AAAI), 5, 23, 37–38

Association for Computing Machinery (ACM), 23

Atlantic, The, 61, 104

automata studies, 241nn8–9

automation: and automated systems, 141, 169–70; of industrial production, 25–26, 34, 74–75, 78; of warfare, 43–44, 57–59

autopoiesis, 194–96: and neoliberalism, 201–2; and war, 213

Azoulay, Ariella Aïsha, 300n1

Azoulay, Roger, 15, 300n1

Baldwin, James, 93

Barbrook, Richard, 156

Baudrillard, Jean, 151

Baupost Group, 263n57

Beer, Stafford, 25, 193, 290n30

Belfer Center, 260n40

Bell Labs, 22

Bell, Trudy E., 246n58

behaviorism, 119, 121–22, 166, 267n46, 269n49, 269n51

Benjamin, Ruha, 285n67

Berkman Klein Center for Internet & Society, 66, 260n39, 261n42

Department of Justice, 114, 135, 142,
   275n39
Descartes, René, 21, 188, 287n7
Desert Storm, 52
DiAngelo, Robin, 171
Domingos, Pedro, 251n99
Dreyfus, Hubert, 33, 172,
   189–93, 198, 203, 206, 238n11,
   244nn37–38, 282n48, 287n11,
   288nn12–13, 288n16, 288n19,
   295n52, 299n79
Dreyfus, Stuart, 191
Dr. Strangelove, 118
Du Bois, W. E. B., 153, 157, 160, 171,
   278n18

eBay, 260n39
economic inequality, 10, 63, 128
economics, 193: and neoliberal
   economics, 201; proximity to
   AI, 23, 30–31, 203, 259n35.
   See also neoliberalism
Edwards, Paul, 21, 37, 239n20
Ekbia, H. R., 242n20, 295n52
electronic battlefield, 58
Embodied Mind, The, 203–6,
   242n20
embodied and situated cognition:
   as alternatives to mainstream
   AI and cognitive science,
   186–88, 299n79; and the
   enactive approach, 294n48; as
   epistemic styles of AI, 242n20;
   epistemic premises of, 203–7,
   291n33, 294n48; militarized
   frame of, 207–10; shortcomings

of, 221–24, 227; social and moral
   visions of, 187, 202, 205; and the
   war industry, 191, 216–21
embodiment: of AI systems, 13; of
   battlefield, 55, 212–16. *See also*
   embodied and situated
   cognition
empire. *See* imperialism
empiricism: in AI narratives,
   106–8, 165; and humanistic
   critique of AI, 13
Endeavor Robotics, 295n55
entrepreneur. *See* neoliberalism
epidemiology, 273n33
epistemic forgeries, 7, 9, 12, 89,
   93: definition of, 5–6, 94;
   service to political projects, 9,
   95; as manifested in AI
   systems, 106–22, 166, 181, 190,
   226–27; rejection of, 123–26,
   185, 224, 229, 234; use in
   affirming white supremacy,
   128, 135, 154, 171–72
epistemic styles, of AI systems,
   5–6, 50, 55–56, 154, 205, 242n20
"ethical" AI, 80, 82, 84, 87, 129, 177,
   226, 284n61
eugenics, 7, 157, 227n14
expert industry: and capitalism,
   74–78, 81–88; carceral-positive
   logic of, 135; neoliberal logic of,
   78–81, 133; formation and
   discourse of, 2–4, 9, 63, 65–68,
   124, 126–28, 228, 225n14; and
   whiteness, 156, 172, 229. *See also*
   critical AI experts

Kissinger, Henry, 61–63, 83–84, 88, 231, 258n33
Klarman, Seth, 263n57
knowledge production, 16, 144, 228
Kubrick, Stanley, 118

labor: in AI narratives, 2, 74–78; in data generation for computing systems, 115–17
Laird, John, 250n93
land accumulation, 9, 85, 87–88. *See also* settler-colonialism
la paperson, 185–186, 239n24, 301n10
Leahey, Thomas H., 267n46
Lebanon, 58
Lederberg, Joshua, 243n30
Lenat, Douglas, 44
Leontief, Wassily, 260n36
liberalism: and liberal policing reforms, 137–38, 146; and liberal view of technology, 290n31; and liberal view of universities, 84, 87
Licklider, Joseph C. R., 96–99, 209, 264nn6–8, 264n10, 265n11
Life 3.0, 75, 258n28
Lighthill, James, 33–34, 171, 244n40
Lincoln, Abraham, 278n19
Lincoln Laboratory, 49, 96, 264n8
LinkedIn, 260n39
Lipsitz, George, 11, 14, 170–71, 229
logic (mathematical): and critique of logicist program in AI, 288n12; in knowledge engineering and expert systems,

26, 50, 103; in narratives about AI, 27, 32, 56, 251n99. *See also* "symbolic" and "statistical" AI
London School of Economics, 294n45
Los Alamos National Lab, 210
love, in alternative streams of cognitive science, 187, 200–2, 205
Lovelock, James, 202

machine learning: in Dartmouth 1956 meeting, 23; as distinct from early AI systems, 30; and "explainable AI," 269n52; in rebranding of AI, 68, 71, 73, 252n107, 254n4, 255n14, 256n15
Macron, Emmanuel, 61
"magical chip" narrative, 60, 164
Massachusetts Institute of Technology (MIT), 13, 22, 44–45, 49–50, 75, 96, 141, 156, 198, 208: and AI propaganda, 38; and corporate-academic hybrids, 175; and early AI laboratories, 24; and Pentagon funding, 25, 37; roles in imperialist projects, 81–86, 88; roles in rebranding AI, 79
makeshift patchwork: AI as a, 9–10; rule by white supremacy as a, 7, 160, 233
manifest destiny: AI as, 42, 159; ALife as, 159, 277n13; in discourse on computing, 158; and imperialist discourse, 61